Garfield
tons of fun

BY: JIM DAVIS

Ballantine Books • New York

Published in the United States by Ballantine Books, a division of Random House, Inc., New York, and simultaneously in Canada by Random House of Canada Limited, Toronto.

Library of Congress Catalog Card Number: 95-95020

ISBN: 0-345-40386-X

Manufactured in the United States of America

First Edition: March 1996

10 9 8 7 6 5 4 3 2 1

6 PRACTICAL USES FOR YOUR CAT

1 DOORSTOP

2 TV ANTENNA
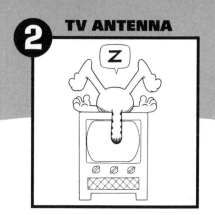

3 PAPERWEIGHT

4 HOOD ORNAMENT

5 LAP WARMER

6 HAT

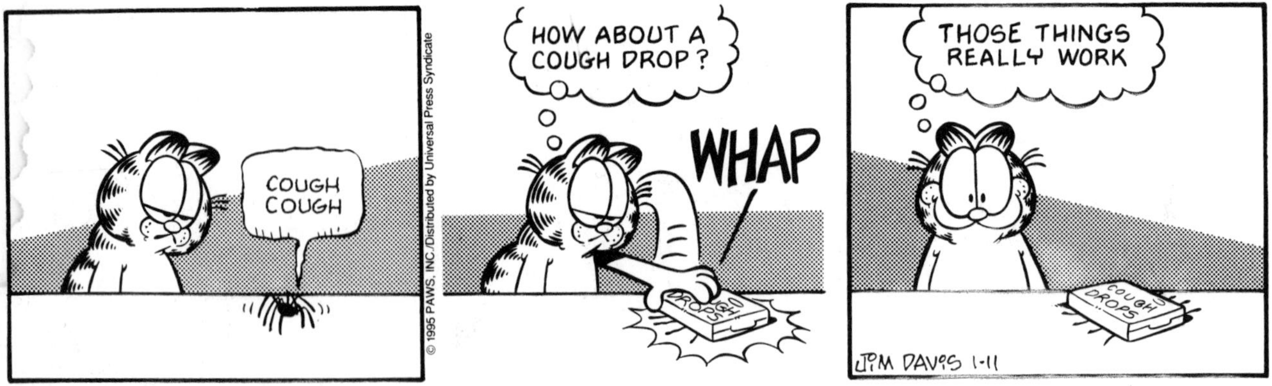
COUGH COUGH
© 1995 PAWS, INC./Distributed by Universal Press Syndicate
HOW ABOUT A COUGH DROP ?
WHAP
COUGH DROPS
THOSE THINGS REALLY WORK
COUGH DROPS
JIM DAVIS 1-11

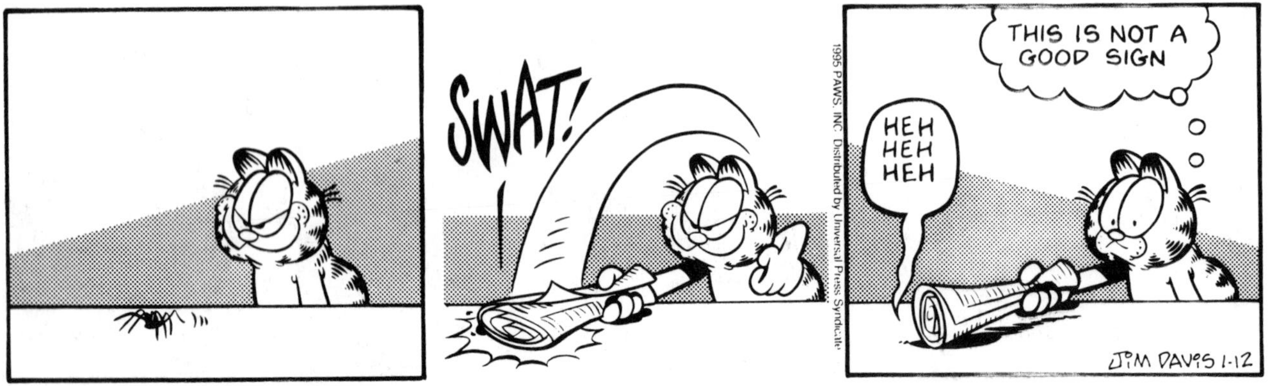
SWAT!
1995 PAWS, INC. Distributed by Universal Press Syndicate
THIS IS NOT A GOOD SIGN
HEH HEH HEH
JIM DAVIS 1-12

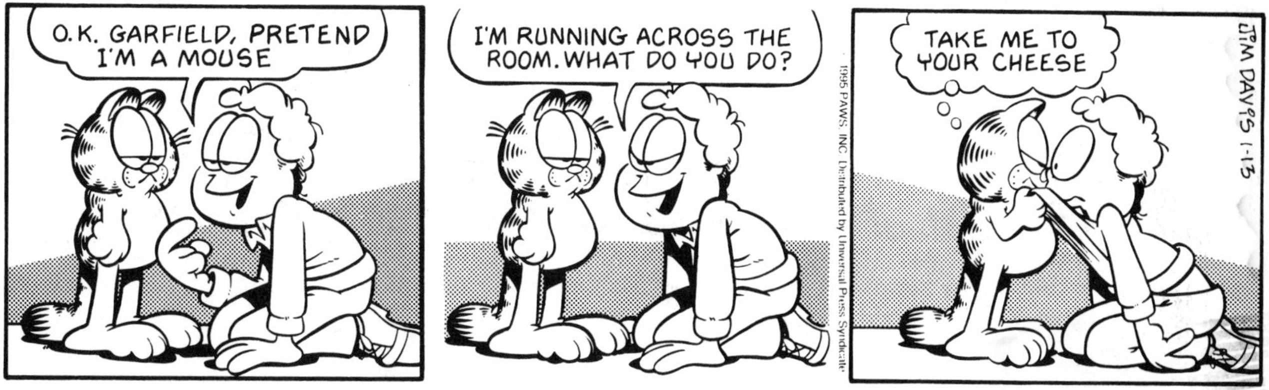
O.K. GARFIELD, PRETEND I'M A MOUSE
I'M RUNNING ACROSS THE ROOM. WHAT DO YOU DO?
© 1995 PAWS, INC. Distributed by Universal Press Syndicate
JIM DAVIS 1-13
TAKE ME TO YOUR CHEESE

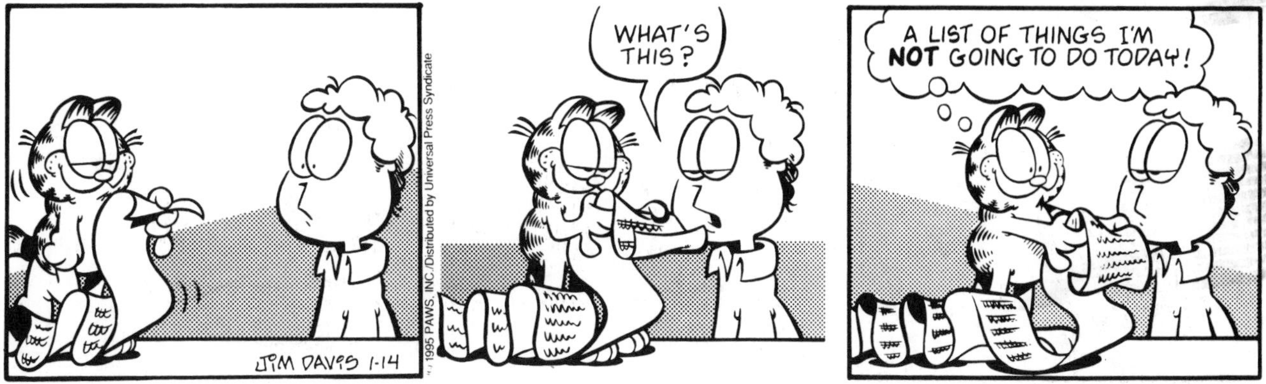
JIM DAVIS 1-14
© 1995 PAWS, INC./Distributed by Universal Press Syndicate
WHAT'S THIS?
A LIST OF THINGS I'M **NOT** GOING TO DO TODAY!

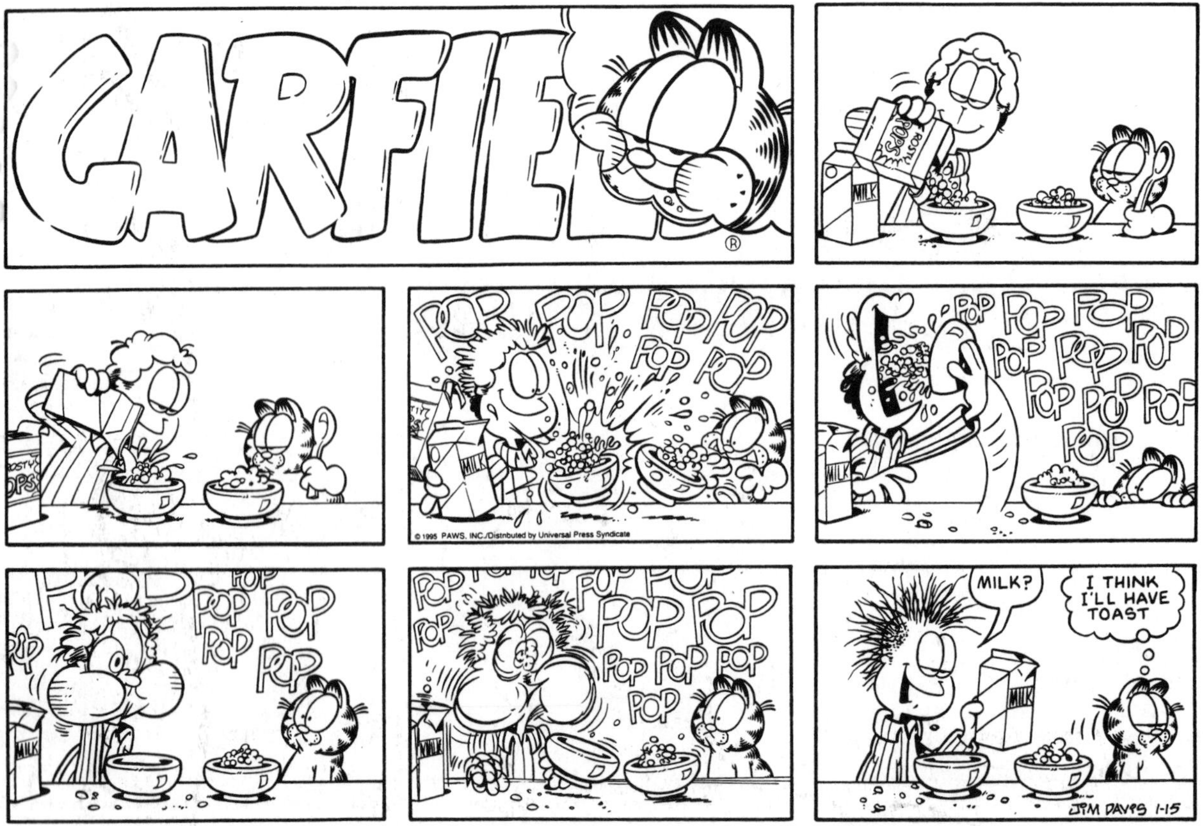
GARFIE
FROSTY POPS
MILK
POP POP POP POP POP POP
© 1995 PAWS, INC./Distributed by Universal Press Syndicate
POP POP POP POP POP POP POP POP POP POP POP
POP POP POP POP POP
POP POP POP POP POP POP POP POP POP POP
MILK?
I THINK I'LL HAVE TOAST
JIM DAVIS 1-15

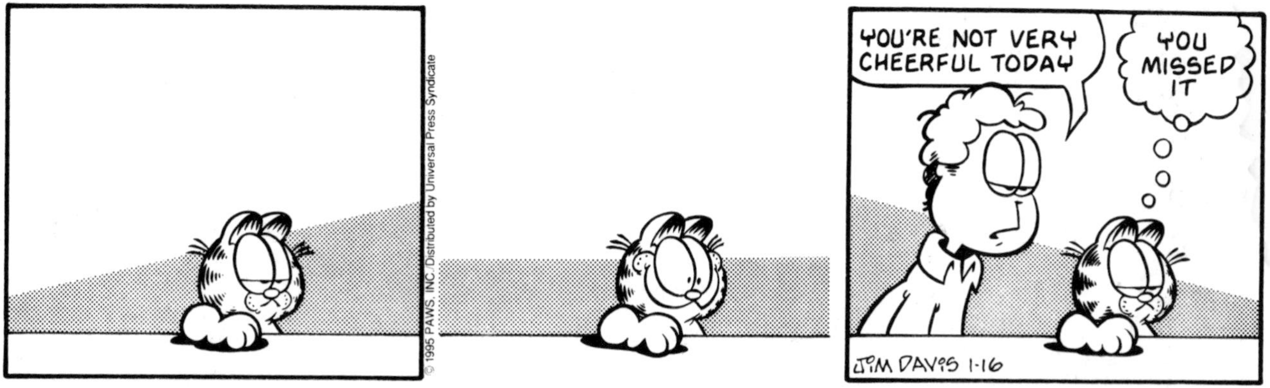
© 1995 PAWS, INC./Distributed by Universal Press Syndicate
YOU'RE NOT VERY CHEERFUL TODAY
YOU MISSED IT
JIM DAVIS 1-16

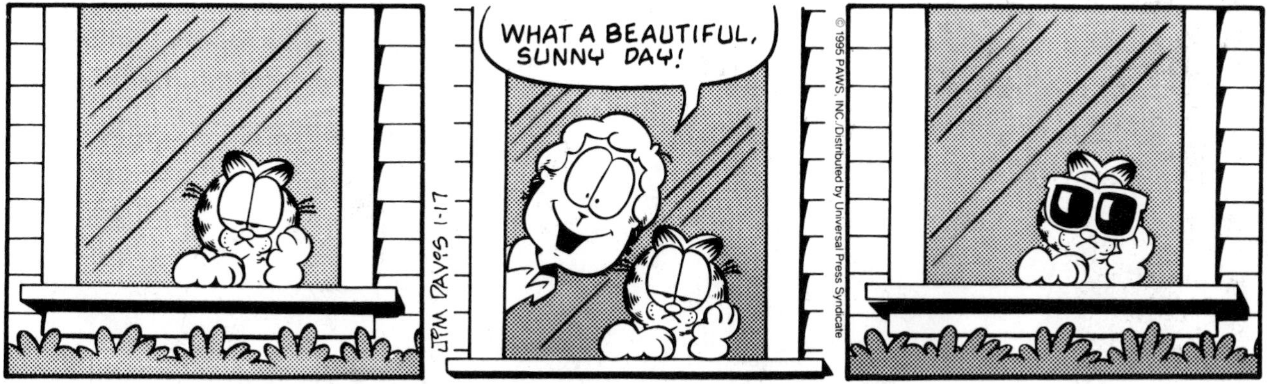
JIM DAVIS 1-17
WHAT A BEAUTIFUL, SUNNY DAY!
© 1995 PAWS, INC./Distributed by Universal Press Syndicate

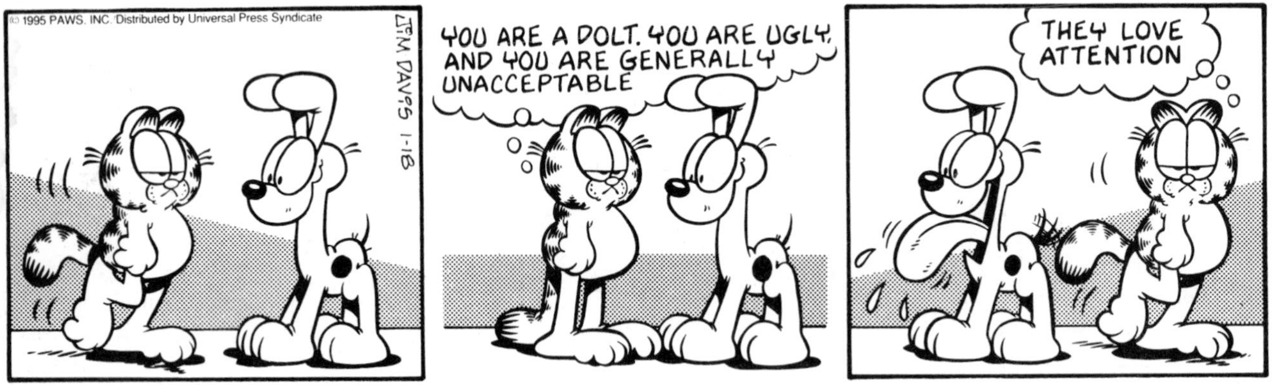
© 1995 PAWS, INC./Distributed by Universal Press Syndicate
JIM DAVIS 1-18
YOU ARE A DOLT. YOU ARE UGLY, AND YOU ARE GENERALLY UNACCEPTABLE
THEY LOVE ATTENTION

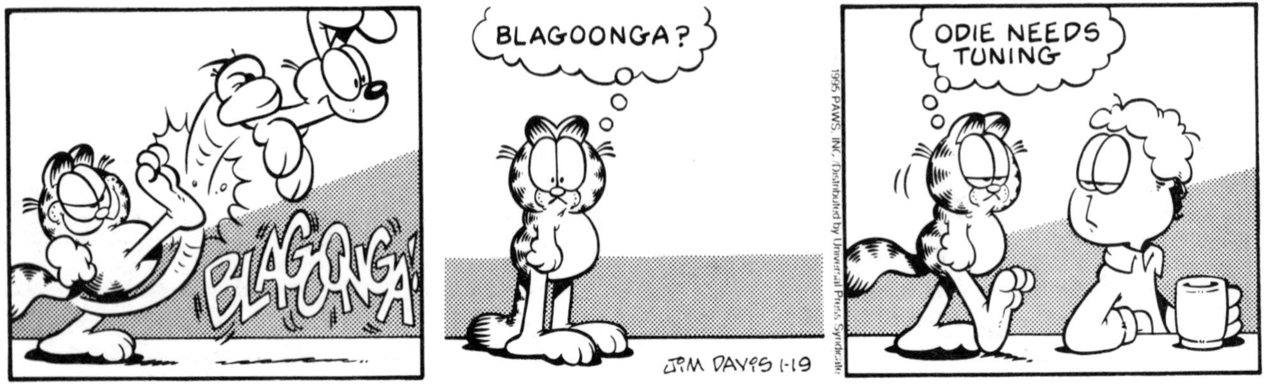
BLAGOONGA!
BLAGOONGA?
JIM DAVIS 1-19
1995 PAWS, INC./Distributed by Universal Press Syndicate
ODIE NEEDS TUNING

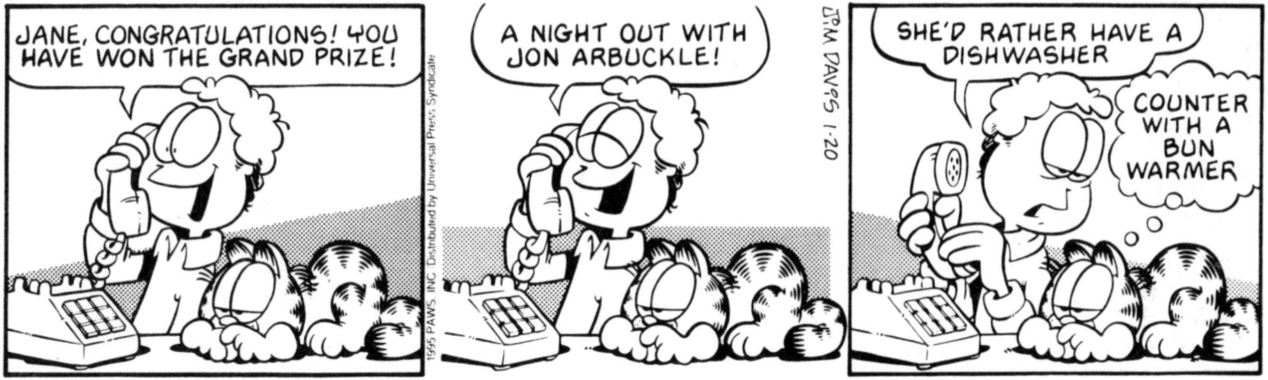
JANE, CONGRATULATIONS! YOU HAVE WON THE GRAND PRIZE!
A NIGHT OUT WITH JON ARBUCKLE!
SHE'D RATHER HAVE A DISHWASHER
COUNTER WITH A BUN WARMER
1995 PAWS, INC. Distributed by Universal Press Syndicate
JIM DAVIS 1-20

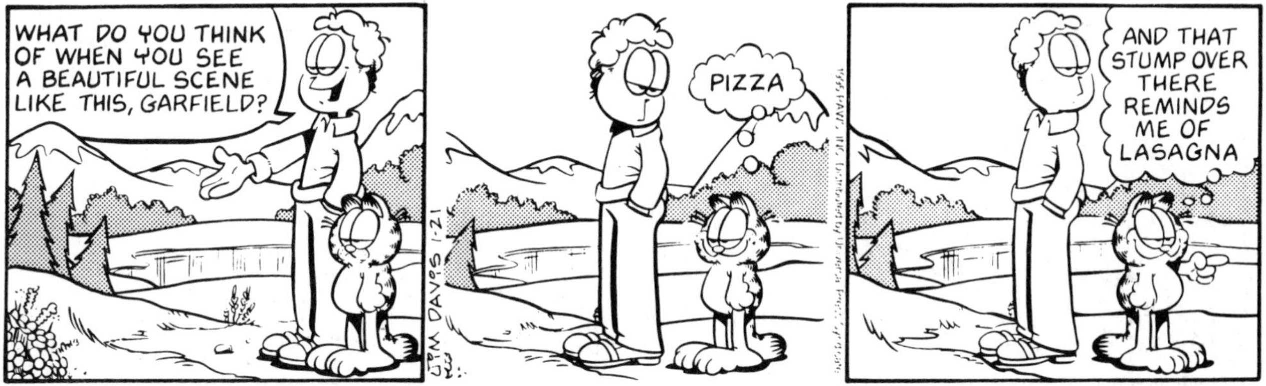
WHAT DO YOU THINK OF WHEN YOU SEE A BEAUTIFUL SCENE LIKE THIS, GARFIELD?
PIZZA
AND THAT STUMP OVER THERE REMINDS ME OF LASAGNA
JIM DAVIS 1-21

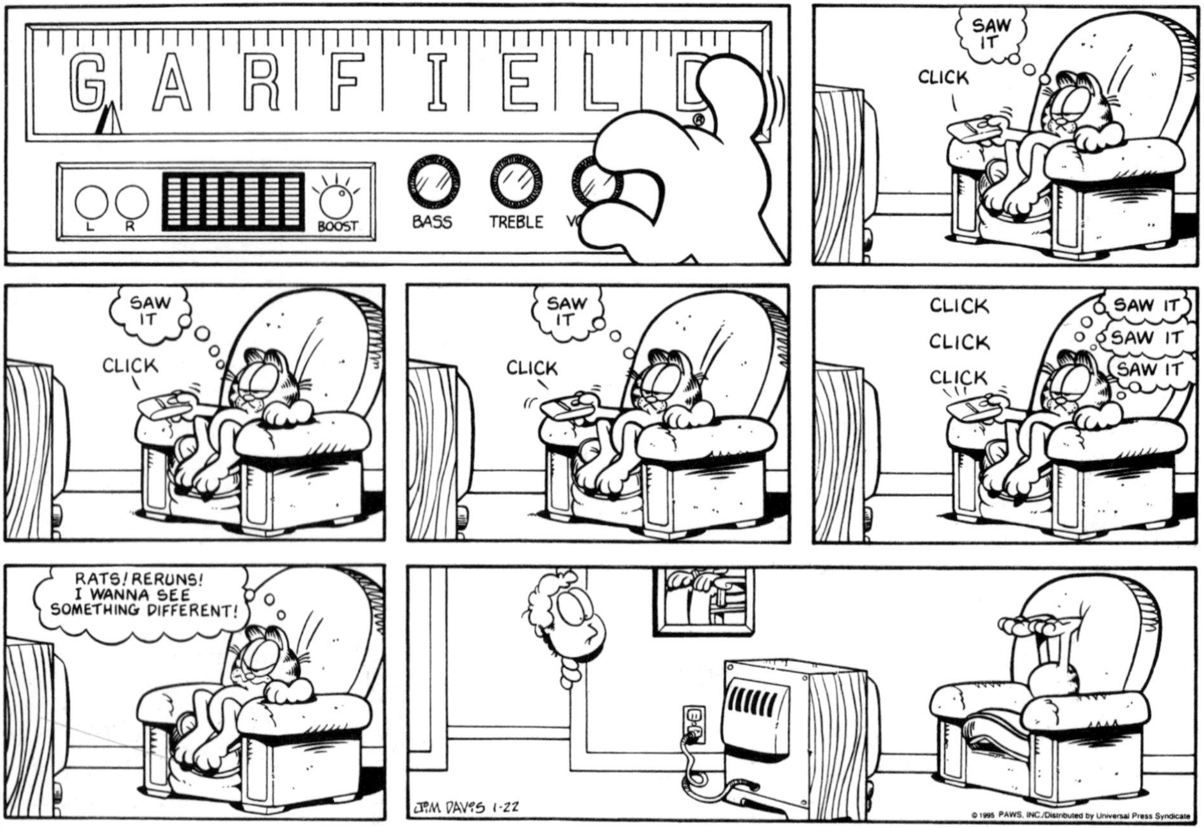
GARFIELD®
L
R
BOOST
BASS
TREBLE
CLICK
SAW IT
CLICK
SAW IT
CLICK
SAW IT
CLICK
CLICK
CLICK
SAW IT
SAW IT
SAW IT
RATS! RERUNS! I WANNA SEE SOMETHING DIFFERENT!
JIM DAVIS 1-22
© 1995 PAWS, INC./Distributed by Universal Press Syndicate

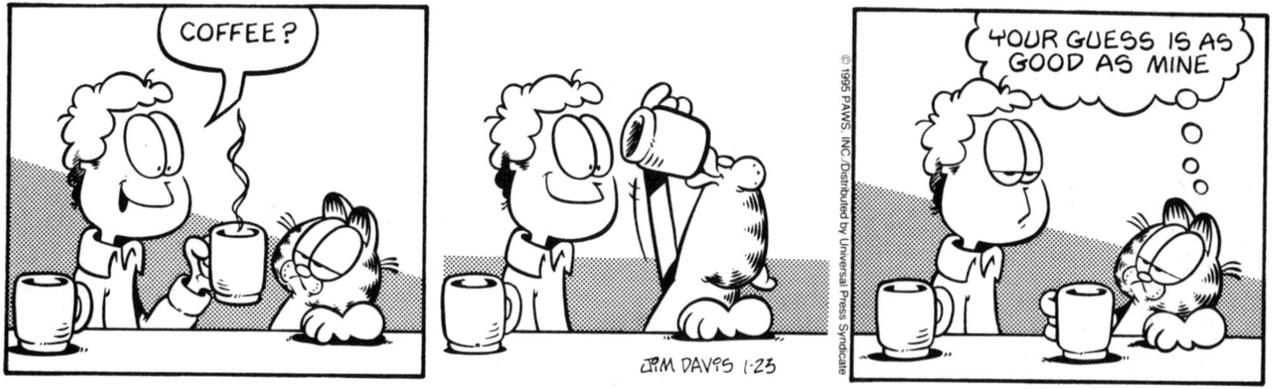
COFFEE?
YOUR GUESS IS AS GOOD AS MINE
JIM DAVIS 1-23

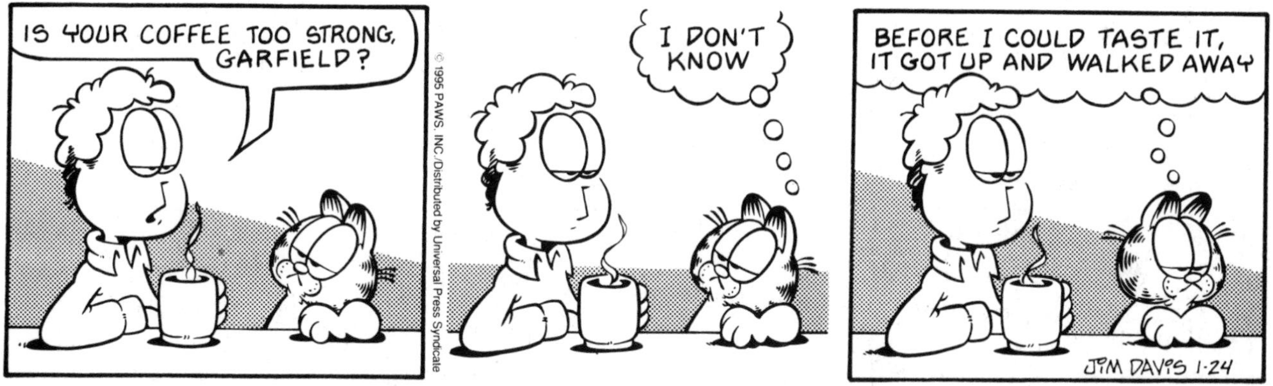
IS YOUR COFFEE TOO STRONG, GARFIELD?
I DON'T KNOW
BEFORE I COULD TASTE IT, IT GOT UP AND WALKED AWAY
JIM DAVIS 1-24

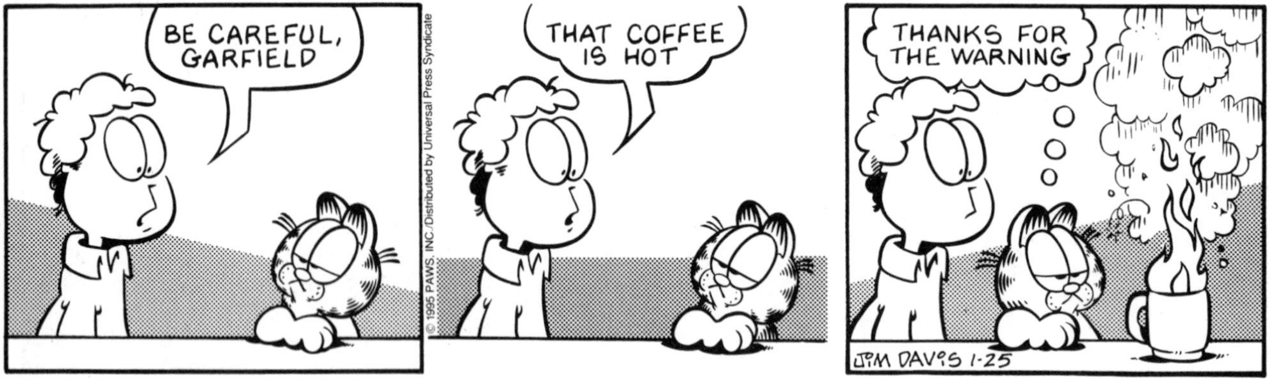
BE CAREFUL, GARFIELD
THAT COFFEE IS HOT
THANKS FOR THE WARNING
© 1995 PAWS, INC./Distributed by Universal Press Syndicate
JIM DAVIS 1-25

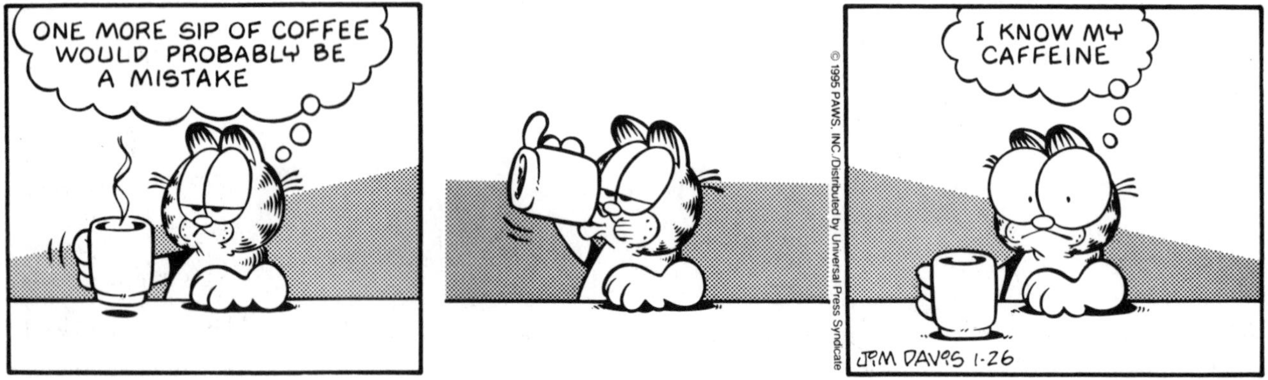
ONE MORE SIP OF COFFEE WOULD PROBABLY BE A MISTAKE
I KNOW MY CAFFEINE
© 1995 PAWS, INC./Distributed by Universal Press Syndicate
JIM DAVIS 1-26

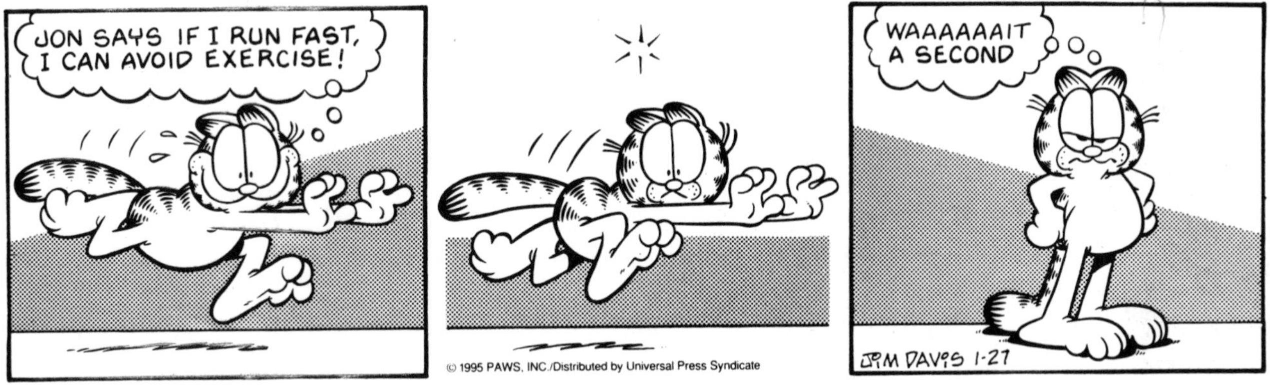
JON SAYS IF I RUN FAST, I CAN AVOID EXERCISE!
WAAAAAAIT A SECOND
© 1995 PAWS, INC./Distributed by Universal Press Syndicate
JIM DAVIS 1-27

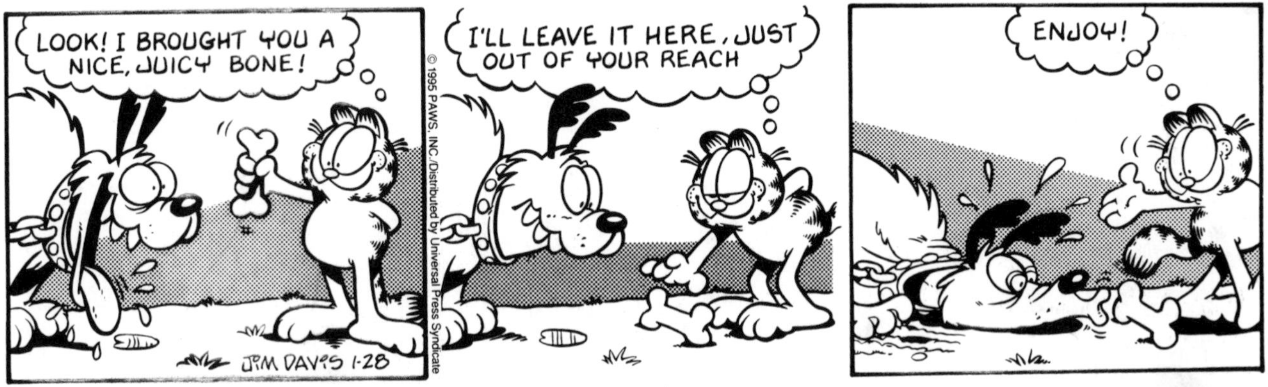
LOOK! I BROUGHT YOU A NICE, JUICY BONE!
JIM DAVIS 1-28
© 1995 PAWS, INC./Distributed by Universal Press Syndicate
I'LL LEAVE IT HERE, JUST OUT OF YOUR REACH
ENJOY!

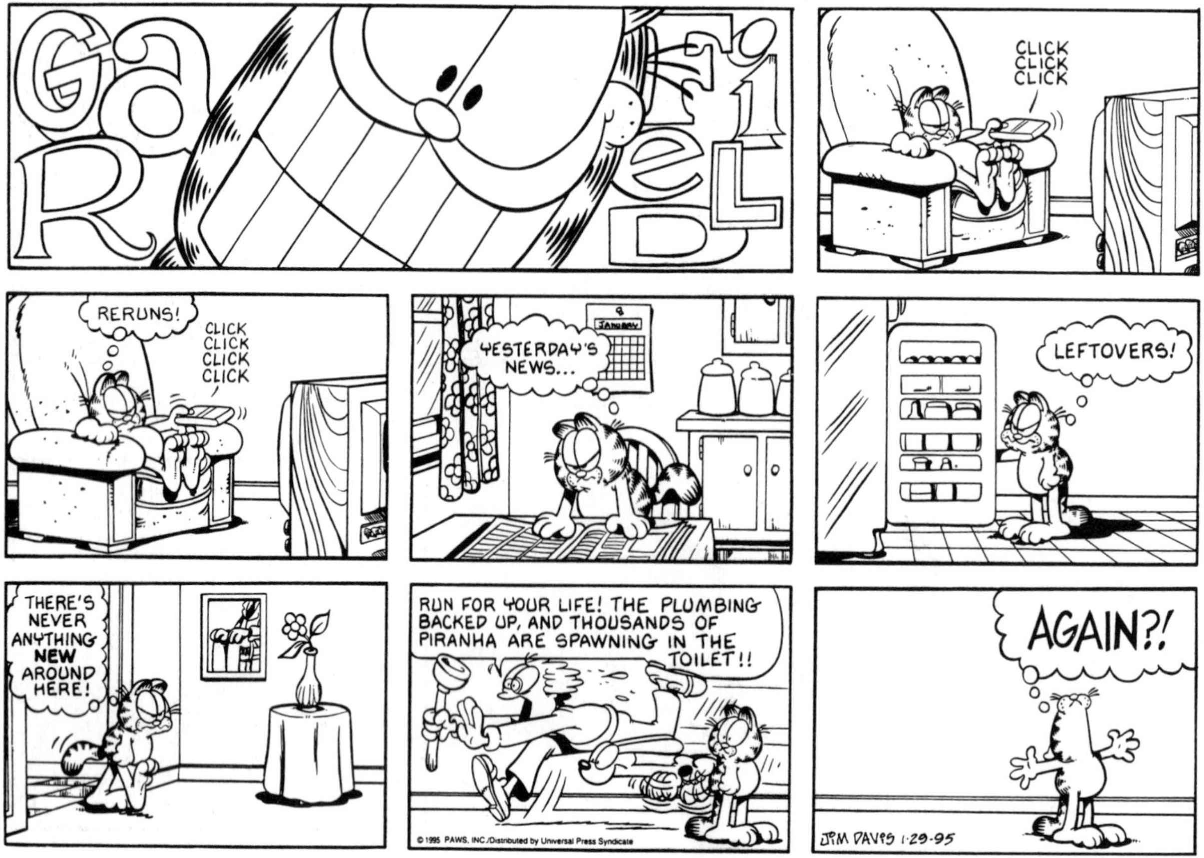
GARFIELD
CLICK CLICK CLICK
RERUNS!
CLICK CLICK CLICK CLICK
YESTERDAY'S NEWS...
LEFTOVERS!
THERE'S NEVER ANYTHING **NEW** AROUND HERE!
RUN FOR YOUR LIFE! THE PLUMBING BACKED UP, AND THOUSANDS OF PIRANHA ARE SPAWNING IN THE TOILET!!
AGAIN?!
© 1995 PAWS, INC./Distributed by Universal Press Syndicate
JIM DAVIS 1-29-95

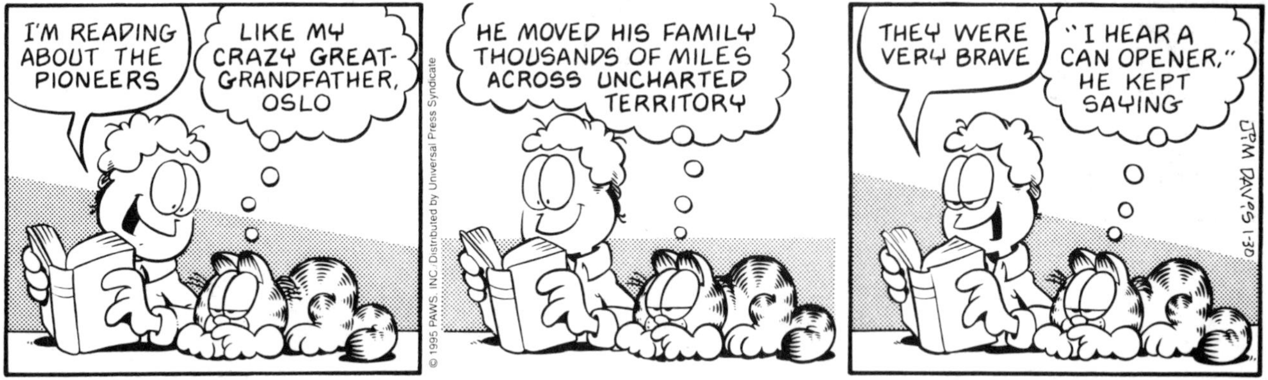
I'M READING ABOUT THE PIONEERS
LIKE MY CRAZY GREAT-GRANDFATHER, OSLO
HE MOVED HIS FAMILY THOUSANDS OF MILES ACROSS UNCHARTED TERRITORY
THEY WERE VERY BRAVE
"I HEAR A CAN OPENER," HE KEPT SAYING
JIM DAVIS 1-30
© 1995 PAWS, INC./Distributed by Universal Press Syndicate

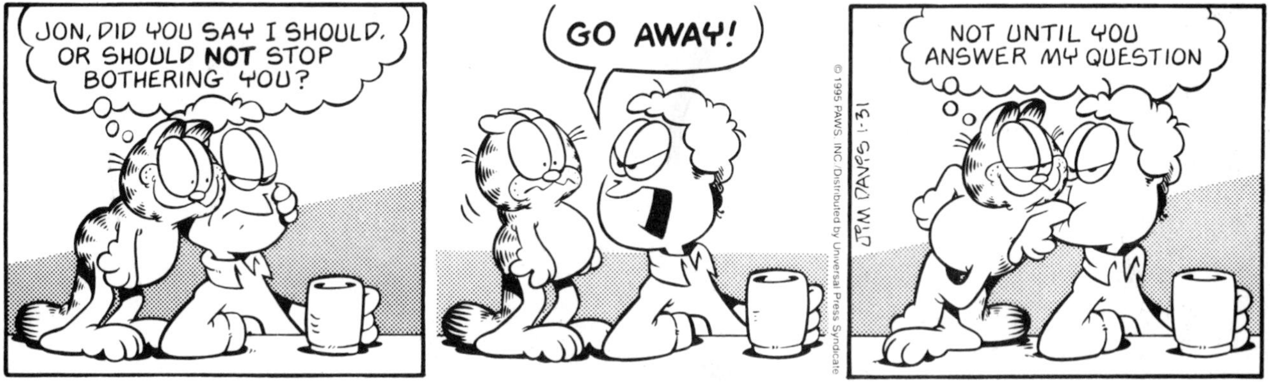
JON, DID YOU SAY I SHOULD, OR SHOULD **NOT** STOP BOTHERING YOU?
GO AWAY!
NOT UNTIL YOU ANSWER MY QUESTION
JIM DAVIS 1-31
© 1995 PAWS, INC./Distributed by Universal Press Syndicate

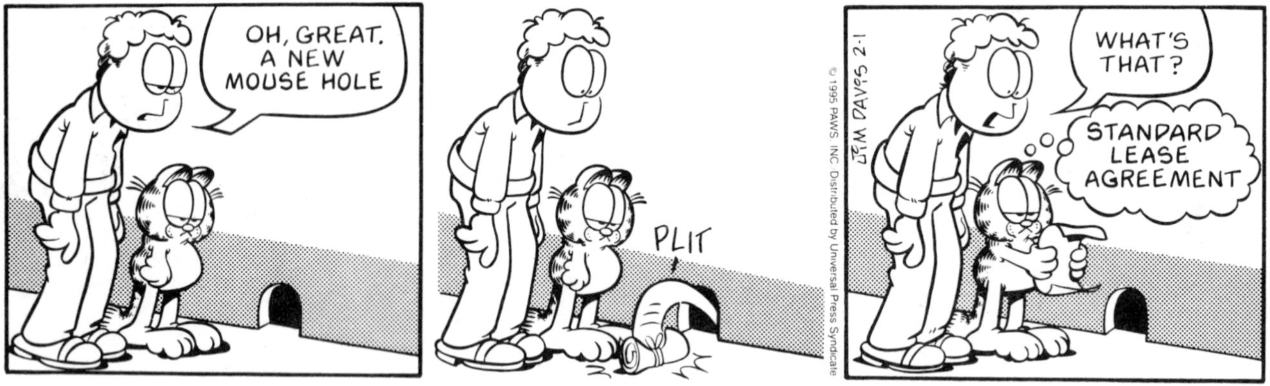
OH, GREAT. A NEW MOUSE HOLE
PLIT
© 1995 PAWS, INC. Distributed by Universal Press Syndicate
JIM DAVIS 2-1
WHAT'S THAT?
STANDARD LEASE AGREEMENT

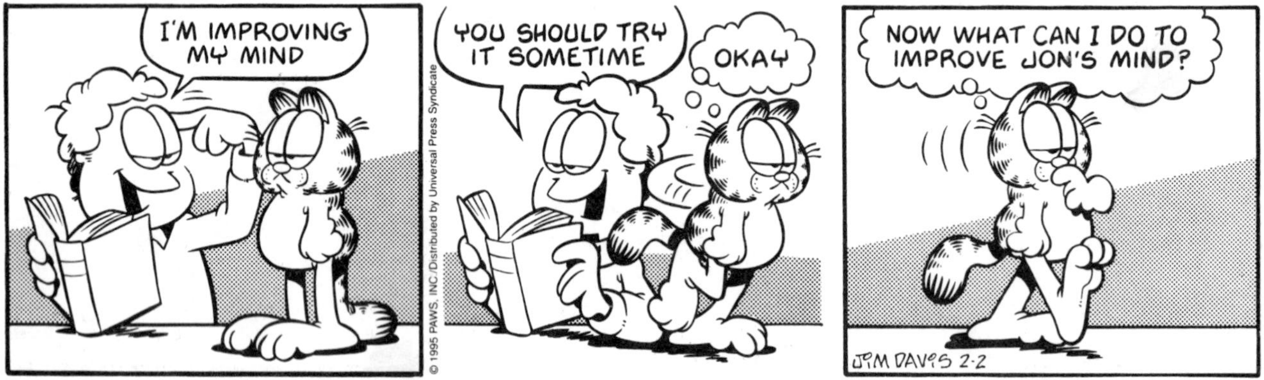
I'M IMPROVING MY MIND
© 1995 PAWS, INC./Distributed by Universal Press Syndicate
YOU SHOULD TRY IT SOMETIME
OKAY
NOW WHAT CAN I DO TO IMPROVE JON'S MIND?
JIM DAVIS 2-2

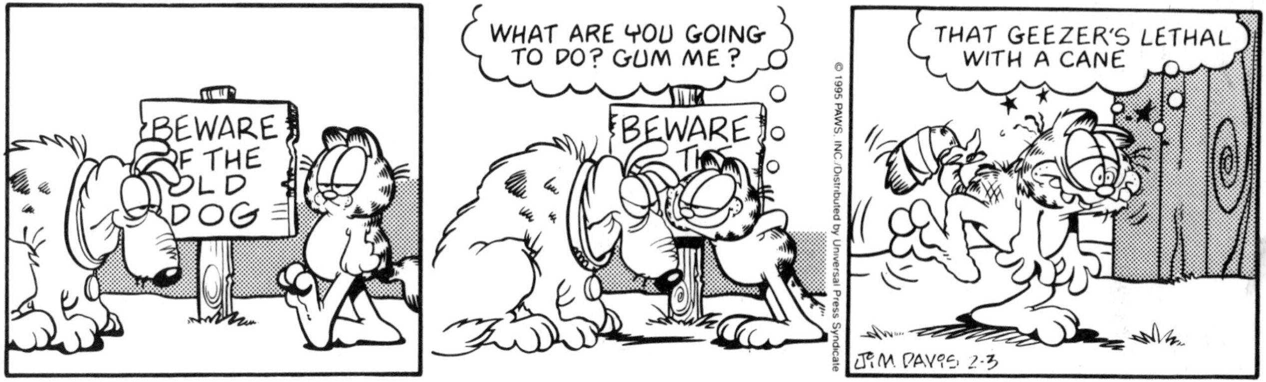
BEWARE
F THE
LD
DOG
WHAT ARE YOU GOING TO DO? GUM ME?
BEWARE
© 1995 PAWS. INC./Distributed by Universal Press Syndicate
THAT GEEZER'S LETHAL WITH A CANE
JIM DAVIS 2-3

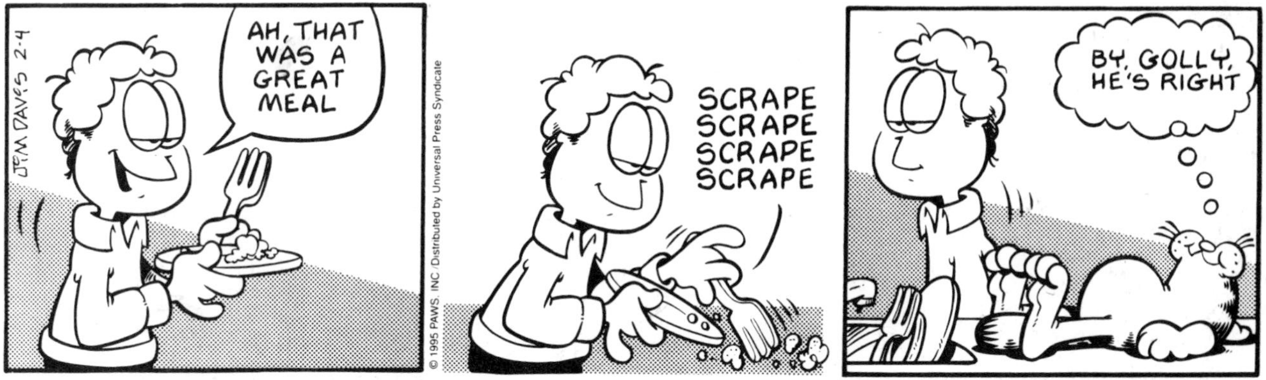
JIM DAVIS 2-4
AH, THAT WAS A GREAT MEAL
© 1995 PAWS. INC./Distributed by Universal Press Syndicate
SCRAPE SCRAPE SCRAPE SCRAPE
BY, GOLLY, HE'S RIGHT

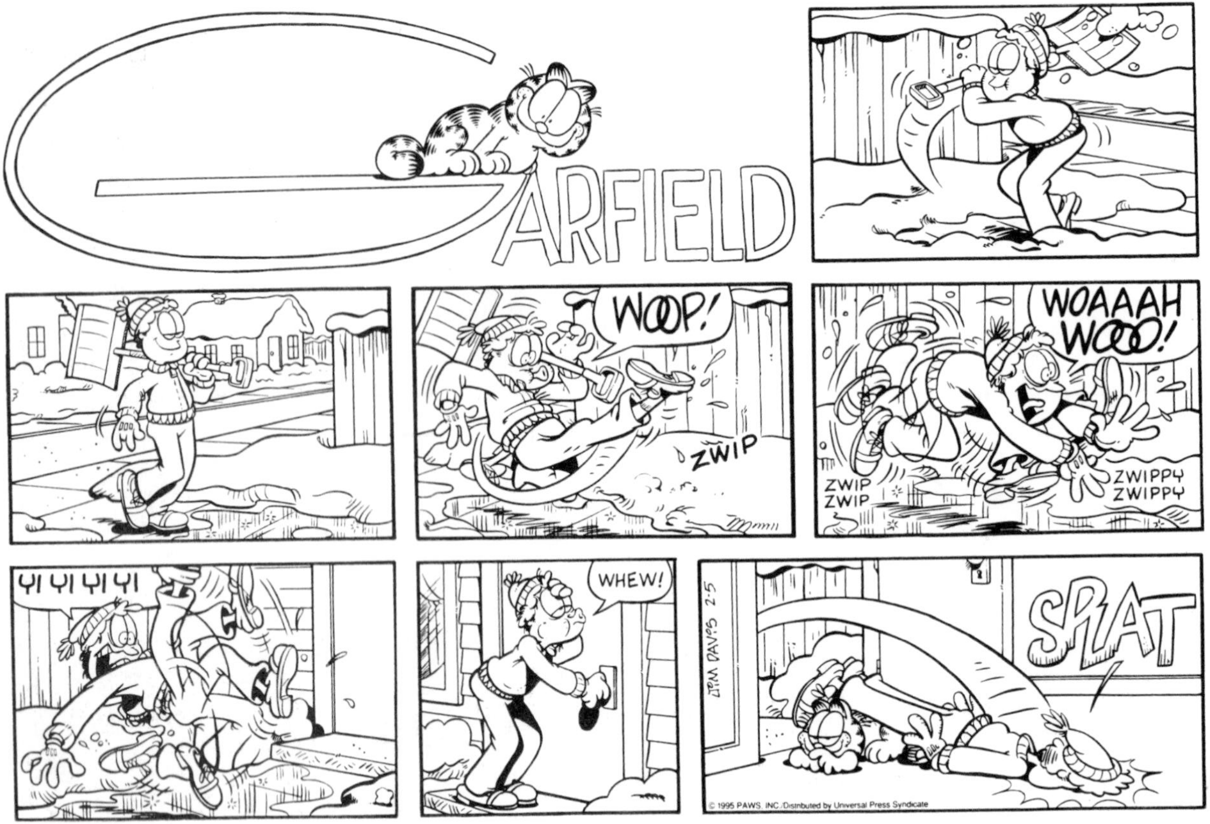
GARFIELD
WOOP!
ZWIP
WOAAAH WOOO!
ZWIP ZWIP
ZWIPPY ZWIPPY
YI YI YI YI
WHEW!
JPM DAVIS 2-5
SPLAT
© 1995 PAWS, INC./Distributed by Universal Press Syndicate

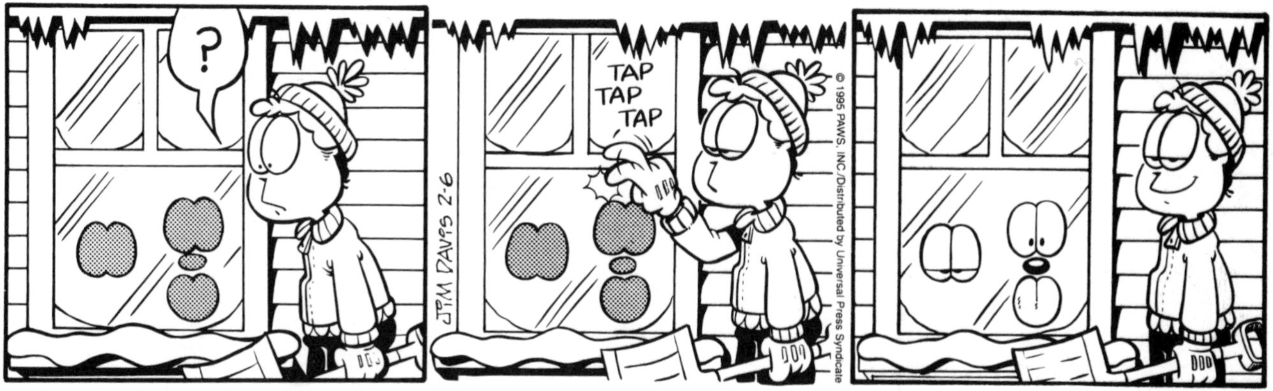
?
TAP
TAP
TAP
JIM DAVIS 2-6
© 1995 PAWS, INC./Distributed by Universal Press Syndicate

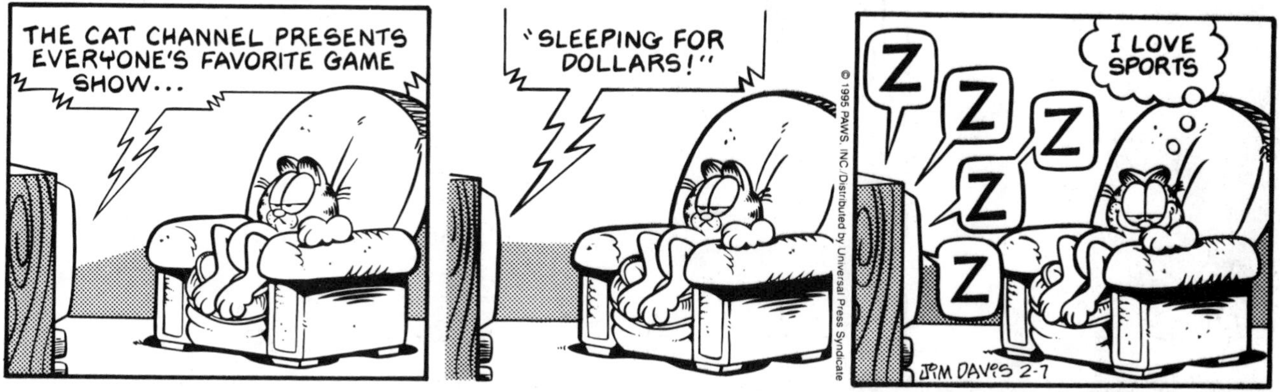
THE CAT CHANNEL PRESENTS EVERYONE'S FAVORITE GAME SHOW...
"SLEEPING FOR DOLLARS!"
Z
Z
Z
Z
Z
I LOVE SPORTS
JIM DAVIS 2-7
© 1995 PAWS, INC./Distributed by Universal Press Syndicate

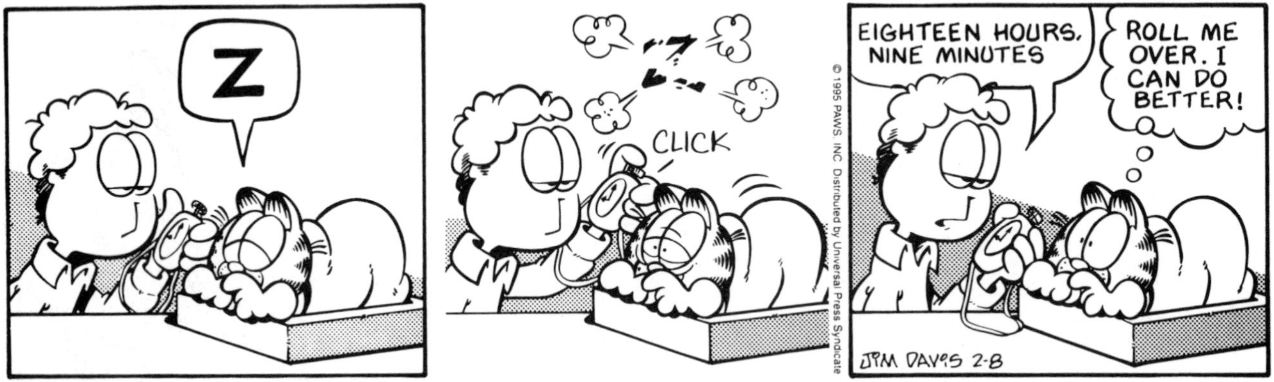
Z
CLICK
EIGHTEEN HOURS, NINE MINUTES
ROLL ME OVER. I CAN DO BETTER!
© 1995 PAWS, INC Distributed by Universal Press Syndicate
JIM DAVIS 2-8

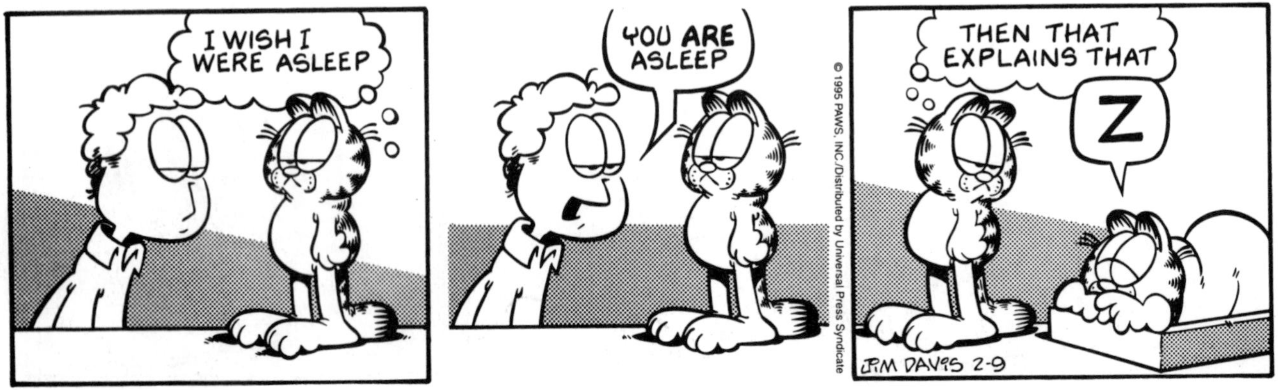
I WISH I WERE ASLEEP
YOU **ARE** ASLEEP
THEN THAT EXPLAINS THAT
Z
© 1995 PAWS, INC/Distributed by Universal Press Syndicate
JIM DAVIS 2-9

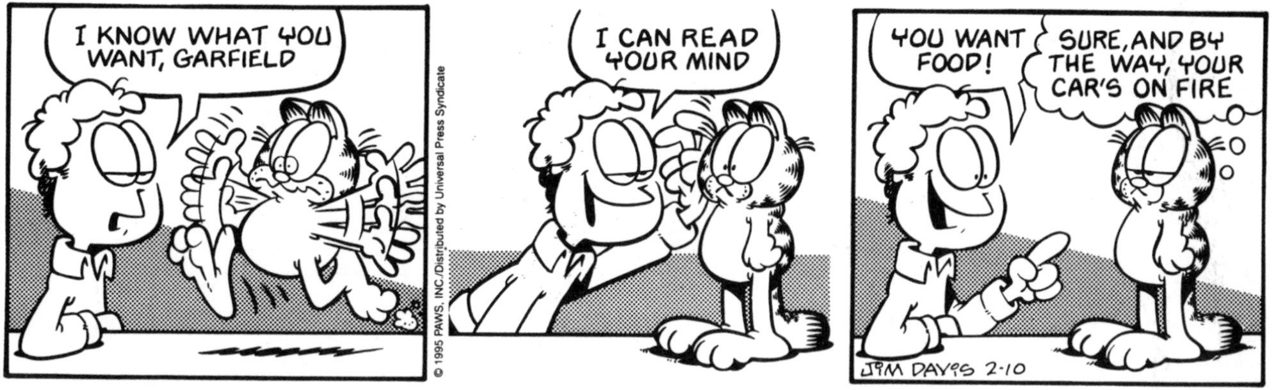
I KNOW WHAT YOU WANT, GARFIELD
I CAN READ YOUR MIND
YOU WANT FOOD!
SURE, AND BY THE WAY, YOUR CAR'S ON FIRE
JIM DAVIS 2-10

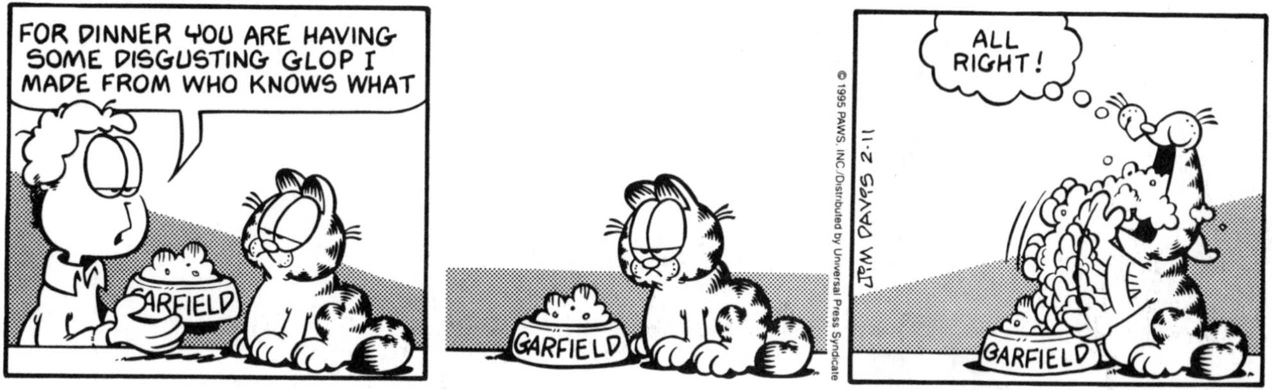
FOR DINNER YOU ARE HAVING SOME DISGUSTING GLOP I MADE FROM WHO KNOWS WHAT
GARFIELD
GARFIELD
ALL RIGHT!
GARFIELD
JIM DAVIS 2-11

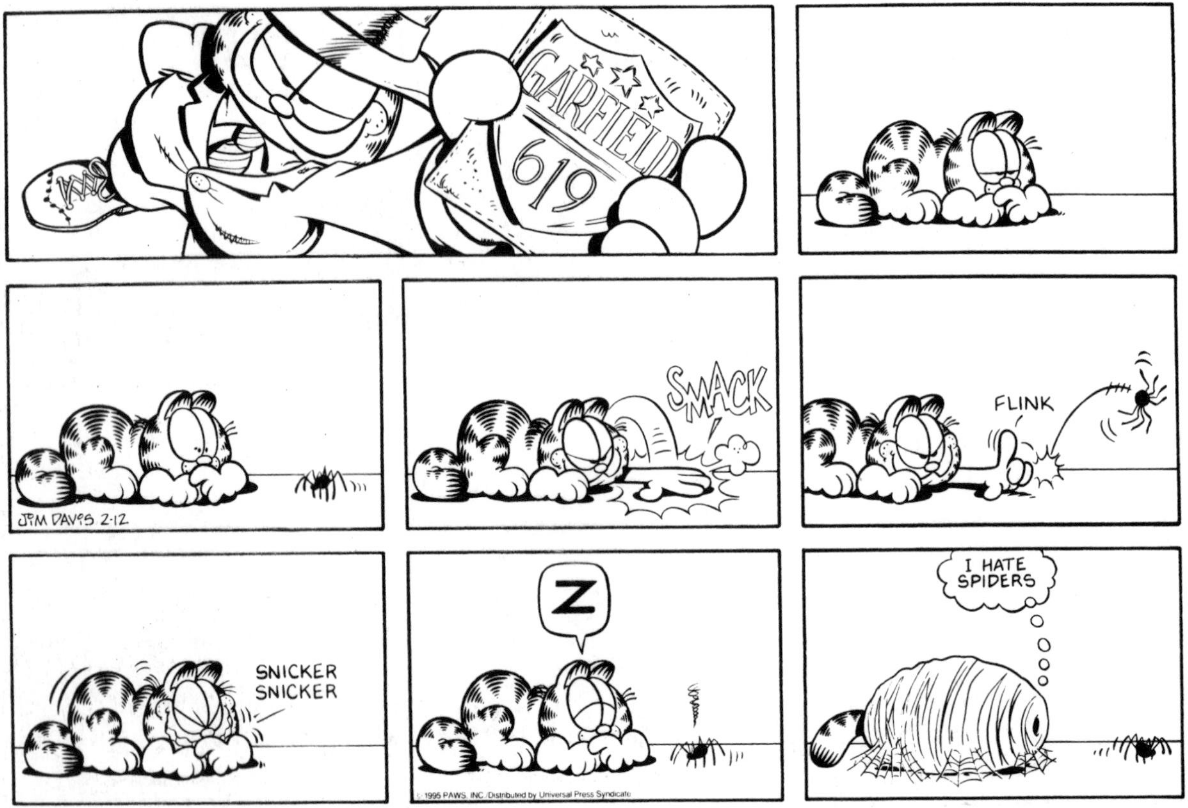
GARFIELD
619
JIM DAVIS 2-12
SMACK
FLINK
SNICKER
SNICKER
Z
© 1995 PAWS, INC./Distributed by Universal Press Syndicate
I HATE SPIDERS

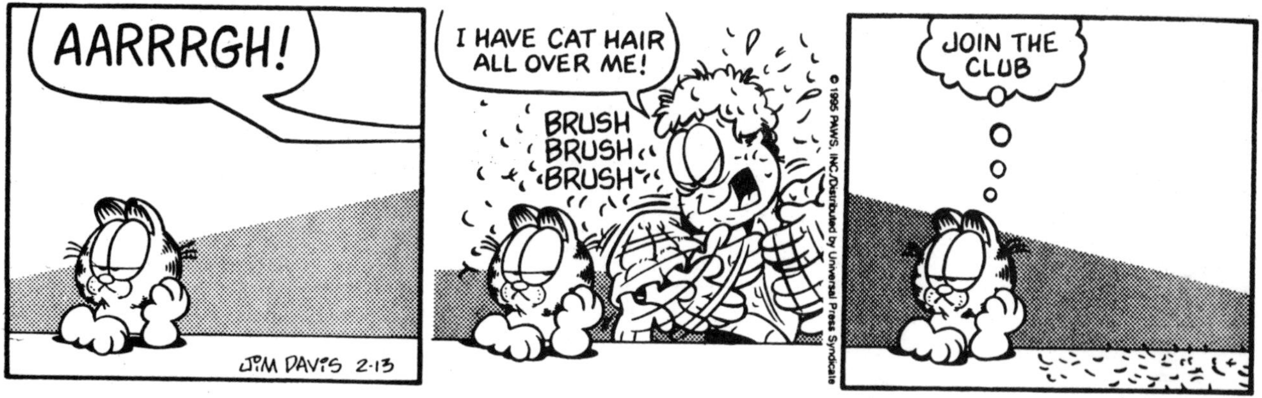
AARRRGH!
JIM DAVIS 2-13
I HAVE CAT HAIR ALL OVER ME!
BRUSH BRUSH BRUSH
© 1995 PAWS, INC./Distributed by Universal Press Syndicate
JOIN THE CLUB

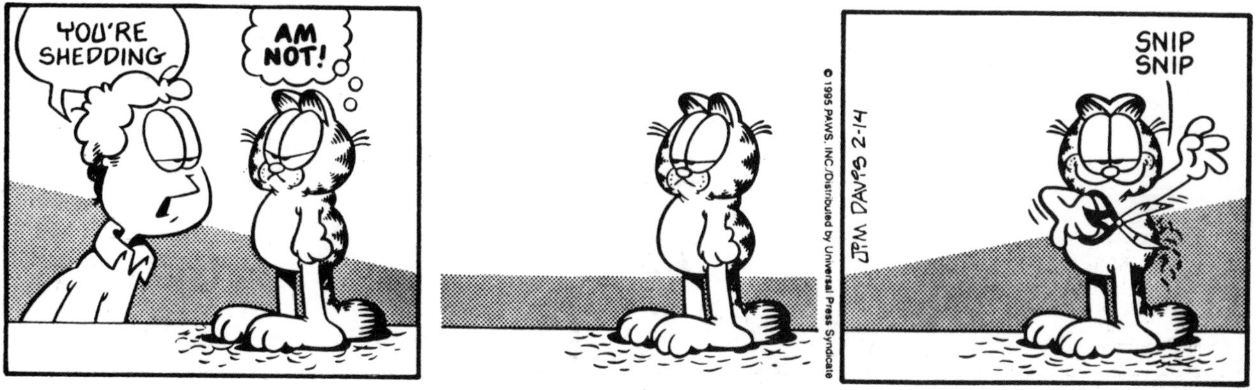
YOU'RE SHEDDING
AM NOT!
JIM DAVIS 2-14
© 1995 PAWS, INC./Distributed by Universal Press Syndicate
SNIP SNIP

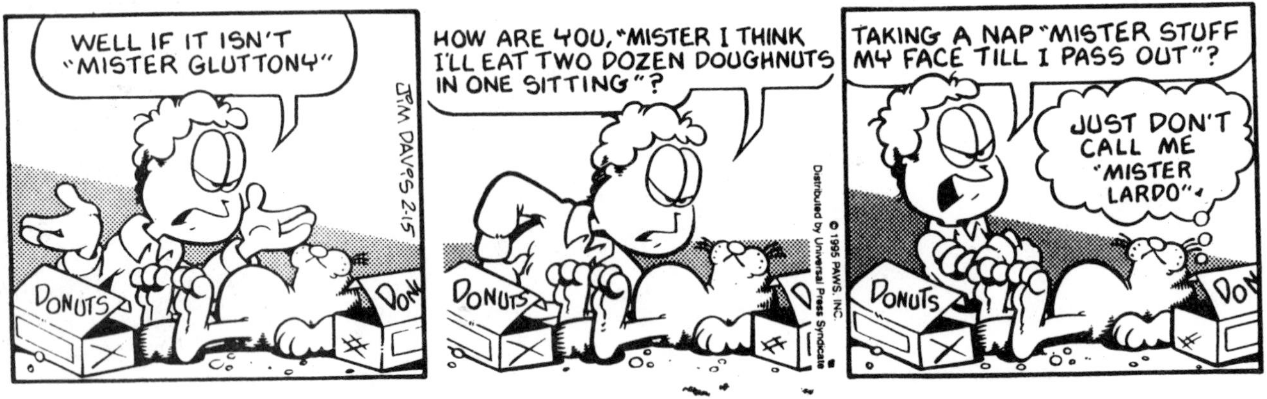
WELL IF IT ISN'T "MISTER GLUTTONY"
JIM DAVIS 2-15
HOW ARE YOU, "MISTER I THINK I'LL EAT TWO DOZEN DOUGHNUTS IN ONE SITTING"?
DONUTS
© 1995 PAWS, INC. Distributed by Universal Press Syndicate
TAKING A NAP "MISTER STUFF MY FACE TILL I PASS OUT"?
JUST DON'T CALL ME "MISTER LARDO"
DONUTS

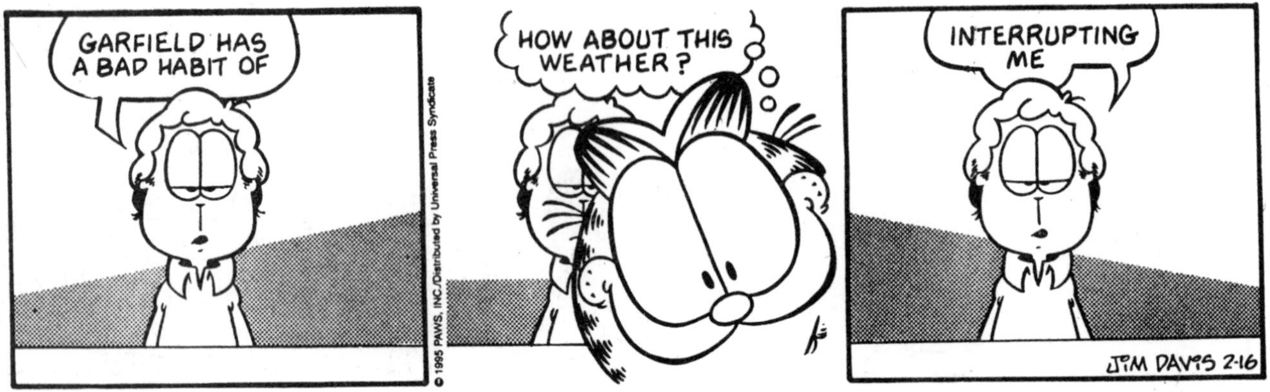
GARFIELD HAS A BAD HABIT OF
© 1995 PAWS, INC./Distributed by Universal Press Syndicate
HOW ABOUT THIS WEATHER?
INTERRUPTING ME
JIM DAVIS 2-16

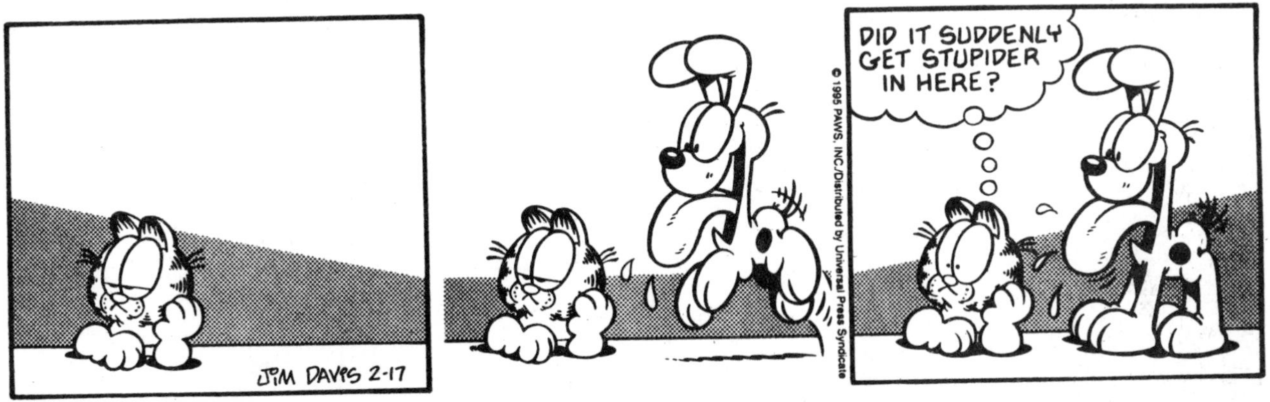
JIM DAVIS 2-17
© 1995 PAWS, INC./Distributed by Universal Press Syndicate
DID IT SUDDENLY GET STUPIDER IN HERE?

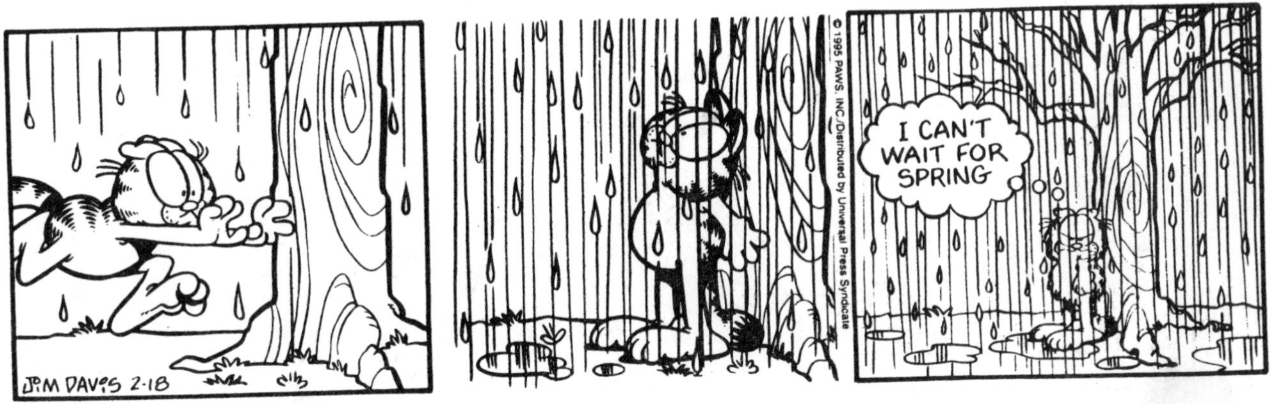
JIM DAVIS 2-18
© 1995 PAWS, INC./Distributed by Universal Press Syndicate
I CAN'T WAIT FOR SPRING

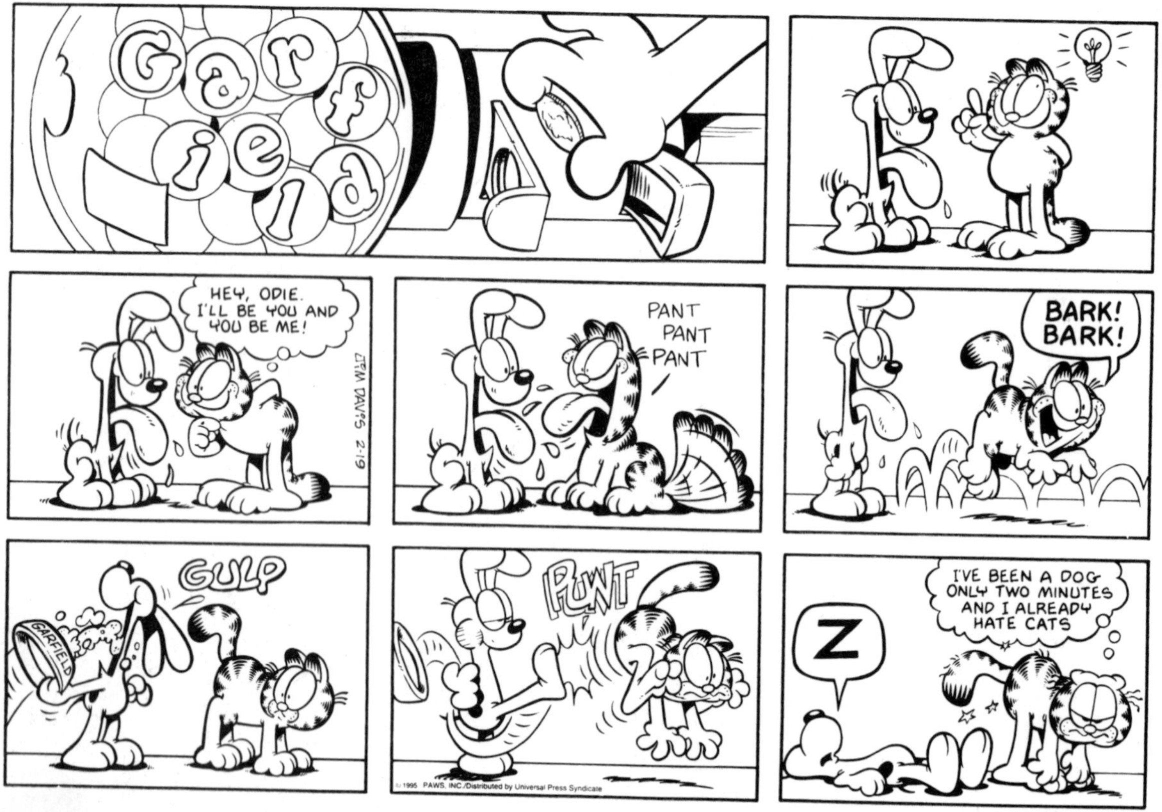
Garfield
HEY, ODIE. I'LL BE YOU AND YOU BE ME!
JIM DAVIS 2-19
PANT PANT PANT
BARK! BARK!
GULP
GARFIELD
PUNT
© 1995 PAWS, INC./Distributed by Universal Press Syndicate
Z
I'VE BEEN A DOG ONLY TWO MINUTES AND I ALREADY HATE CATS

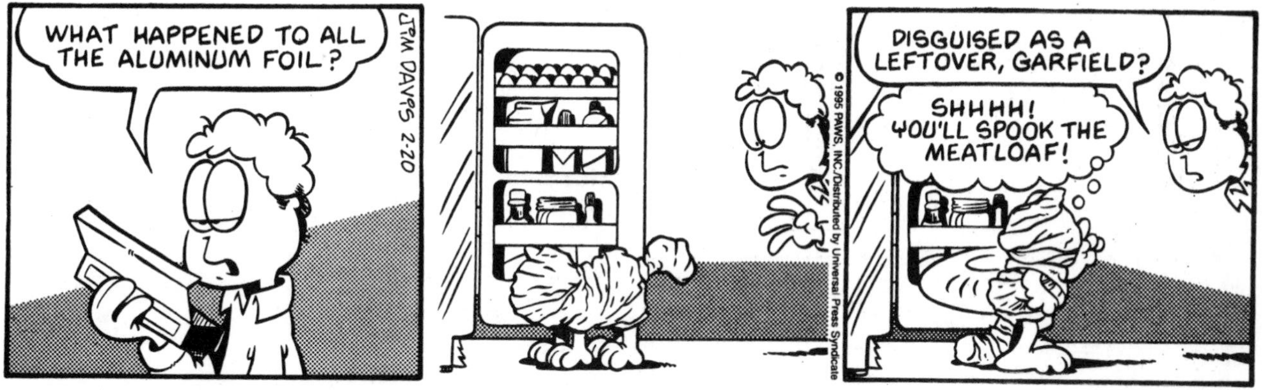
WHAT HAPPENED TO ALL THE ALUMINUM FOIL?
JIM DAVIS 2-20
© 1995 PAWS, INC./Distributed by Universal Press Syndicate
DISGUISED AS A LEFTOVER, GARFIELD?
SHHHH! YOU'LL SPOOK THE MEATLOAF!

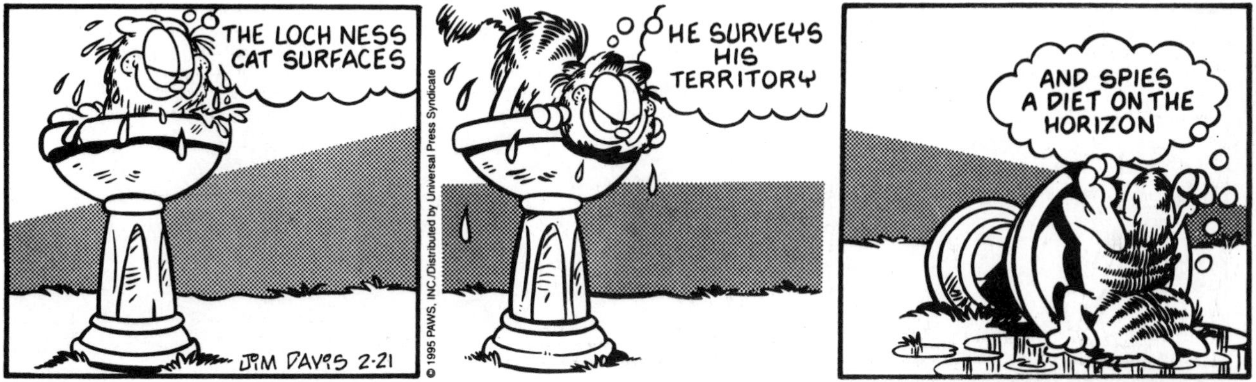
THE LOCH NESS CAT SURFACES
JIM DAVIS 2-21
© 1995 PAWS, INC./Distributed by Universal Press Syndicate
HE SURVEYS HIS TERRITORY
AND SPIES A DIET ON THE HORIZON

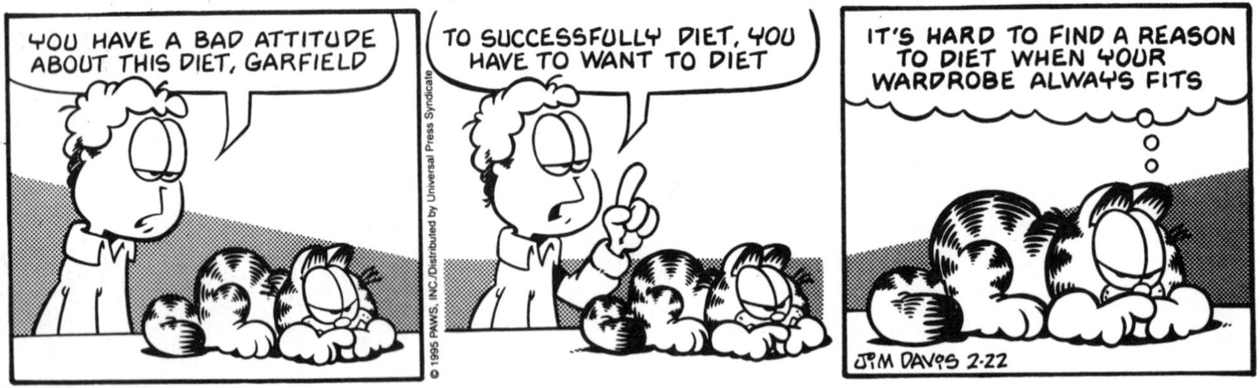
YOU HAVE A BAD ATTITUDE ABOUT THIS DIET, GARFIELD
TO SUCCESSFULLY DIET, YOU HAVE TO WANT TO DIET
IT'S HARD TO FIND A REASON TO DIET WHEN YOUR WARDROBE ALWAYS FITS
JIM DAVIS 2·22
© 1995 PAWS, INC./Distributed by Universal Press Syndicate

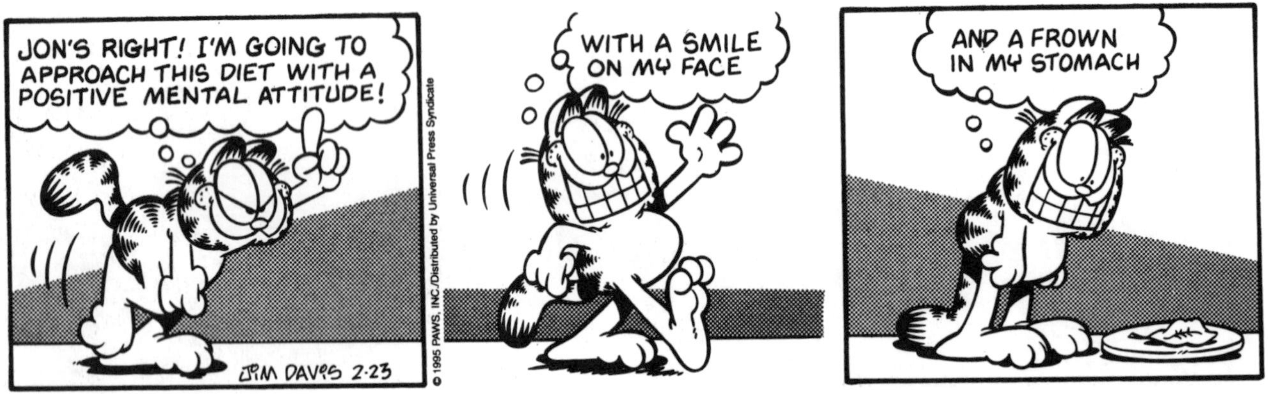
JON'S RIGHT! I'M GOING TO APPROACH THIS DIET WITH A POSITIVE MENTAL ATTITUDE!
WITH A SMILE ON MY FACE
AND A FROWN IN MY STOMACH
JIM DAVIS 2·23
© 1995 PAWS, INC./Distributed by Universal Press Syndicate

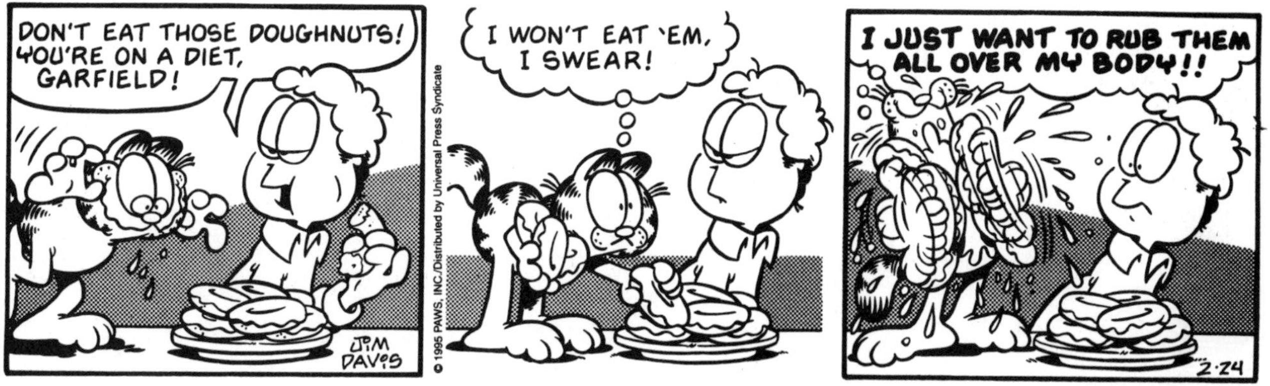

DON'T EAT THOSE DOUGHNUTS! YOU'RE ON A DIET, GARFIELD!
JIM DAVIS
© 1995 PAWS, INC./Distributed by Universal Press Syndicate
I WON'T EAT 'EM, I SWEAR!
I JUST WANT TO RUB THEM ALL OVER MY BODY!!
2·24

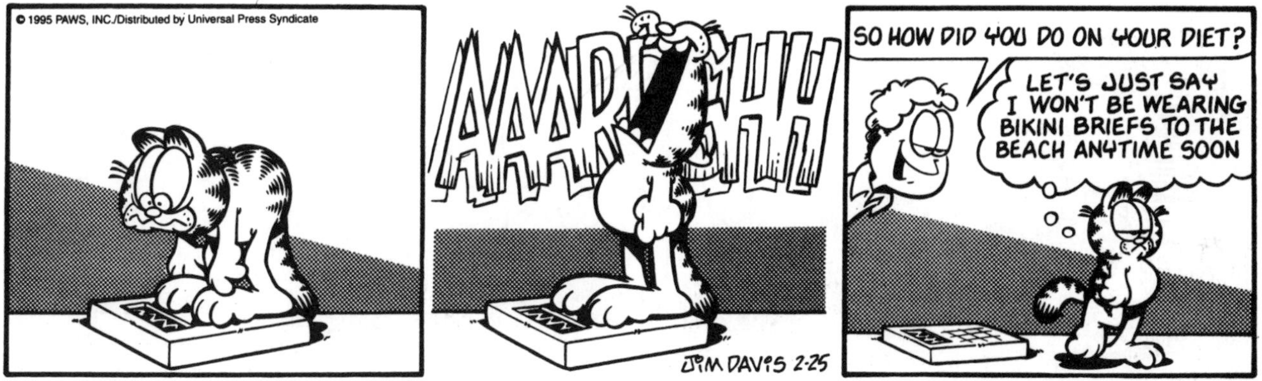

© 1995 PAWS, INC./Distributed by Universal Press Syndicate
JIM DAVIS 2·25
SO HOW DID YOU DO ON YOUR DIET?
LET'S JUST SAY I WON'T BE WEARING BIKINI BRIEFS TO THE BEACH ANYTIME SOON

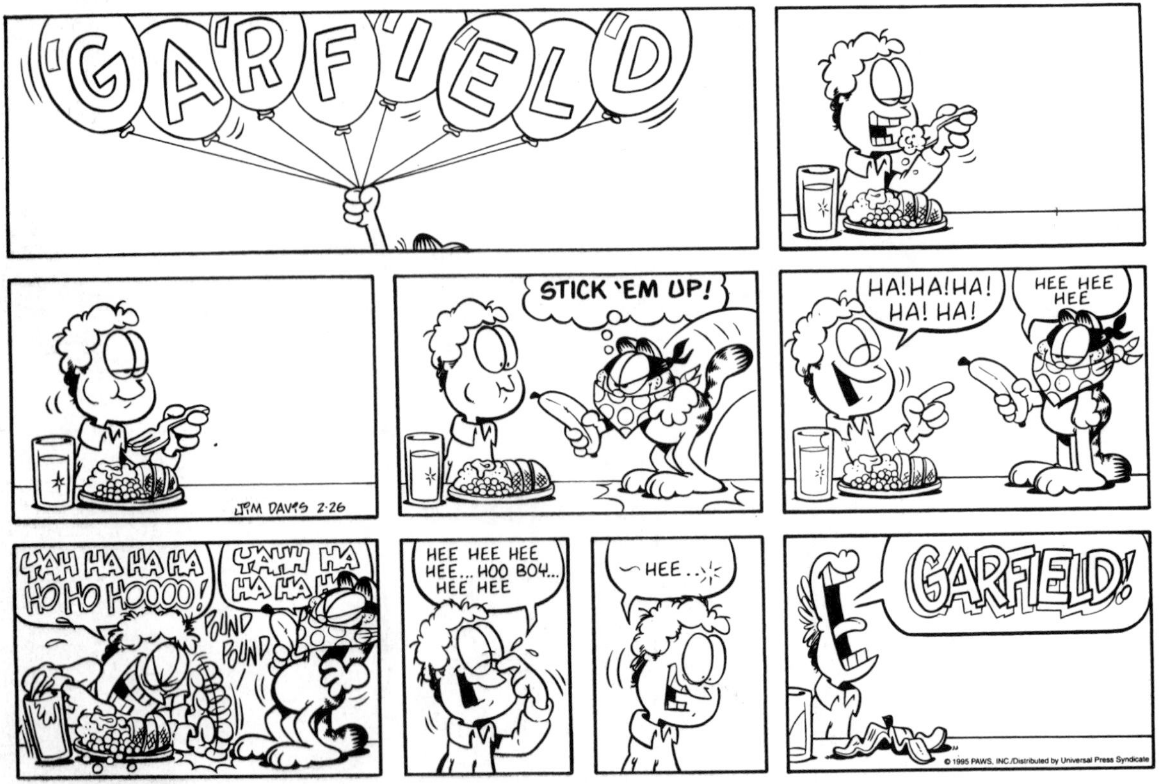
GARFIELD
JIM DAVIS 2·26
STICK 'EM UP!
HA! HA! HA! HA! HA!
HEE HEE HEE
YAH HA HA HA HO HO HOOOO!
YAHH HA HA HA H
POUND POUND
HEE HEE HEE HEE... HOO BOY... HEE HEE
HEE..
GARFIELD!
© 1995 PAWS, INC./Distributed by Universal Press Syndicate

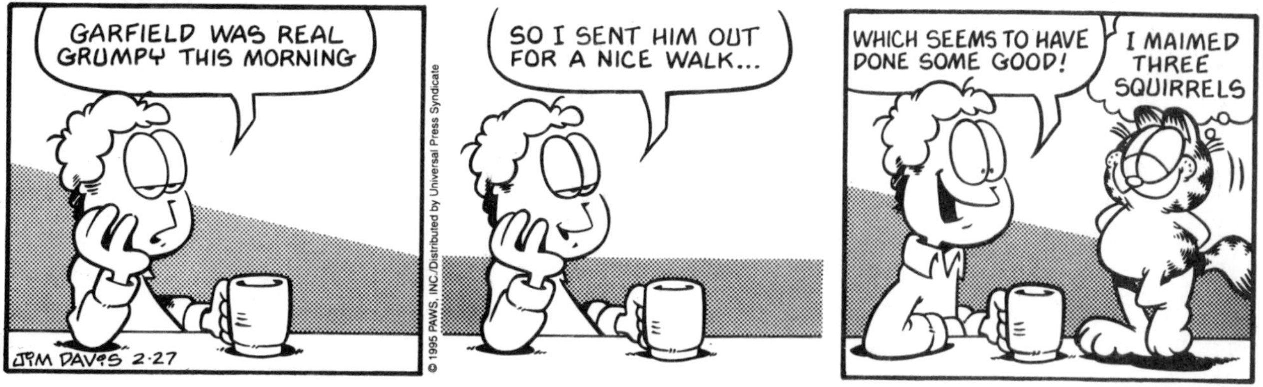
GARFIELD WAS REAL GRUMPY THIS MORNING
SO I SENT HIM OUT FOR A NICE WALK...
WHICH SEEMS TO HAVE DONE SOME GOOD!
I MAIMED THREE SQUIRRELS
JIM DAVIS 2·27

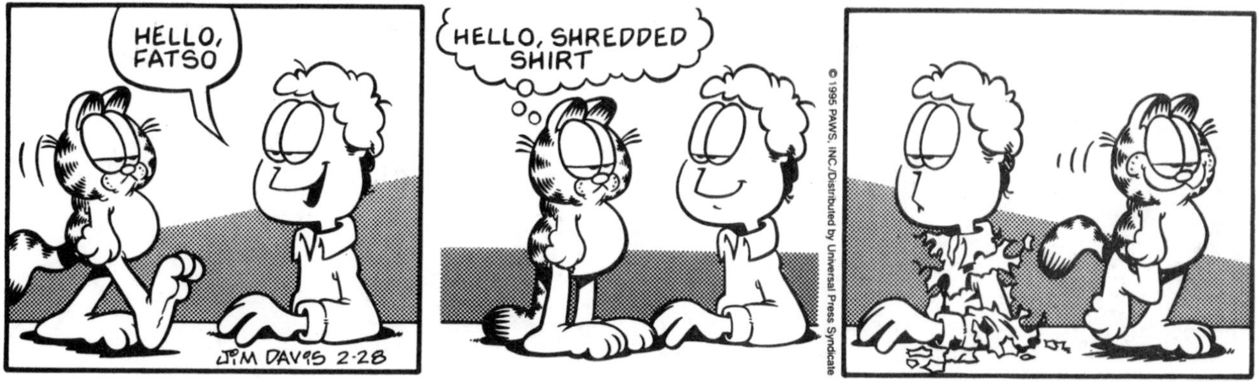
HELLO, FATSO
HELLO, SHREDDED SHIRT
JIM DAVIS 2·28

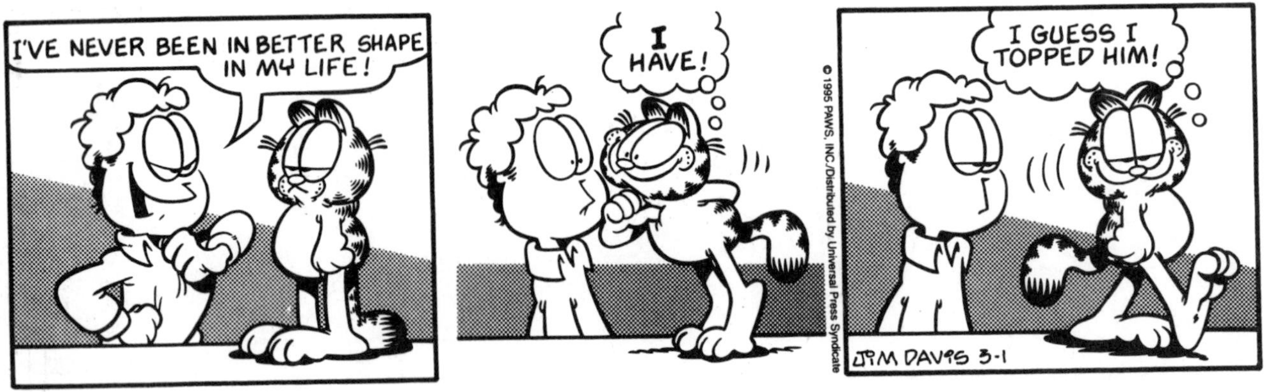
I'VE NEVER BEEN IN BETTER SHAPE IN MY LIFE!
I HAVE!
I GUESS I TOPPED HIM!
© 1995 PAWS, INC./Distributed by Universal Press Syndicate
JIM DAVIS 3-1

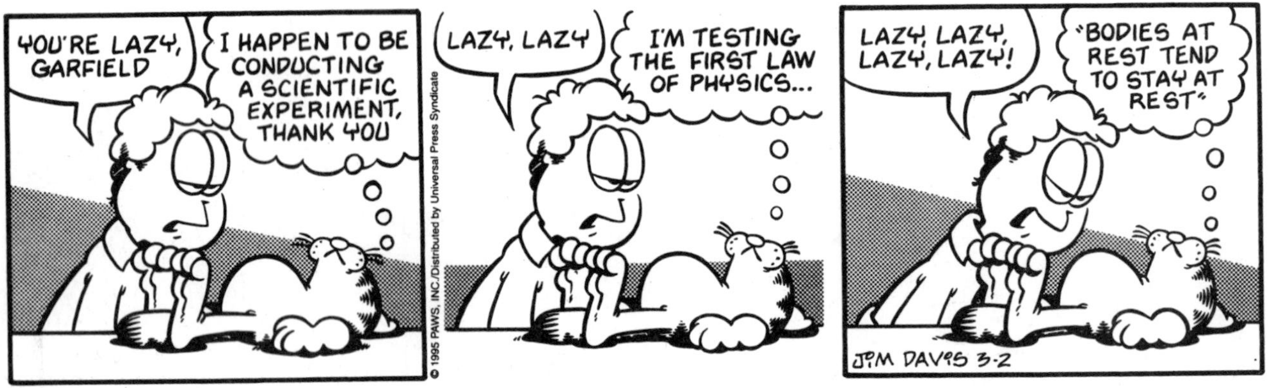
YOU'RE LAZY, GARFIELD
I HAPPEN TO BE CONDUCTING A SCIENTIFIC EXPERIMENT, THANK YOU
© 1995 PAWS, INC./Distributed by Universal Press Syndicate
LAZY, LAZY
I'M TESTING THE FIRST LAW OF PHYSICS...
LAZY, LAZY, LAZY, LAZY!
"BODIES AT REST TEND TO STAY AT REST"
JIM DAVIS 3-2

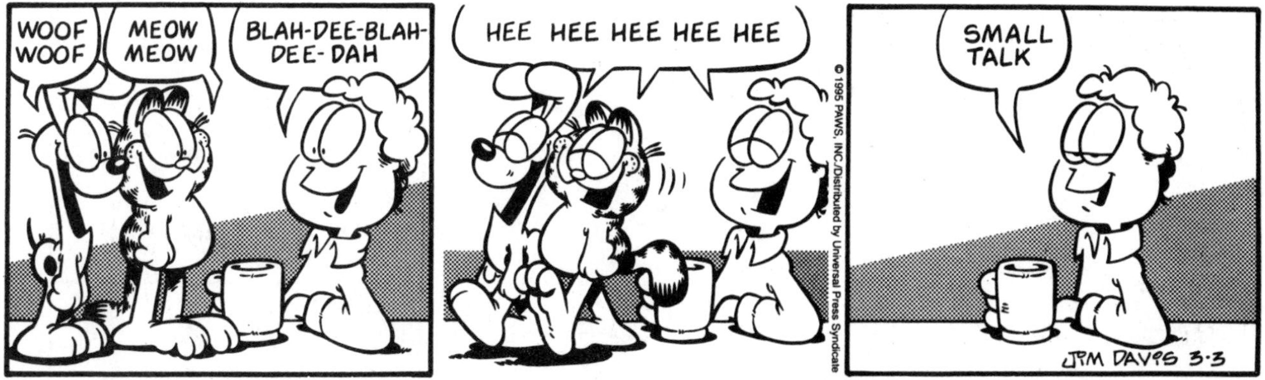
WOOF WOOF
MEOW MEOW
BLAH-DEE-BLAH-DEE-DAH
HEE HEE HEE HEE HEE
© 1995 PAWS, INC./Distributed by Universal Press Syndicate
SMALL TALK
JIM DAVIS 3-3

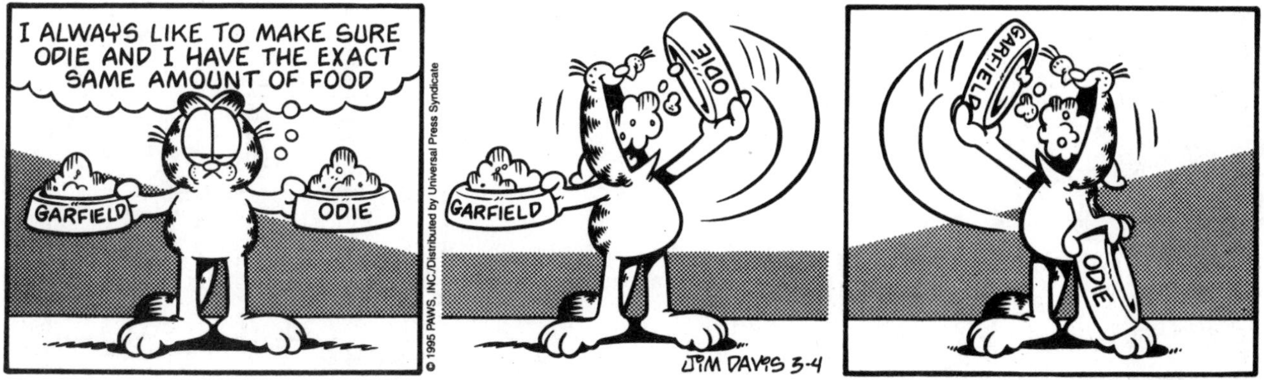
I ALWAYS LIKE TO MAKE SURE ODIE AND I HAVE THE EXACT SAME AMOUNT OF FOOD
GARFIELD
ODIE
© 1995 PAWS, INC./Distributed by Universal Press Syndicate
GARFIELD
ODIE
JIM DAVIS 3-4
GARFIELD
ODIE

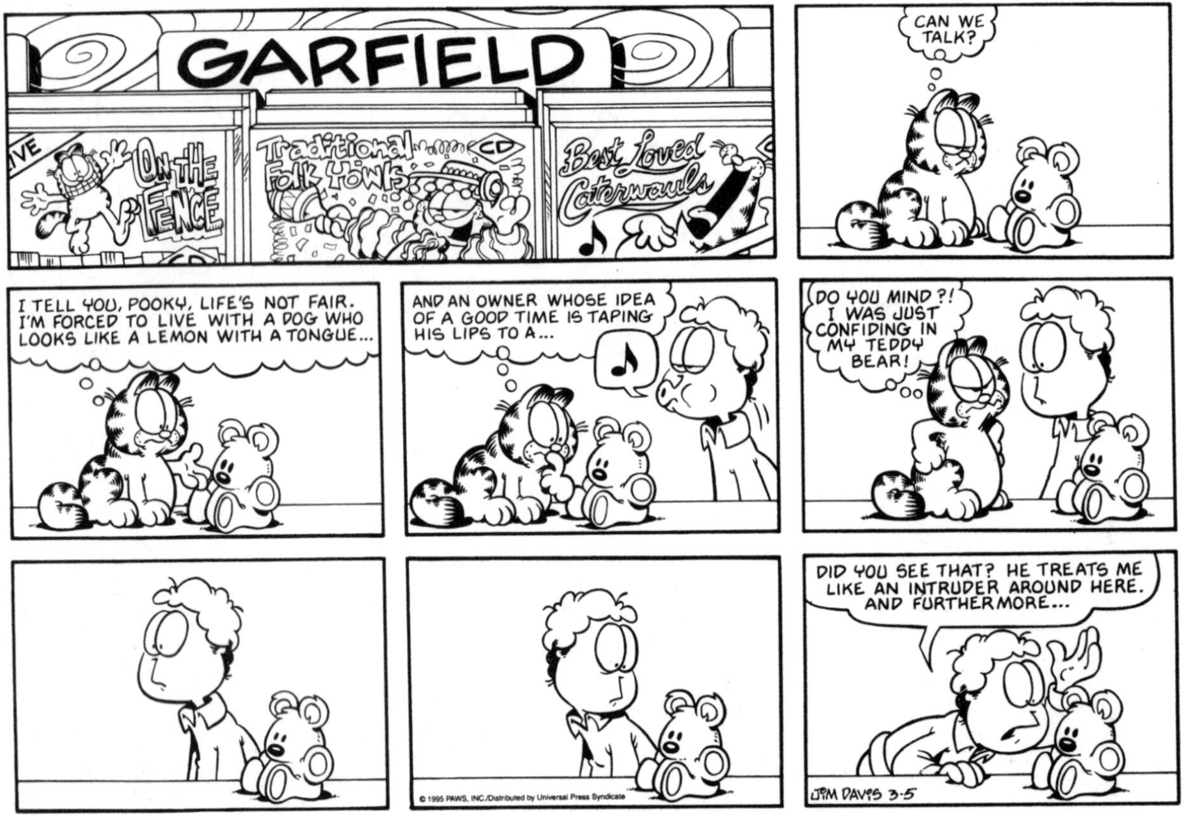
GARFIELD
LIVE
ON THE FENCE
Traditional Folk Yowls
CD
Best Loved Caterwauls
CAN WE TALK?
I TELL YOU, POOKY, LIFE'S NOT FAIR. I'M FORCED TO LIVE WITH A DOG WHO LOOKS LIKE A LEMON WITH A TONGUE...
AND AN OWNER WHOSE IDEA OF A GOOD TIME IS TAPING HIS LIPS TO A...
♪
DO YOU MIND?! I WAS JUST CONFIDING IN MY TEDDY BEAR!
© 1995 PAWS, INC./Distributed by Universal Press Syndicate
DID YOU SEE THAT? HE TREATS ME LIKE AN INTRUDER AROUND HERE. AND FURTHERMORE...
JIM DAVIS 3-5

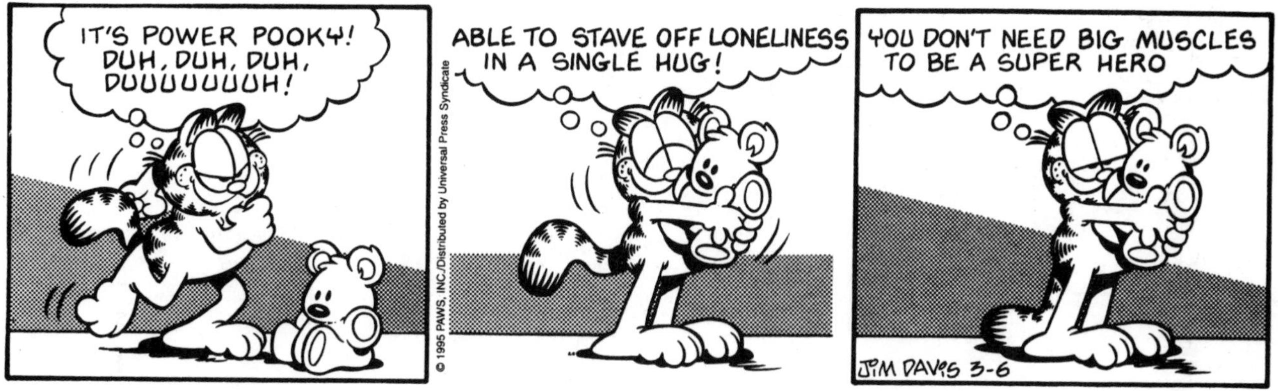
IT'S POWER POOKY! DUH, DUH, DUH, DUUUUUUUH!
© 1995 PAWS, INC./Distributed by Universal Press Syndicate
ABLE TO STAVE OFF LONELINESS IN A SINGLE HUG!
YOU DON'T NEED BIG MUSCLES TO BE A SUPER HERO
JIM DAVIS 3-6

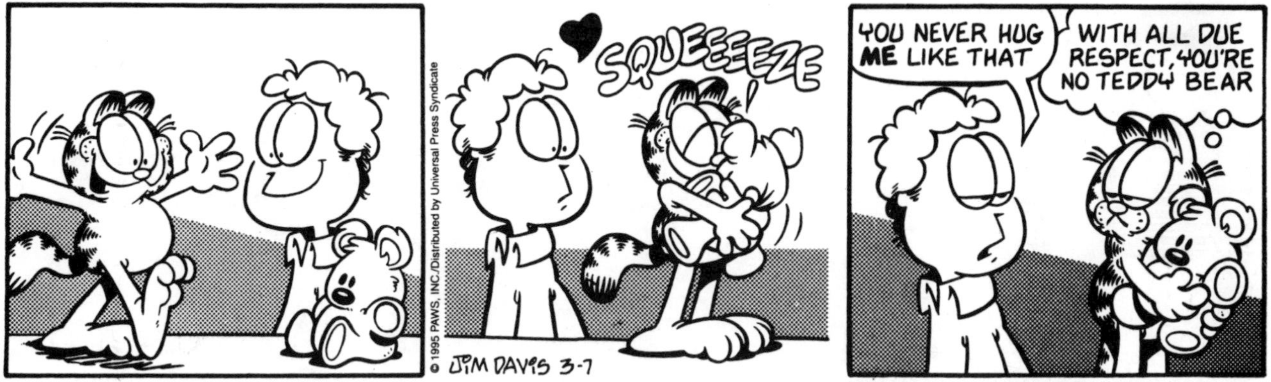
© 1995 PAWS, INC./Distributed by Universal Press Syndicate
SQUEEEEEZE
JIM DAVIS 3-7
YOU NEVER HUG **ME** LIKE THAT
WITH ALL DUE RESPECT, YOU'RE NO TEDDY BEAR

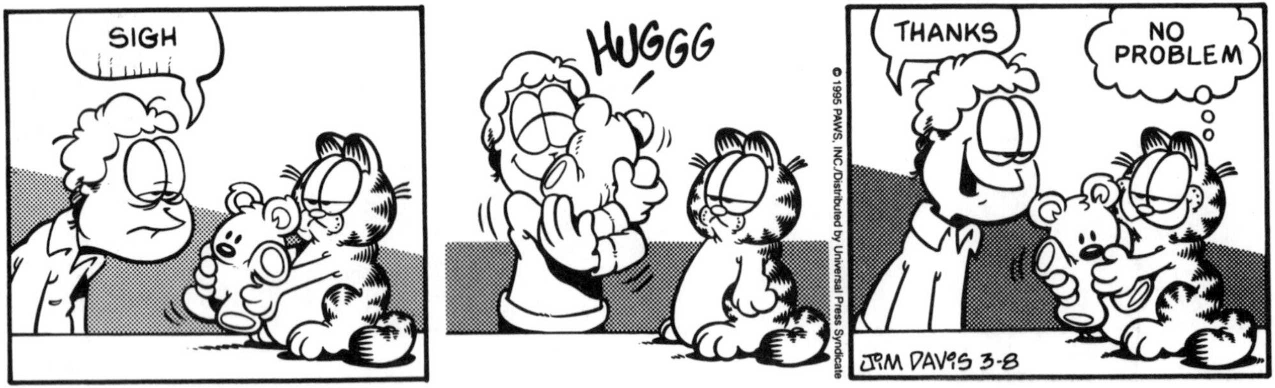
SIGH
HUGGG
THANKS
NO PROBLEM
JIM DAVIS 3-8
© 1995 PAWS, INC./Distributed by Universal Press Syndicate

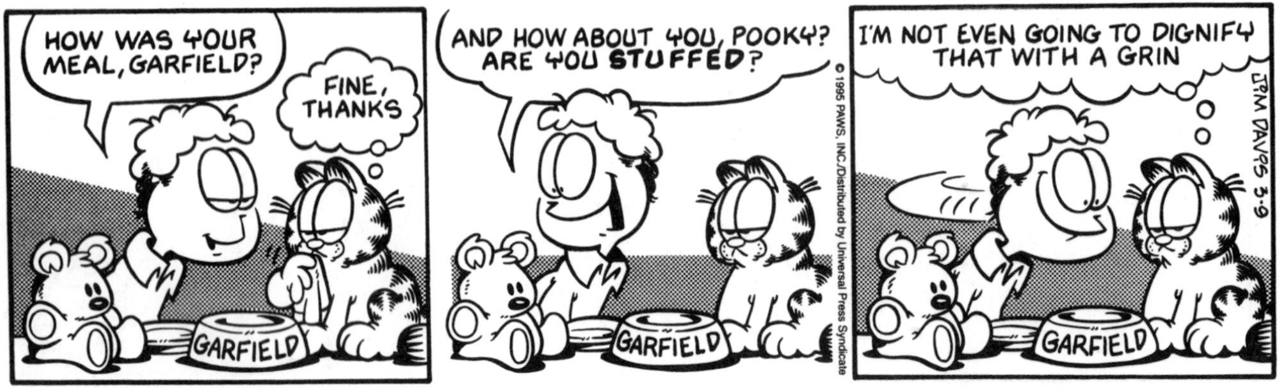
HOW WAS YOUR MEAL, GARFIELD?
FINE, THANKS
AND HOW ABOUT YOU, POOKY? ARE YOU **STUFFED**?
I'M NOT EVEN GOING TO DIGNIFY THAT WITH A GRIN
GARFIELD
GARFIELD
GARFIELD
JIM DAVIS 3-9
© 1995 PAWS, INC./Distributed by Universal Press Syndicate

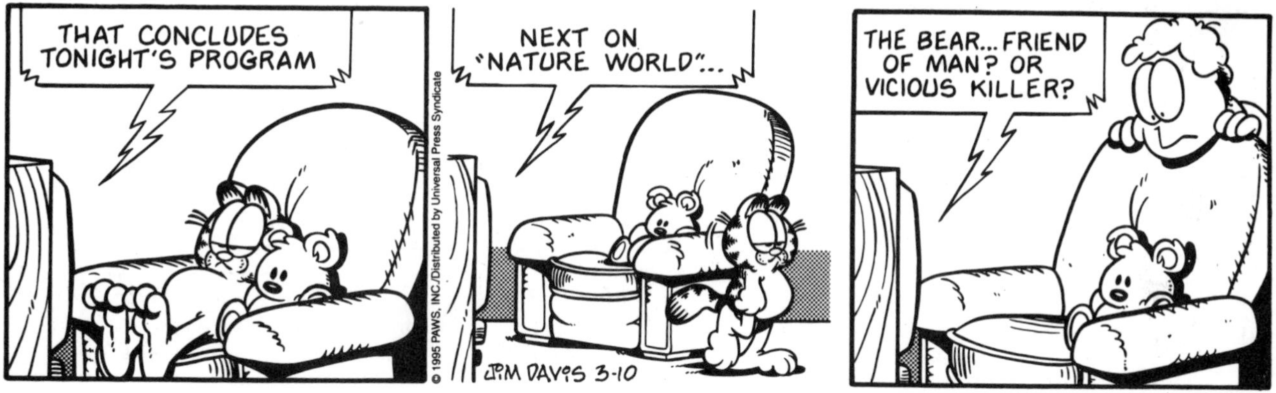
THAT CONCLUDES TONIGHT'S PROGRAM
NEXT ON "NATURE WORLD"...
THE BEAR... FRIEND OF MAN? OR VICIOUS KILLER?
JIM DAVIS 3-10

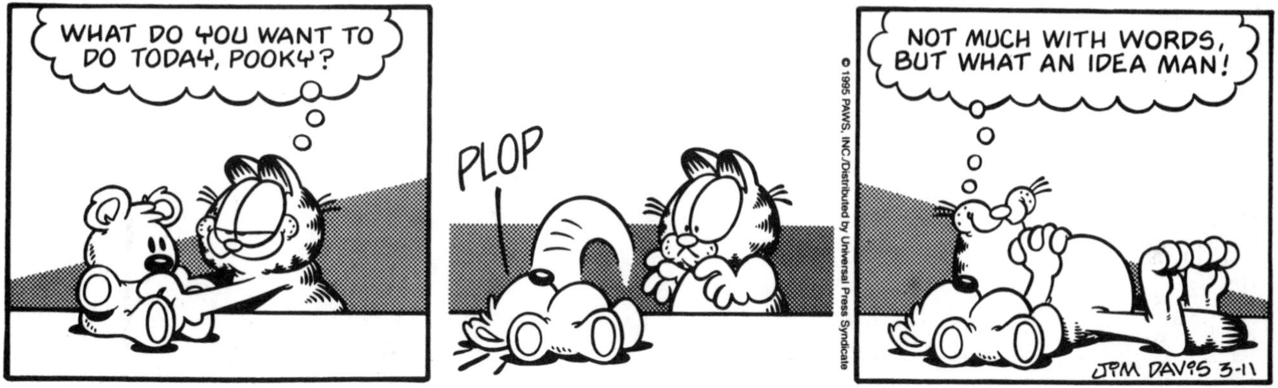
WHAT DO YOU WANT TO DO TODAY, POOKY?
PLOP
NOT MUCH WITH WORDS, BUT WHAT AN IDEA MAN!
JIM DAVIS 3-11

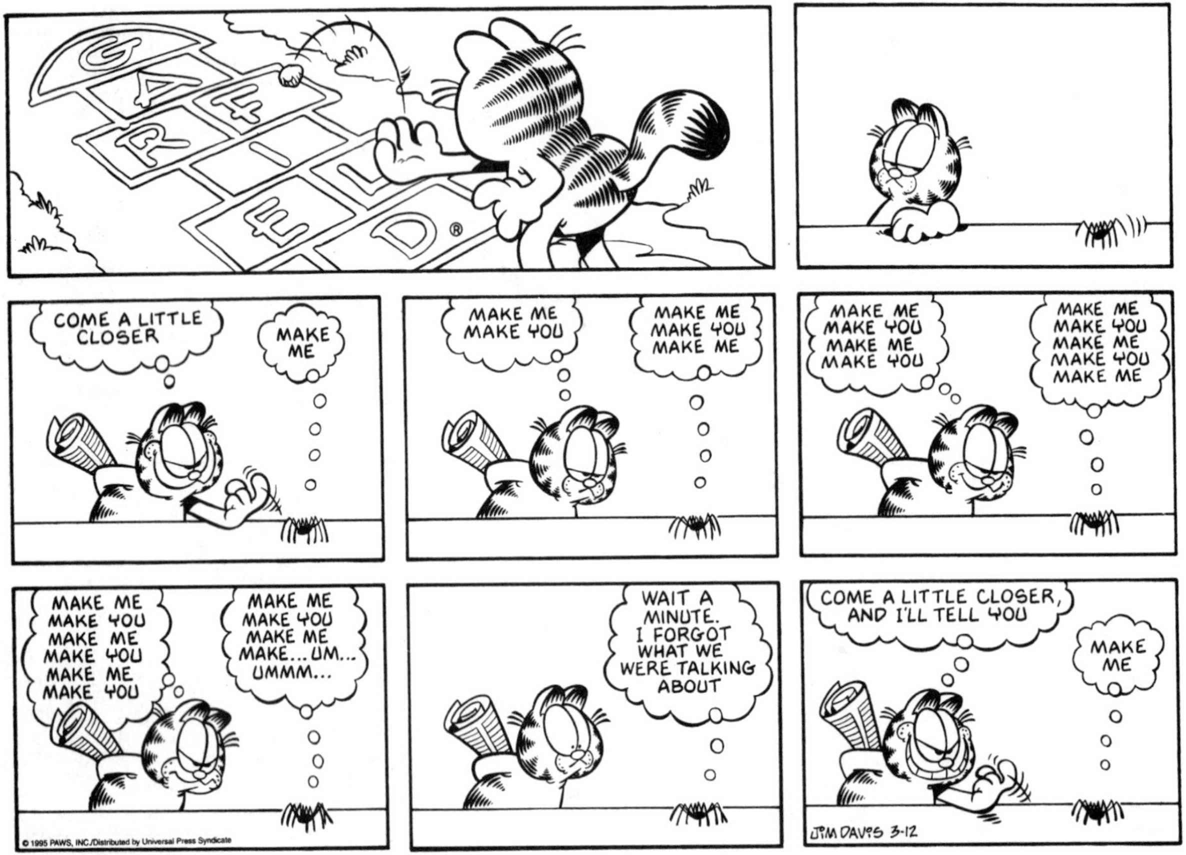
GARFIELD®
COME A LITTLE CLOSER
MAKE ME
MAKE ME MAKE YOU
MAKE ME MAKE YOU MAKE ME
MAKE ME MAKE YOU MAKE ME MAKE YOU
MAKE ME MAKE YOU MAKE ME MAKE YOU MAKE ME
MAKE ME MAKE YOU MAKE ME MAKE YOU MAKE ME MAKE YOU
MAKE ME MAKE YOU MAKE ME MAKE... UM... UMMM...
WAIT A MINUTE. I FORGOT WHAT WE WERE TALKING ABOUT
COME A LITTLE CLOSER, AND I'LL TELL YOU
MAKE ME
JIM DAVIS 3-12

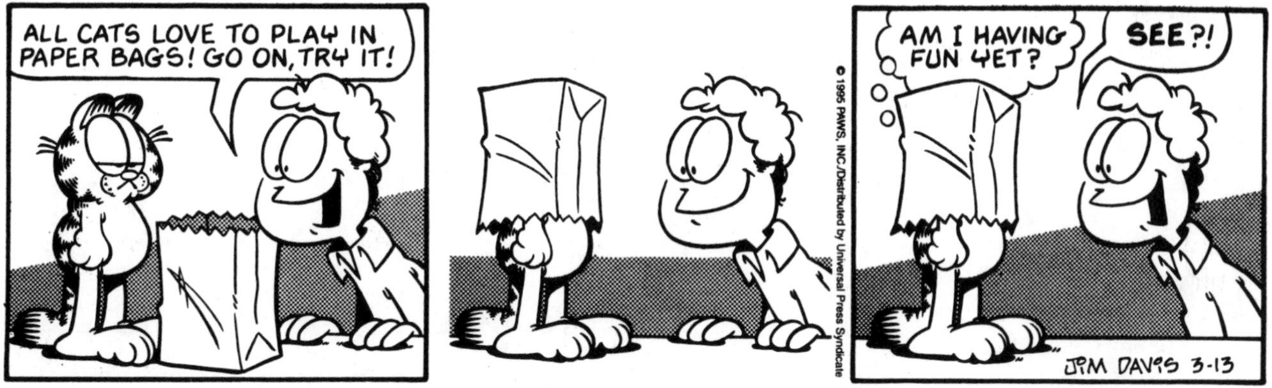
ALL CATS LOVE TO PLAY IN PAPER BAGS! GO ON, TRY IT!
© 1995 PAWS, INC./Distributed by Universal Press Syndicate
AM I HAVING FUN YET?
SEE?!
JIM DAVIS 3-13

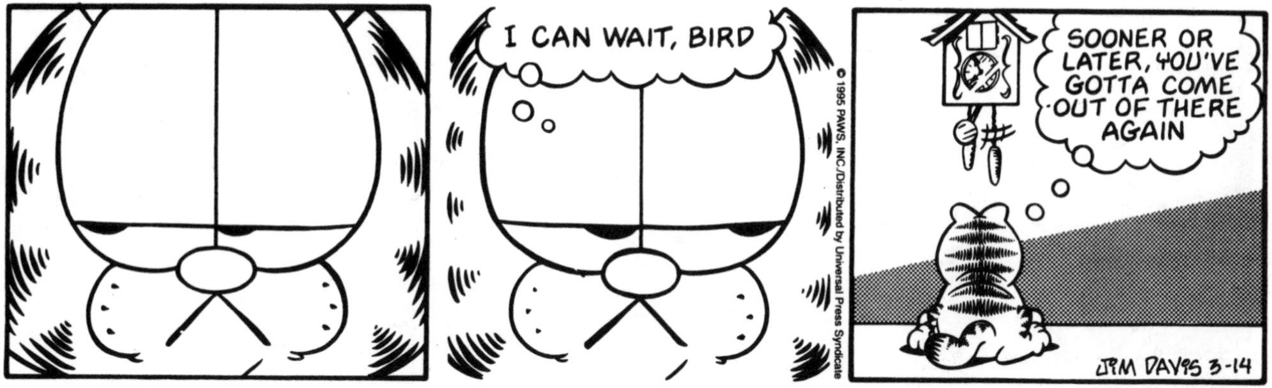
I CAN WAIT, BIRD
© 1995 PAWS, INC./Distributed by Universal Press Syndicate
SOONER OR LATER, YOU'VE GOTTA COME OUT OF THERE AGAIN
JIM DAVIS 3-14

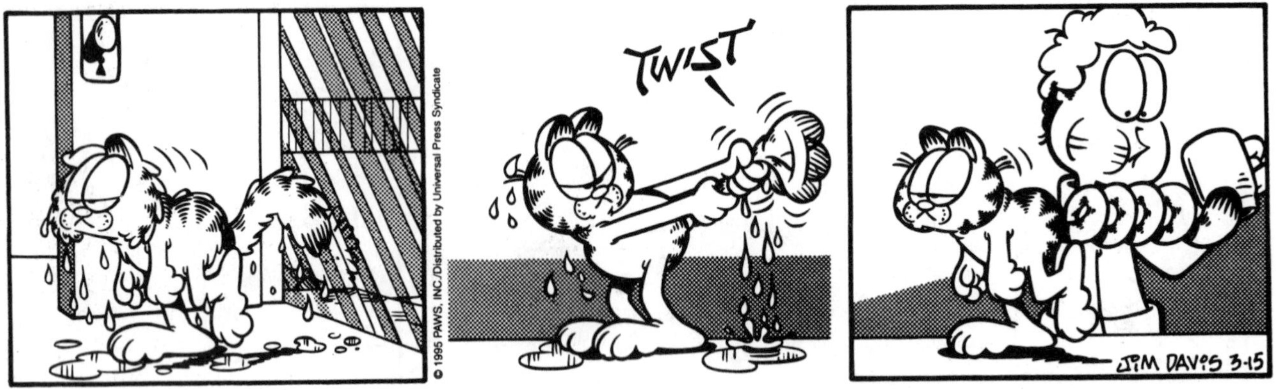
© 1995 PAWS, INC./Distributed by Universal Press Syndicate
TWIST
JIM DAVIS 3-15

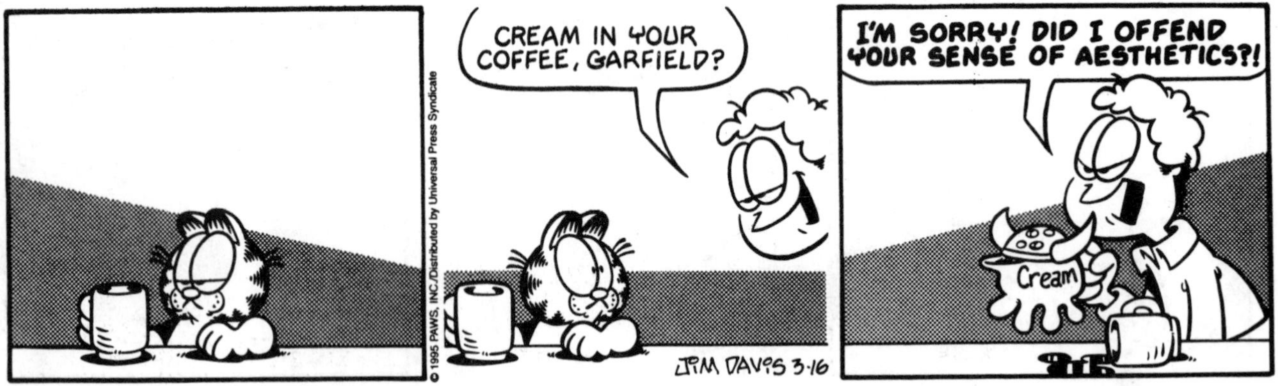
© 1995 PAWS, INC./Distributed by Universal Press Syndicate
CREAM IN YOUR COFFEE, GARFIELD?
JIM DAVIS 3-16
I'M SORRY! DID I OFFEND YOUR SENSE OF AESTHETICS?!
Cream

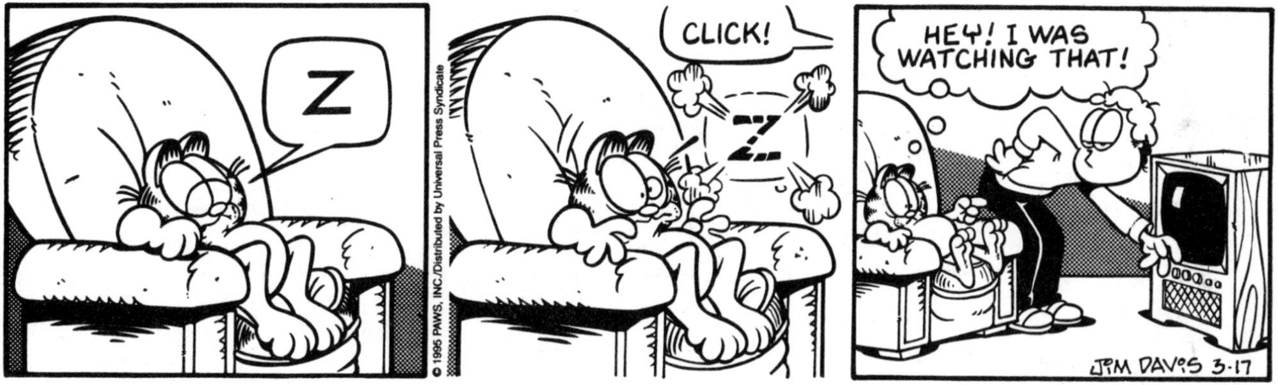
Z
CLICK!
HEY! I WAS WATCHING THAT!
JIM DAVIS 3-17
© 1995 PAWS, INC./Distributed by Universal Press Syndicate

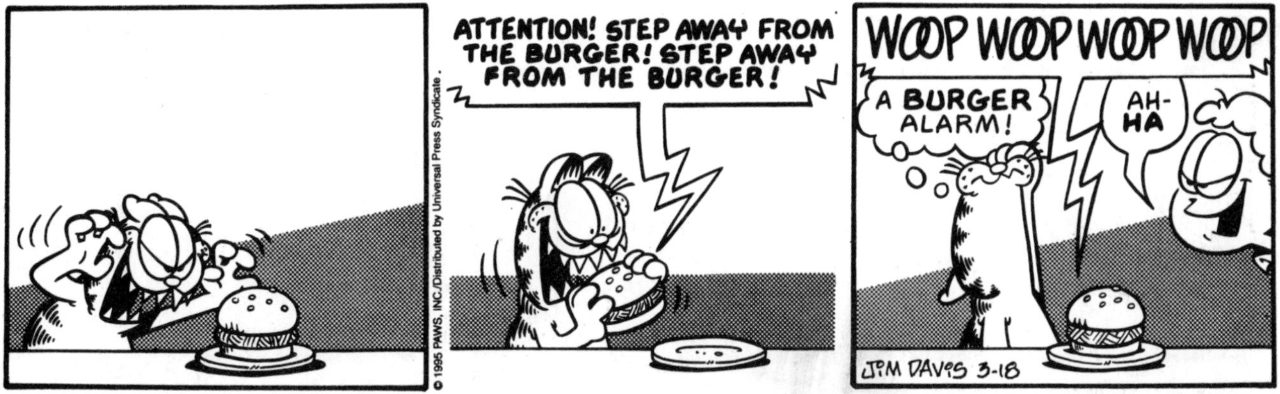
ATTENTION! STEP AWAY FROM THE BURGER! STEP AWAY FROM THE BURGER!
WOOP WOOP WOOP WOOP
A BURGER ALARM!
AH-HA
JIM DAVIS 3-18
© 1995 PAWS, INC./Distributed by Universal Press Syndicate.

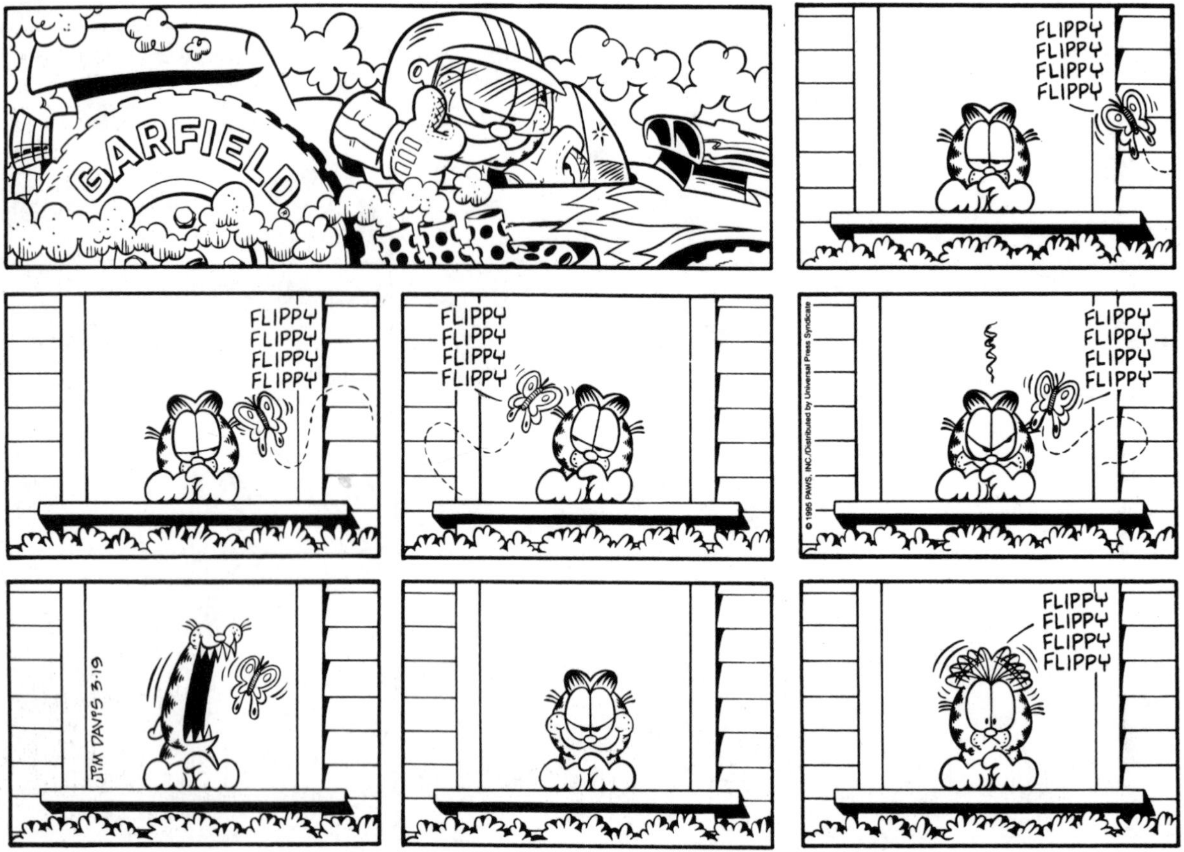
GARFIELD
FLIPPY
FLIPPY
FLIPPY
FLIPPY
FLIPPY
FLIPPY
FLIPPY
FLIPPY
FLIPPY
FLIPPY
FLIPPY
FLIPPY
FLIPPY
FLIPPY
FLIPPY
FLIPPY
JIM DAVIS 3-19
FLIPPY
FLIPPY
FLIPPY
FLIPPY

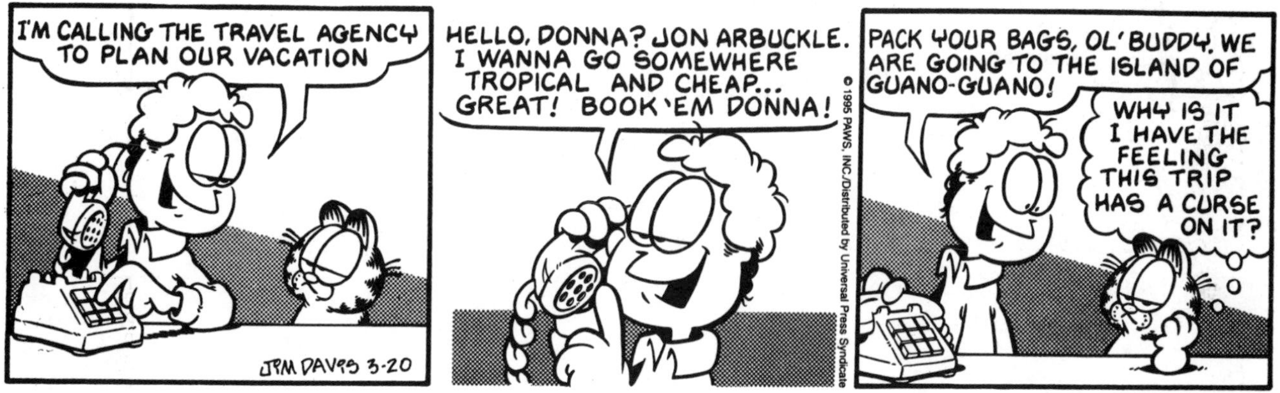
I'M CALLING THE TRAVEL AGENCY TO PLAN OUR VACATION
JIM DAVIS 3-20
HELLO, DONNA? JON ARBUCKLE. I WANNA GO SOMEWHERE TROPICAL AND CHEAP... GREAT! BOOK 'EM DONNA!
© 1995 PAWS, INC./Distributed by Universal Press Syndicate
PACK YOUR BAGS, OL' BUDDY. WE ARE GOING TO THE ISLAND OF GUANO-GUANO!
WHY IS IT I HAVE THE FEELING THIS TRIP HAS A CURSE ON IT?

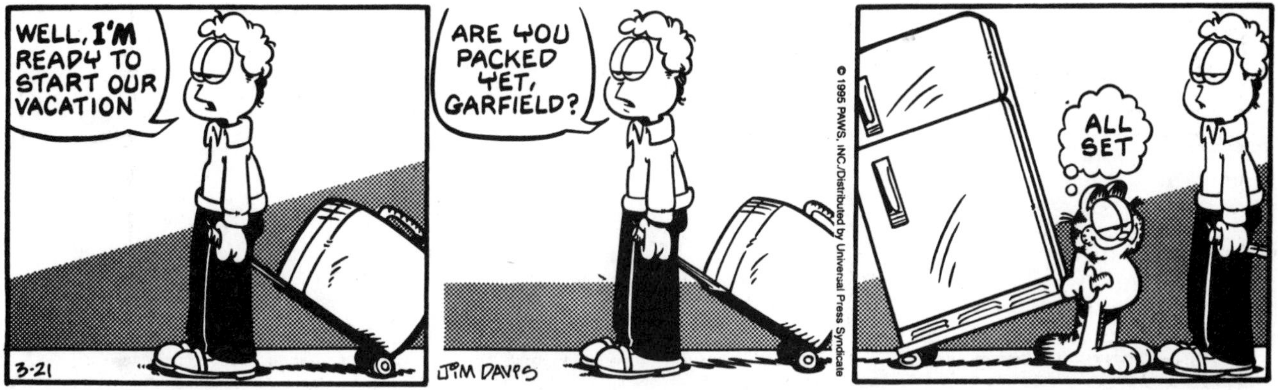
WELL, I'M READY TO START OUR VACATION
3-21
ARE YOU PACKED YET, GARFIELD?
JIM DAVIS
© 1995 PAWS, INC./Distributed by Universal Press Syndicate
ALL SET

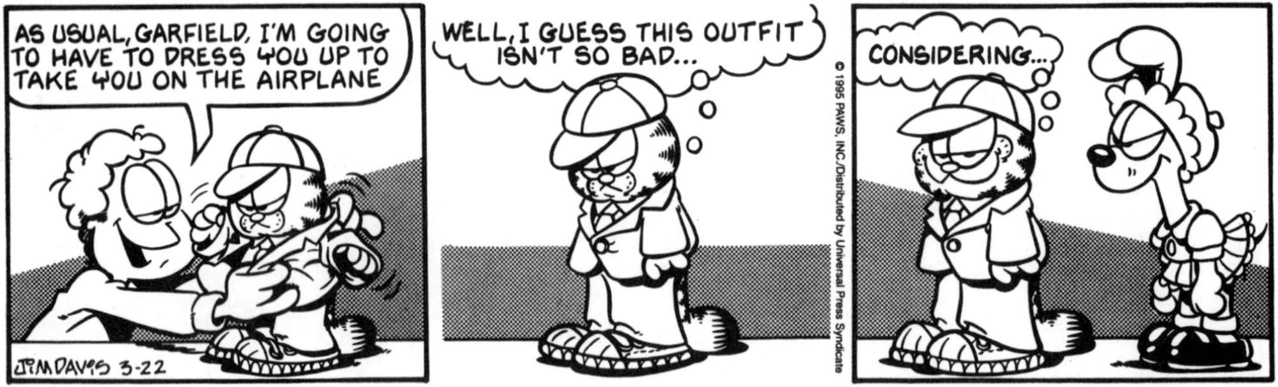
AS USUAL, GARFIELD, I'M GOING TO HAVE TO DRESS YOU UP TO TAKE YOU ON THE AIRPLANE
JIM DAVIS 3-22
WELL, I GUESS THIS OUTFIT ISN'T SO BAD...
© 1995 PAWS, INC./Distributed by Universal Press Syndicate
CONSIDERING...

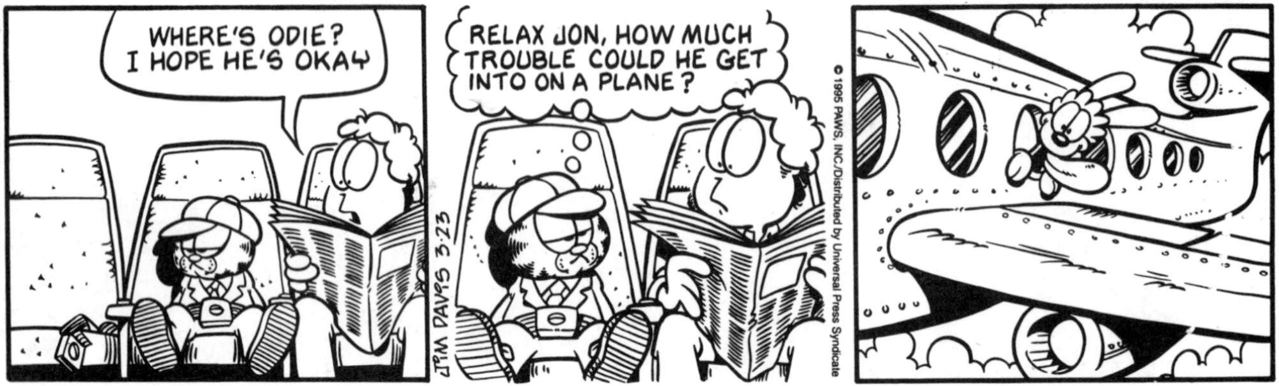
WHERE'S ODIE? I HOPE HE'S OKAY
JIM DAVIS 3-23
RELAX JON, HOW MUCH TROUBLE COULD HE GET INTO ON A PLANE?
© 1995 PAWS, INC./Distributed by Universal Press Syndicate

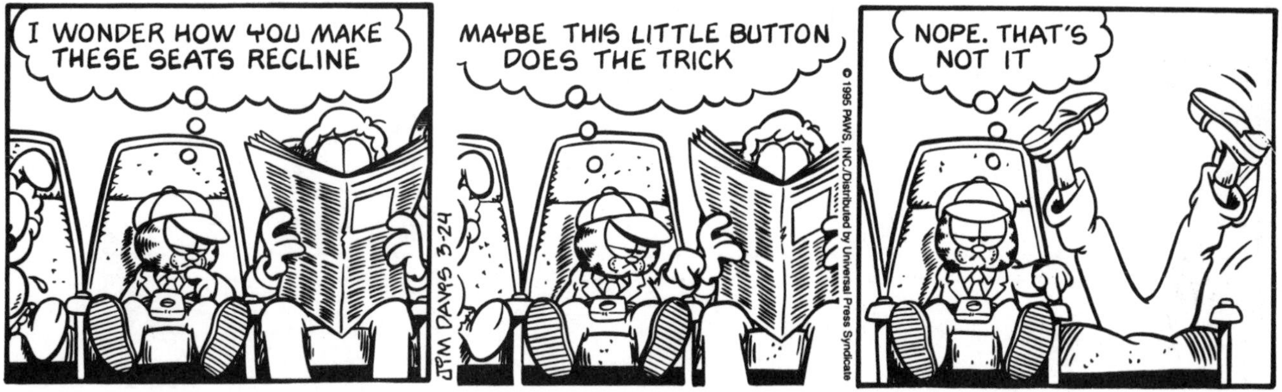
I WONDER HOW YOU MAKE THESE SEATS RECLINE
JIM DAVIS 3-24
MAYBE THIS LITTLE BUTTON DOES THE TRICK
© 1995 PAWS, INC./Distributed by Universal Press Syndicate
NOPE. THAT'S NOT IT

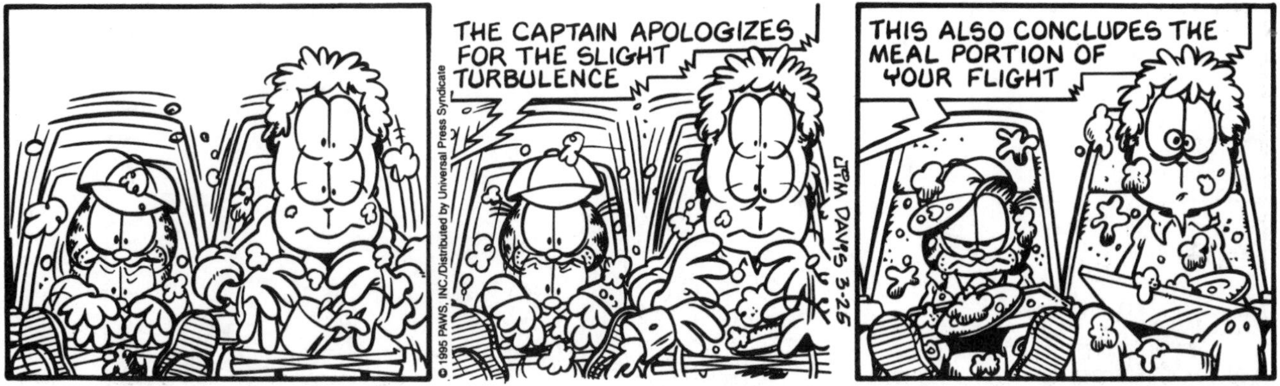
© 1995 PAWS, INC./Distributed by Universal Press Syndicate
THE CAPTAIN APOLOGIZES FOR THE SLIGHT TURBULENCE
JIM DAVIS 3-25
THIS ALSO CONCLUDES THE MEAL PORTION OF YOUR FLIGHT

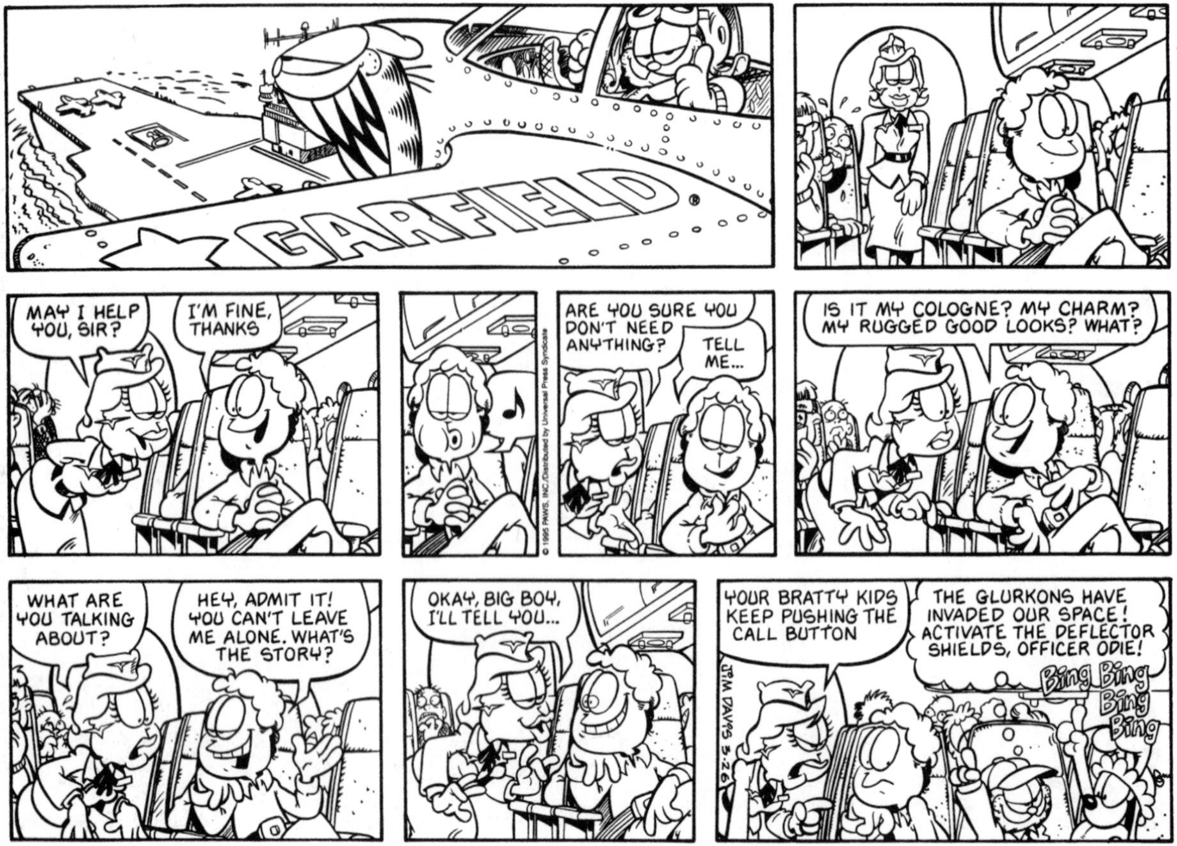
GARFIELD®
MAY I HELP YOU, SIR?
I'M FINE, THANKS
© 1995 PAWS, INC./Distributed by Universal Press Syndicate
ARE YOU SURE YOU DON'T NEED ANYTHING?
TELL ME...
IS IT MY COLOGNE? MY CHARM? MY RUGGED GOOD LOOKS? WHAT?
WHAT ARE YOU TALKING ABOUT?
HEY, ADMIT IT! YOU CAN'T LEAVE ME ALONE. WHAT'S THE STORY?
OKAY, BIG BOY, I'LL TELL YOU...
JIM DAVIS 3-26
YOUR BRATTY KIDS KEEP PUSHING THE CALL BUTTON
THE GLURKONS HAVE INVADED OUR SPACE! ACTIVATE THE DEFLECTOR SHIELDS, OFFICER ODIE!
Bing Bing Bing Bing

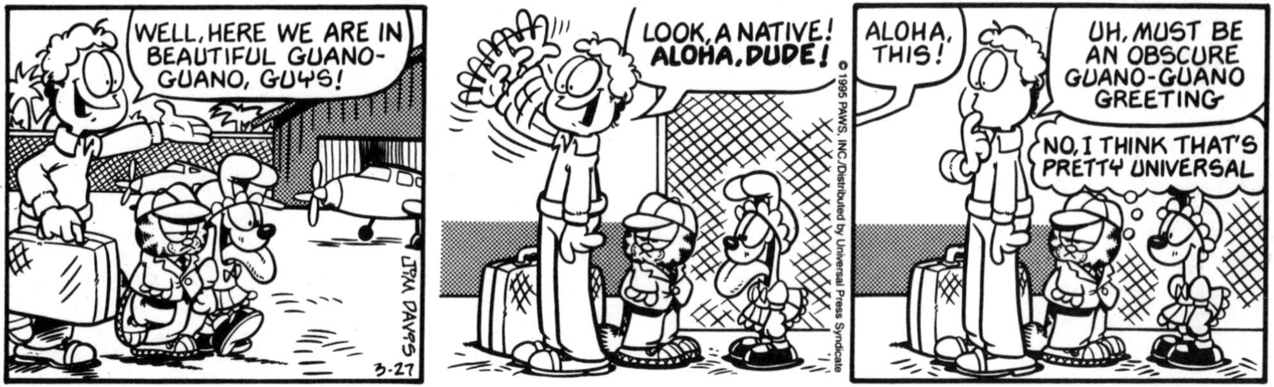
WELL, HERE WE ARE IN BEAUTIFUL GUANO-GUANO, GUYS!
JIM DAVIS 3-27
LOOK, A NATIVE! ALOHA, DUDE!
© 1995 PAWS, INC./Distributed by Universal Press Syndicate
ALOHA, THIS!
UH, MUST BE AN OBSCURE GUANO-GUANO GREETING
NO, I THINK THAT'S PRETTY UNIVERSAL

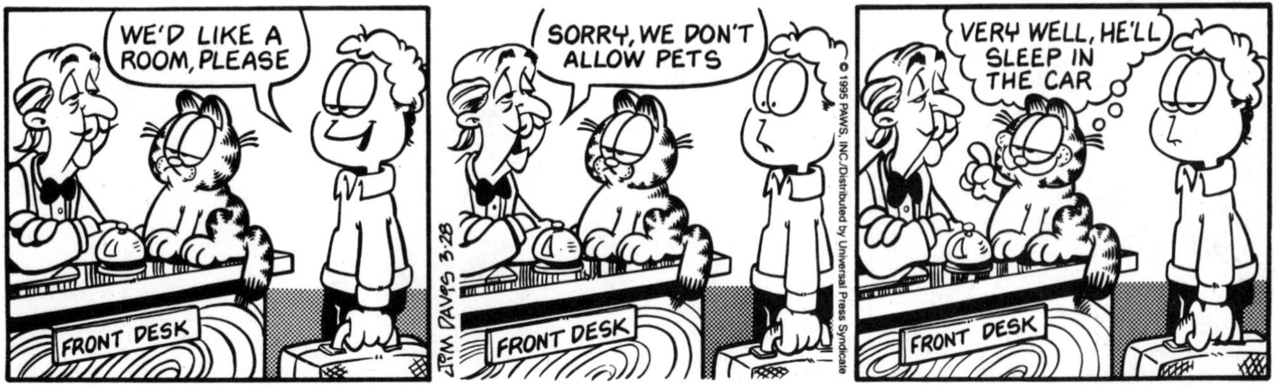
WE'D LIKE A ROOM, PLEASE
FRONT DESK
JIM DAVIS 3-28
SORRY, WE DON'T ALLOW PETS
FRONT DESK
© 1995 PAWS, INC./Distributed by Universal Press Syndicate
VERY WELL, HE'LL SLEEP IN THE CAR
FRONT DESK

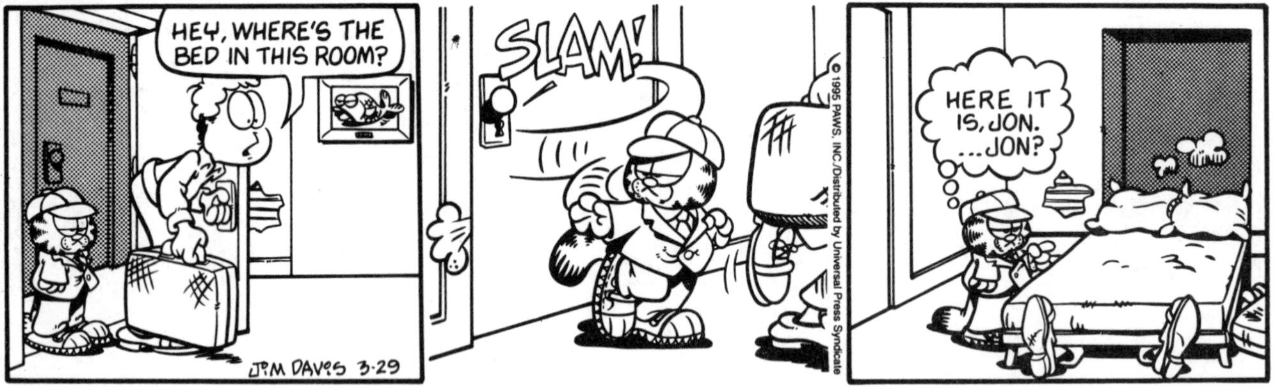
HEY, WHERE'S THE BED IN THIS ROOM?
JIM DAVIS 3-29
SLAM!
© 1995 PAWS, INC./Distributed by Universal Press Syndicate
HERE IT IS, JON. ...JON?

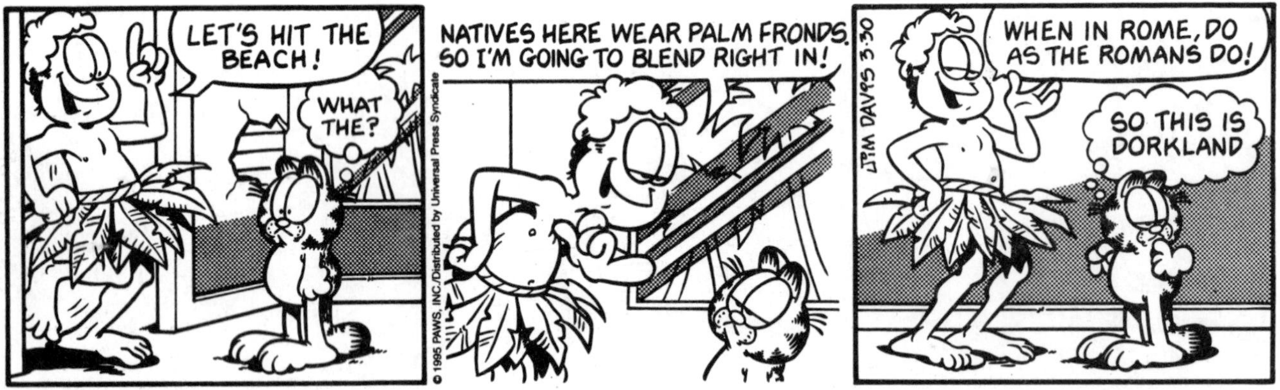
LET'S HIT THE BEACH!
WHAT THE?
© 1995 PAWS, INC./Distributed by Universal Press Syndicate
NATIVES HERE WEAR PALM FRONDS. SO I'M GOING TO BLEND RIGHT IN!
JIM DAVIS 3-30
WHEN IN ROME, DO AS THE ROMANS DO!
SO THIS IS DORKLAND

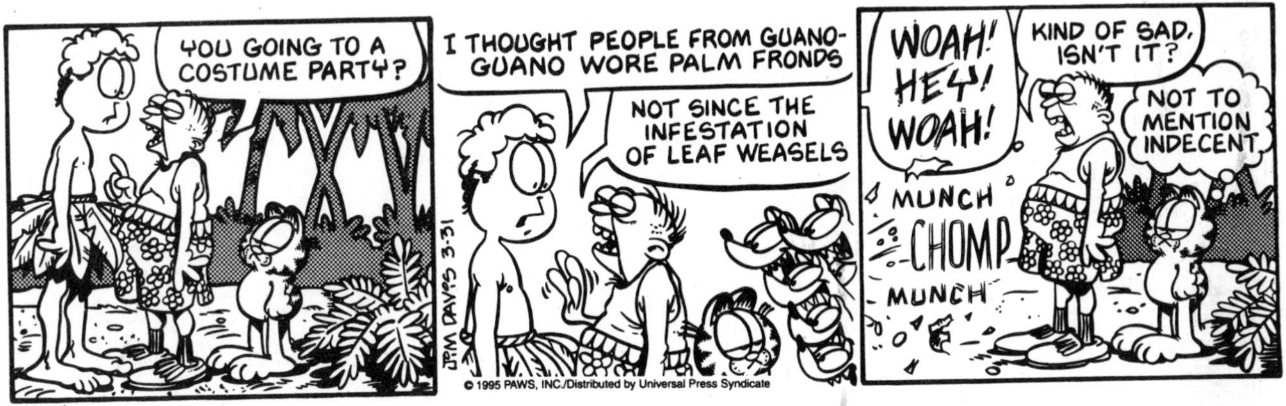
YOU GOING TO A COSTUME PARTY?
I THOUGHT PEOPLE FROM GUANO-GUANO WORE PALM FRONDS
NOT SINCE THE INFESTATION OF LEAF WEASELS
WOAH! HEY! WOAH!
MUNCH
CHOMP
MUNCH
KIND OF SAD, ISN'T IT?
NOT TO MENTION INDECENT
JIM DAVIS 3-31
© 1995 PAWS, INC./Distributed by Universal Press Syndicate

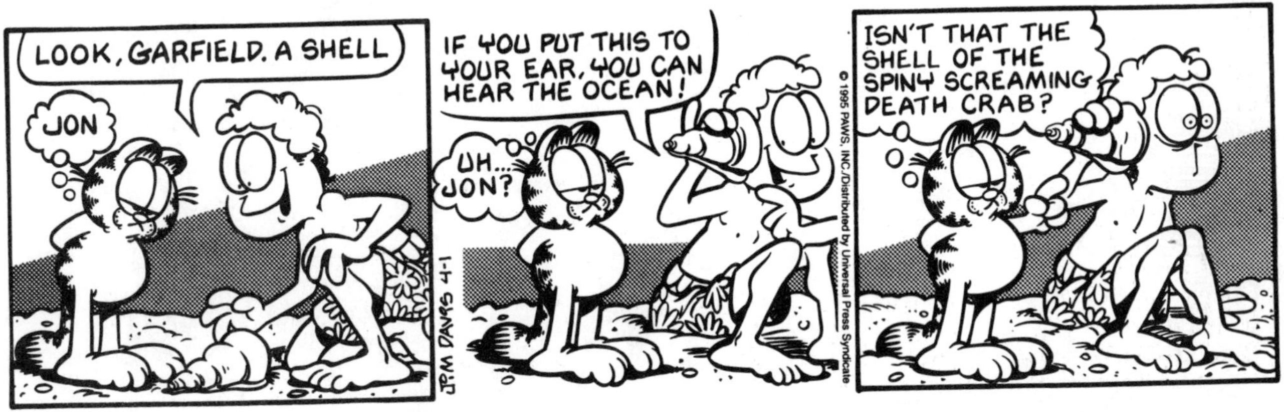
LOOK, GARFIELD. A SHELL
JON
IF YOU PUT THIS TO YOUR EAR, YOU CAN HEAR THE OCEAN!
UH... JON?
ISN'T THAT THE SHELL OF THE SPINY SCREAMING DEATH CRAB?
JIM DAVIS 4-1
© 1995 PAWS, INC./Distributed by Universal Press Syndicate

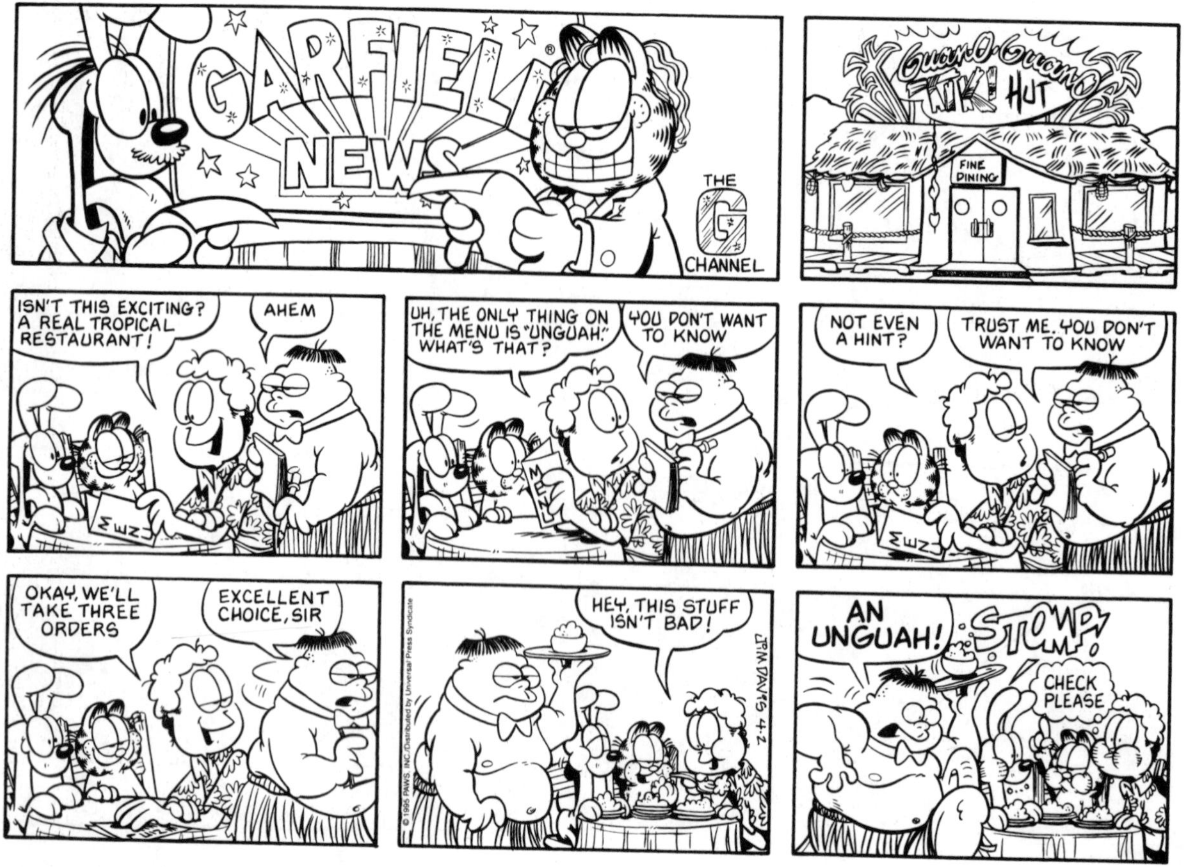
GARFIELD®
NEWS
THE G CHANNEL
Guan-O-Guano TIKI HUT
FINE DINING
ISN'T THIS EXCITING? A REAL TROPICAL RESTAURANT!
AHEM
MENU
UH, THE ONLY THING ON THE MENU IS "UNGUAH." WHAT'S THAT?
YOU DON'T WANT TO KNOW
NOT EVEN A HINT?
TRUST ME. YOU DON'T WANT TO KNOW
OKAY, WE'LL TAKE THREE ORDERS
EXCELLENT CHOICE, SIR
© 1995 PAWS, INC./Distributed by Universal Press Syndicate
HEY, THIS STUFF ISN'T BAD!
JIM DAVIS 4-2
AN UNGUAH!
STOMP
CHECK PLEASE

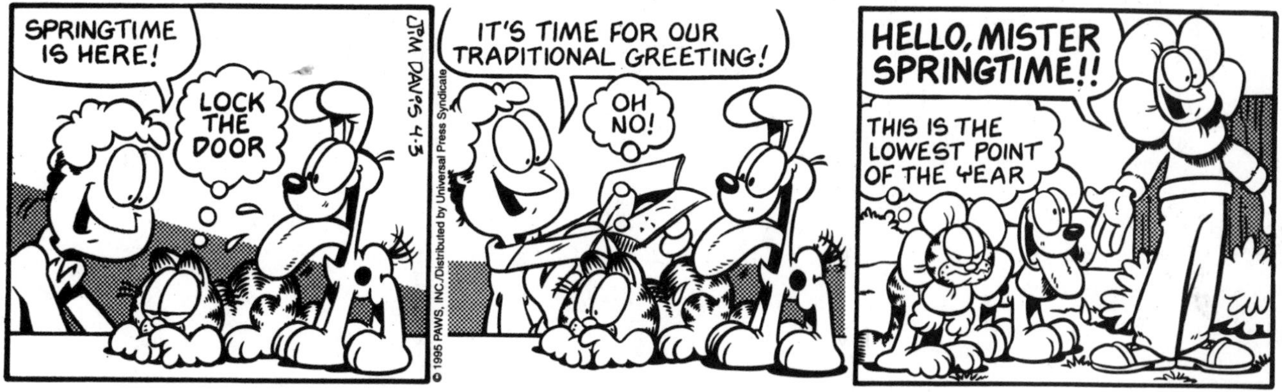
SPRINGTIME IS HERE!
LOCK THE DOOR
JIM DAVIS 95 4-3
IT'S TIME FOR OUR TRADITIONAL GREETING!
OH NO!
© 1995 PAWS, INC./Distributed by Universal Press Syndicate
HELLO, MISTER SPRINGTIME!!
THIS IS THE LOWEST POINT OF THE YEAR

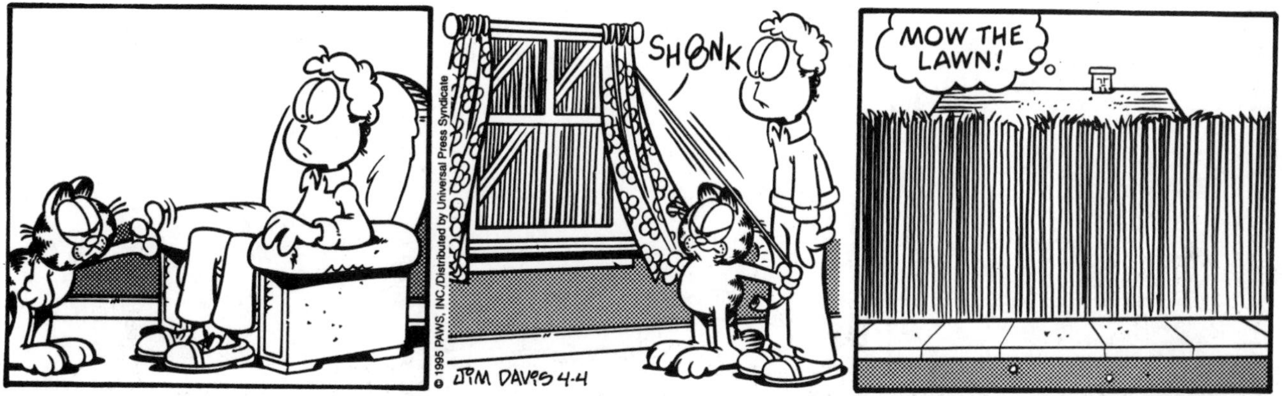
© 1995 PAWS, INC./Distributed by Universal Press Syndicate
SHONK
JIM DAVIS 4-4
MOW THE LAWN!

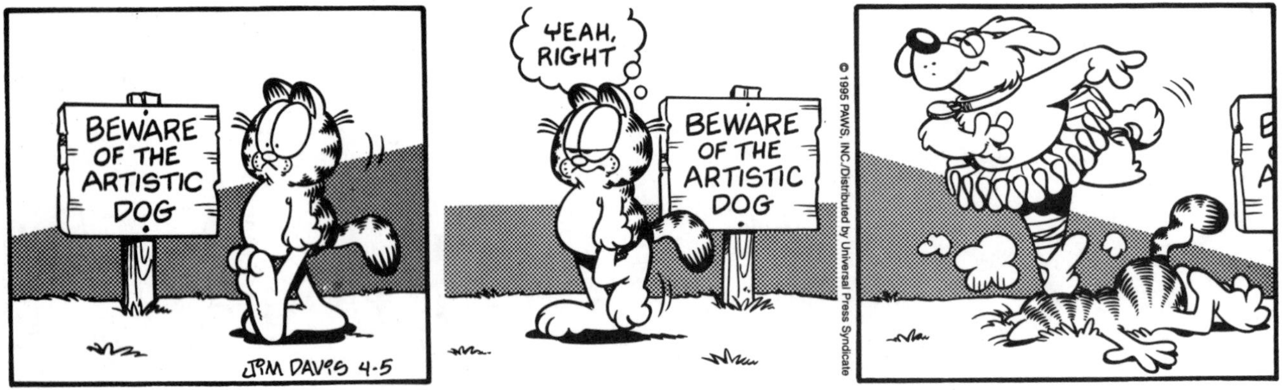
BEWARE OF THE ARTISTIC DOG
JIM DAVIS 4-5
YEAH, RIGHT
BEWARE OF THE ARTISTIC DOG
© 1995 PAWS, INC./Distributed by Universal Press Syndicate

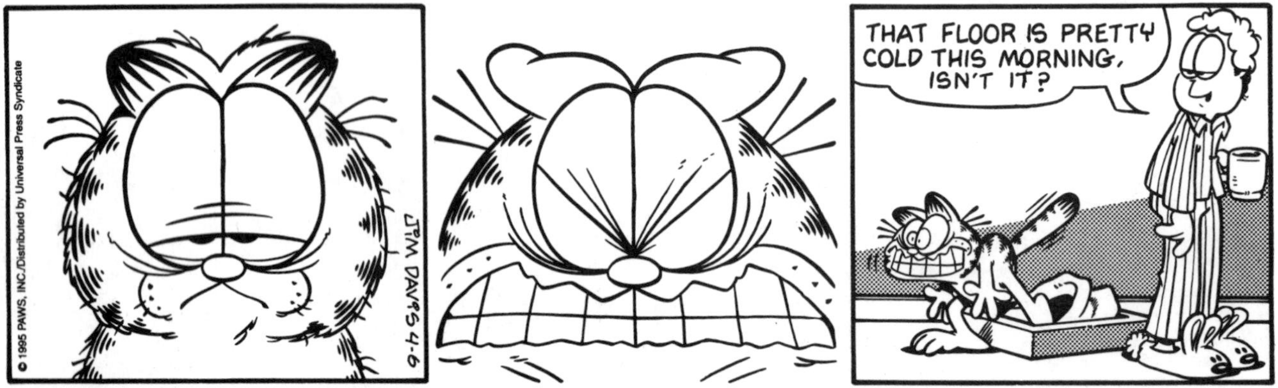
© 1995 PAWS, INC./Distributed by Universal Press Syndicate
JIM DAVIS 4-6
THAT FLOOR IS PRETTY COLD THIS MORNING, ISN'T IT?

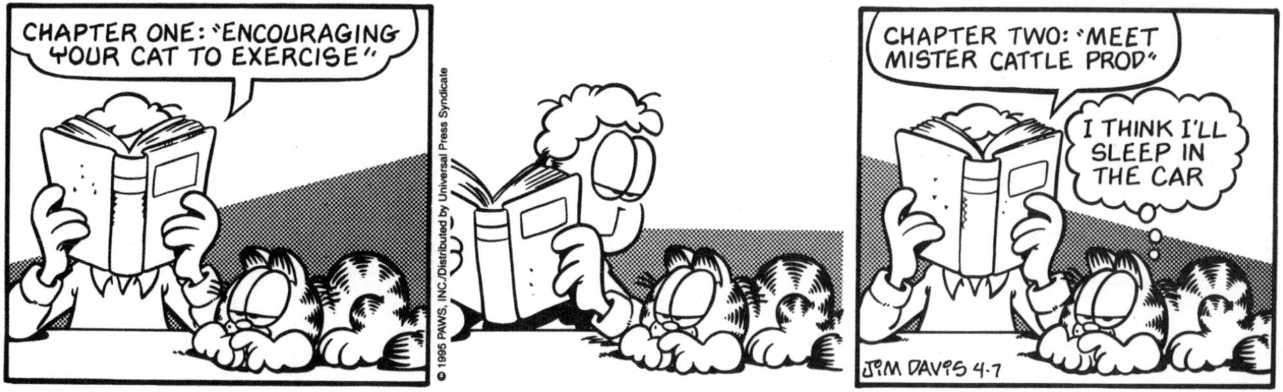
CHAPTER ONE: "ENCOURAGING YOUR CAT TO EXERCISE"
CHAPTER TWO: "MEET MISTER CATTLE PROD"
I THINK I'LL SLEEP IN THE CAR
JIM DAVIS 4-7

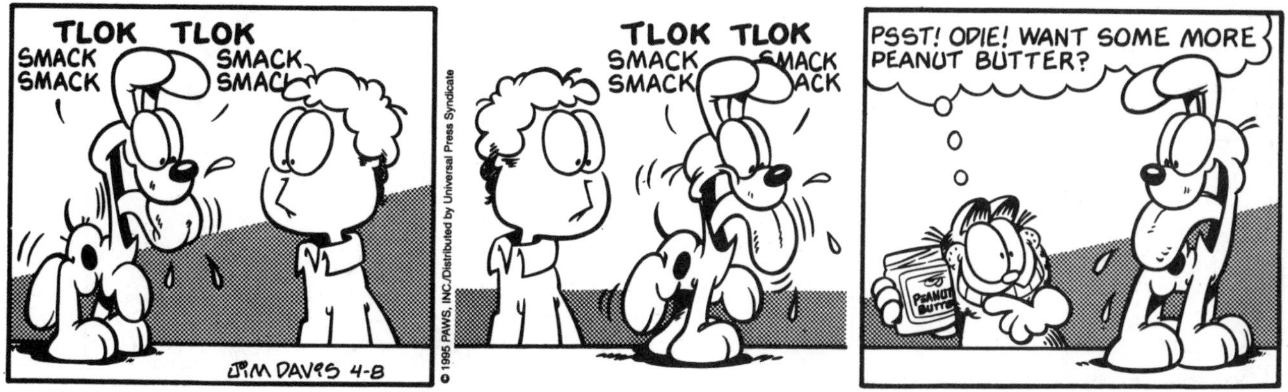
TLOK TLOK
SMACK SMACK
SMACK SMACK
JIM DAVIS 4-8
TLOK TLOK
SMACK SMACK
SMACK SMACK
PSST! ODIE! WANT SOME MORE PEANUT BUTTER?
PEANUT BUTTER

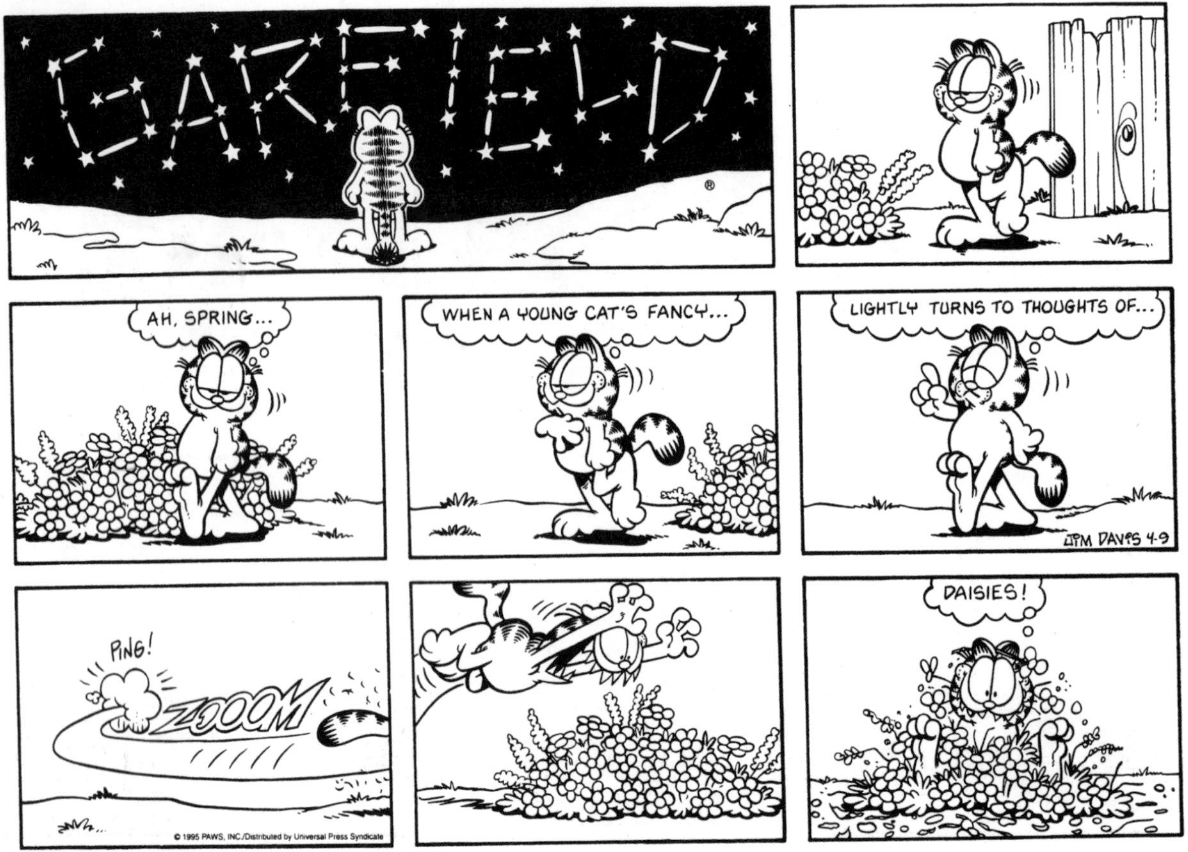
GARFIELD
AH, SPRING...
WHEN A YOUNG CAT'S FANCY...
LIGHTLY TURNS TO THOUGHTS OF...
JIM DAVIS 4-9
PING!
ZOOOM
DAISIES!
© 1995 PAWS, INC./Distributed by Universal Press Syndicate

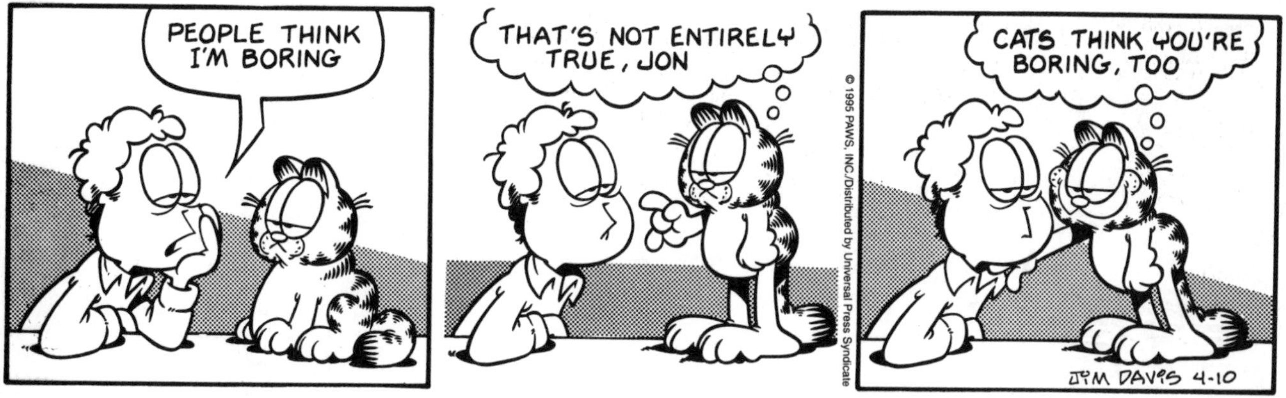
PEOPLE THINK I'M BORING
THAT'S NOT ENTIRELY TRUE, JON
CATS THINK YOU'RE BORING, TOO
JIM DAVIS 4-10
© 1995 PAWS, INC./Distributed by Universal Press Syndicate

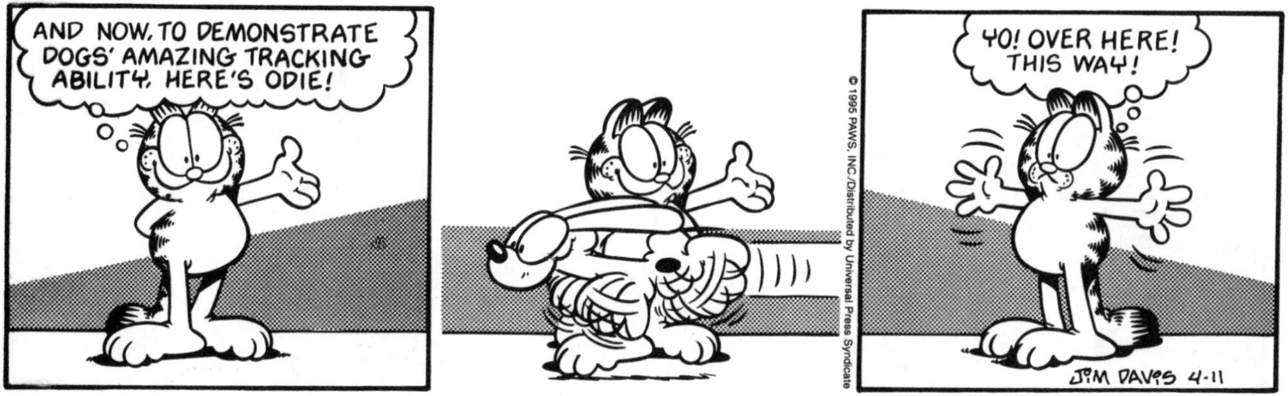
AND NOW, TO DEMONSTRATE DOGS' AMAZING TRACKING ABILITY, HERE'S ODIE!
YO! OVER HERE! THIS WAY!
JIM DAVIS 4-11
© 1995 PAWS, INC./Distributed by Universal Press Syndicate

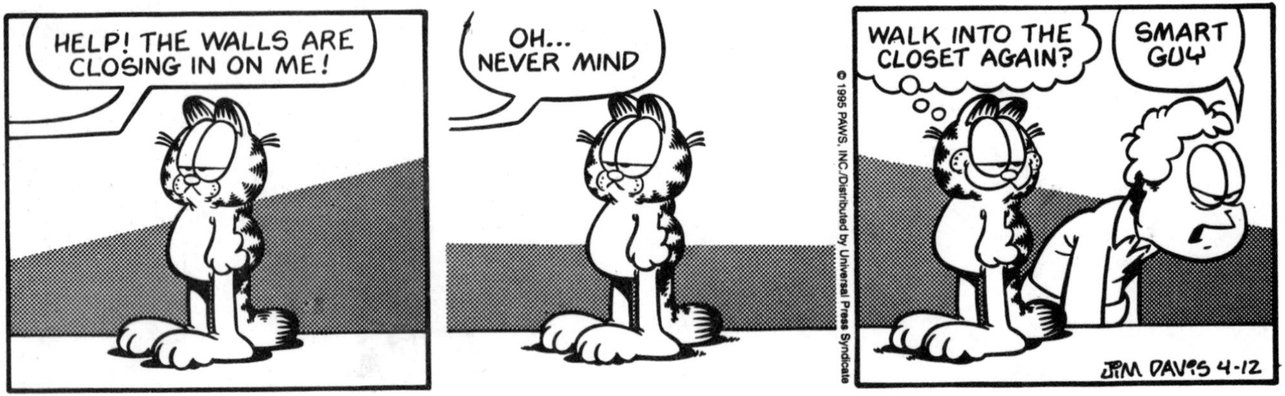
HELP! THE WALLS ARE CLOSING IN ON ME!
OH... NEVER MIND
WALK INTO THE CLOSET AGAIN?
SMART GUY
JIM DAVIS 4-12
© 1995 PAWS, INC./Distributed by Universal Press Syndicate

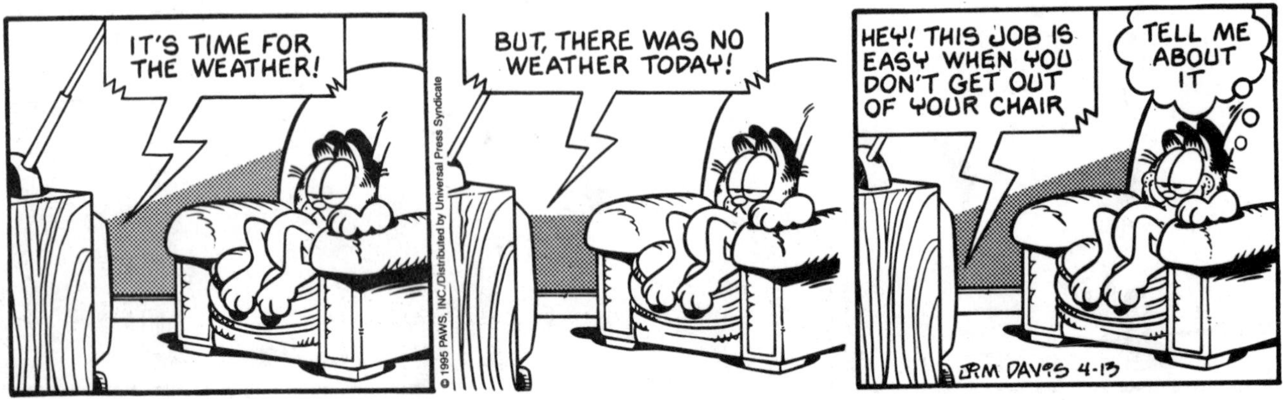
IT'S TIME FOR THE WEATHER!
BUT, THERE WAS NO WEATHER TODAY!
HEY! THIS JOB IS EASY WHEN YOU DON'T GET OUT OF YOUR CHAIR
TELL ME ABOUT IT
JIM DAVIS 4-13
© 1995 PAWS, INC./Distributed by Universal Press Syndicate

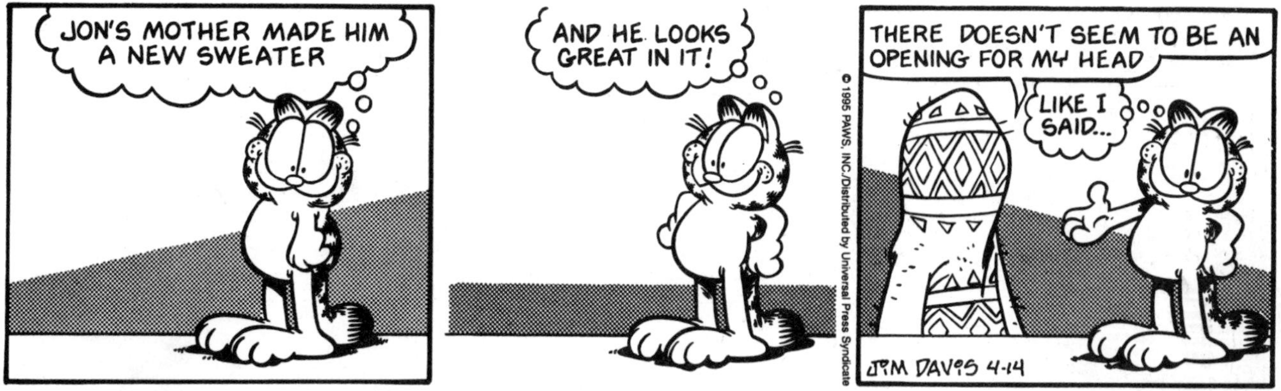
JON'S MOTHER MADE HIM A NEW SWEATER
AND HE LOOKS GREAT IN IT!
THERE DOESN'T SEEM TO BE AN OPENING FOR MY HEAD
LIKE I SAID...
© 1995 PAWS, INC./Distributed by Universal Press Syndicate
JIM DAVIS 4-14

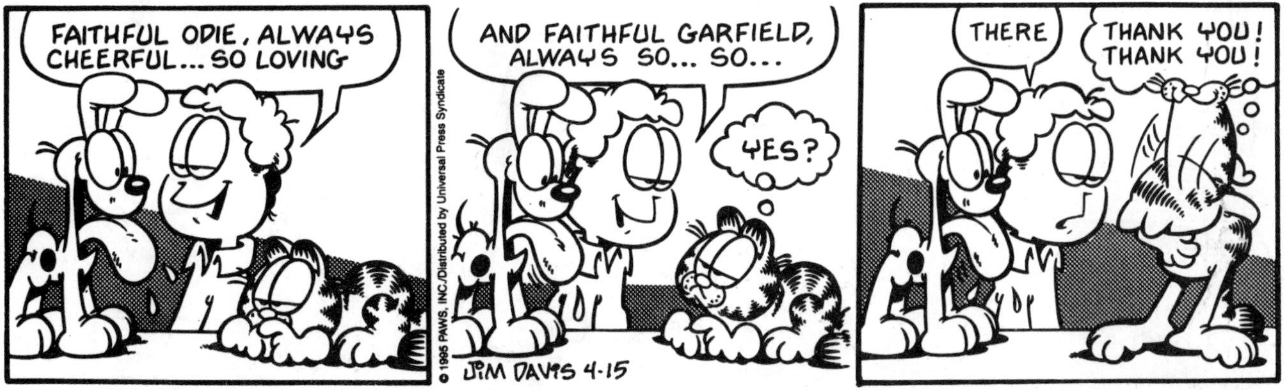
FAITHFUL ODIE, ALWAYS CHEERFUL... SO LOVING
© 1995 PAWS, INC./Distributed by Universal Press Syndicate
AND FAITHFUL GARFIELD, ALWAYS SO... SO...
YES?
JIM DAVIS 4-15
THERE
THANK YOU! THANK YOU!

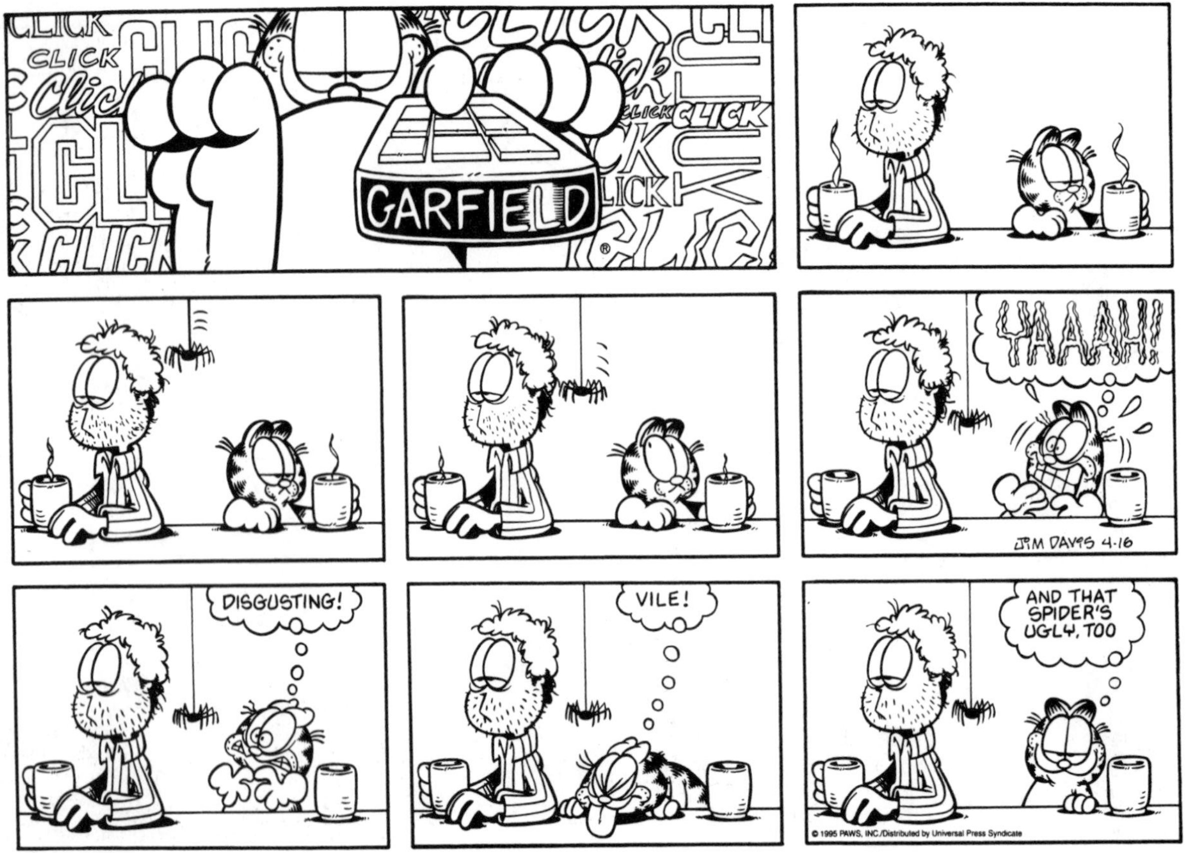
CLICK
GARFIELD
HAAAH!
JIM DAVIS 4-16
DISGUSTING!
VILE!
AND THAT SPIDER'S UGLY, TOO
© 1995 PAWS, INC./Distributed by Universal Press Syndicate

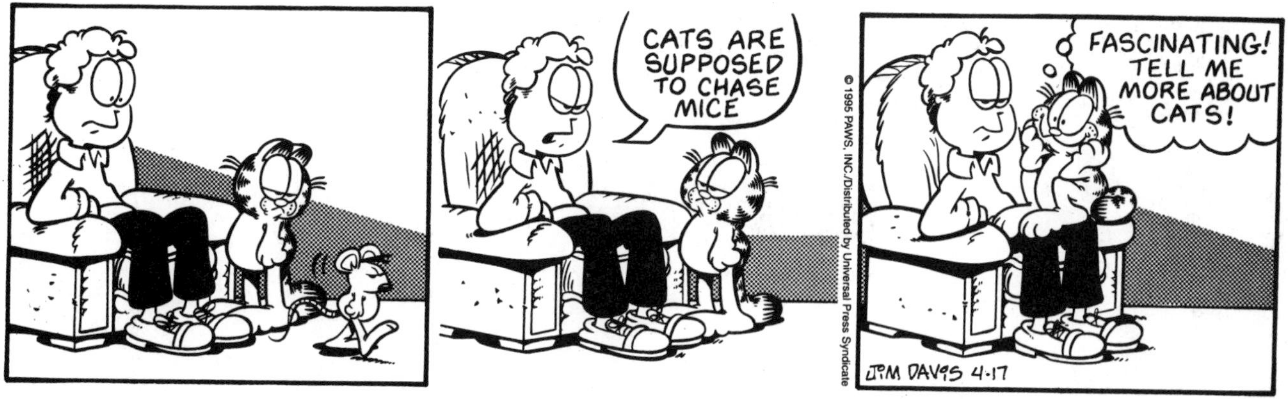
CATS ARE SUPPOSED TO CHASE MICE
© 1995 PAWS, INC./Distributed by Universal Press Syndicate
FASCINATING! TELL ME MORE ABOUT CATS!
JIM DAVIS 4-17

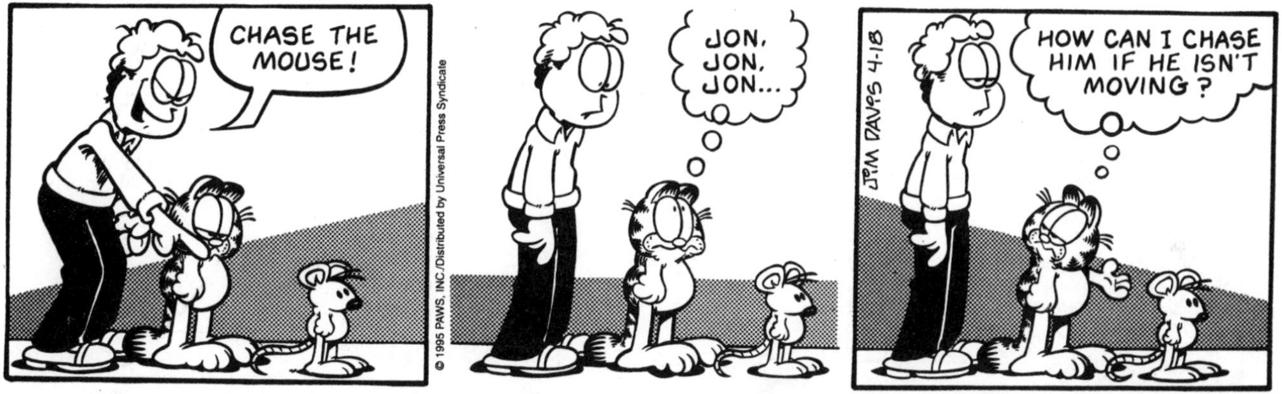
CHASE THE MOUSE!
© 1995 PAWS, INC./Distributed by Universal Press Syndicate
JON, JON, JON...
JIM DAVIS 4-18
HOW CAN I CHASE HIM IF HE ISN'T MOVING?

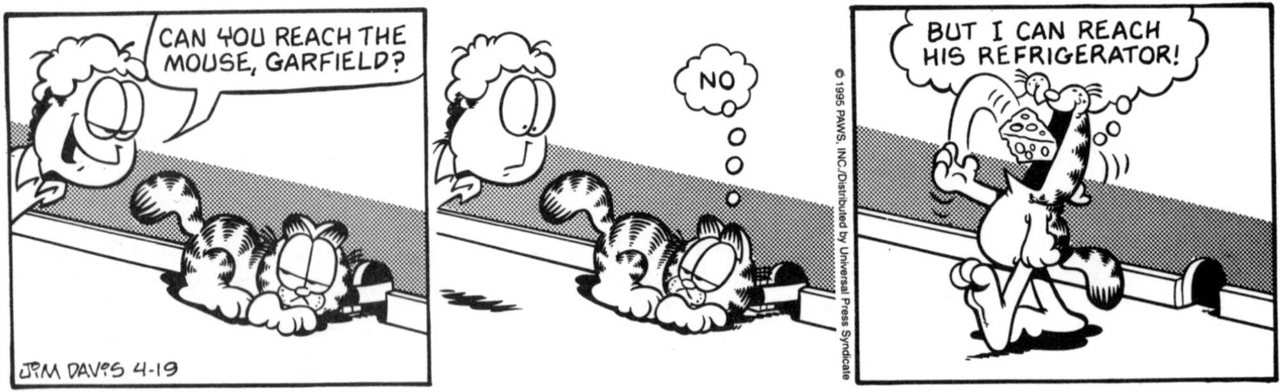
CAN YOU REACH THE MOUSE, GARFIELD?
JIM DAVIS 4-19
NO
© 1995 PAWS, INC./Distributed by Universal Press Syndicate
BUT I CAN REACH HIS REFRIGERATOR!

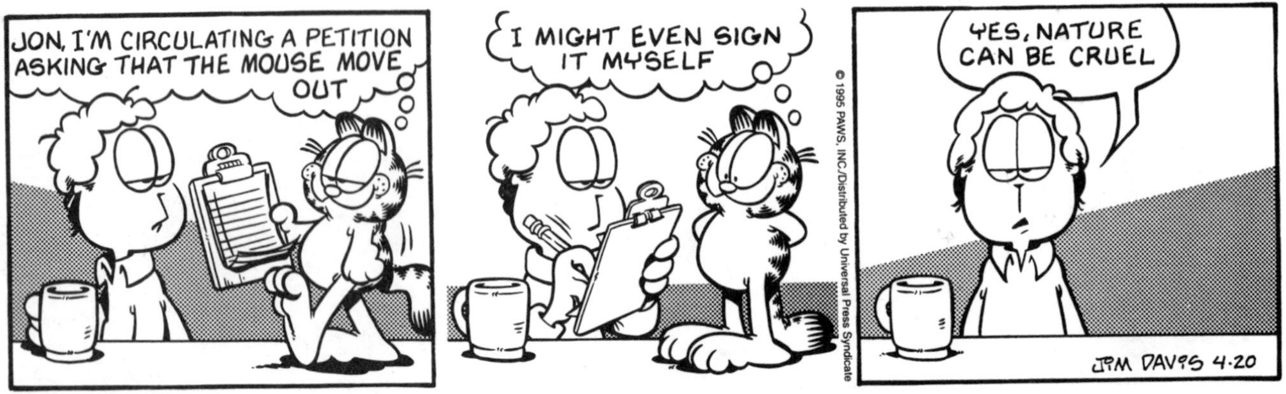
JON, I'M CIRCULATING A PETITION ASKING THAT THE MOUSE MOVE OUT
I MIGHT EVEN SIGN IT MYSELF
© 1995 PAWS, INC./Distributed by Universal Press Syndicate
YES, NATURE CAN BE CRUEL
JIM DAVIS 4-20

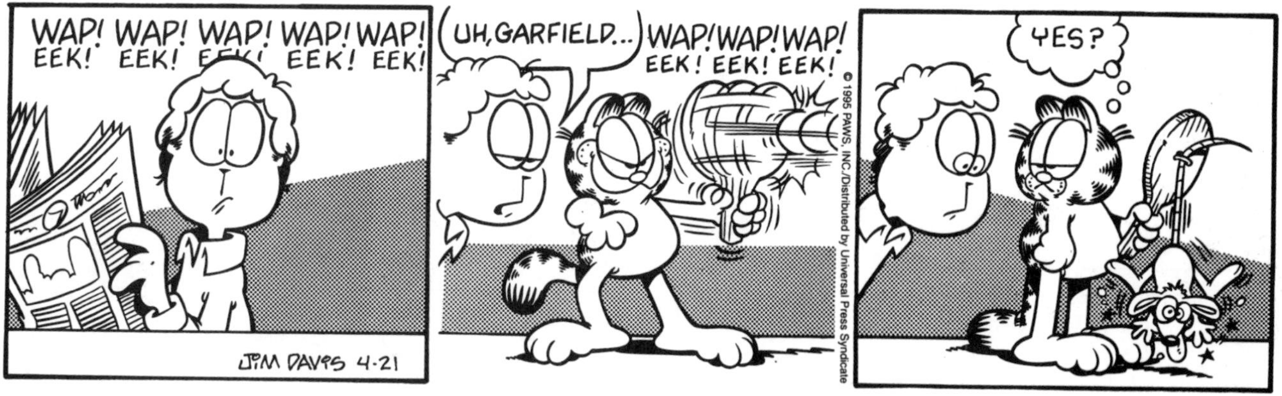
WAP! WAP! WAP! WAP! WAP!
EEK! EEK! EEK! EEK!
JIM DAVIS 4-21
UH, GARFIELD...
WAP! WAP! WAP!
EEK! EEK! EEK!
YES?

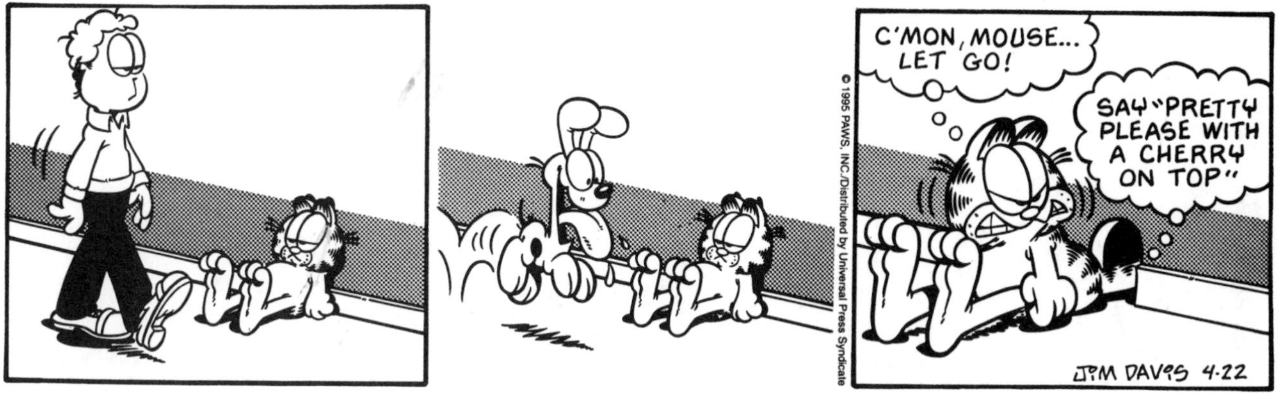
C'MON, MOUSE... LET GO!
SAY "PRETTY PLEASE WITH A CHERRY ON TOP"
JIM DAVIS 4-22

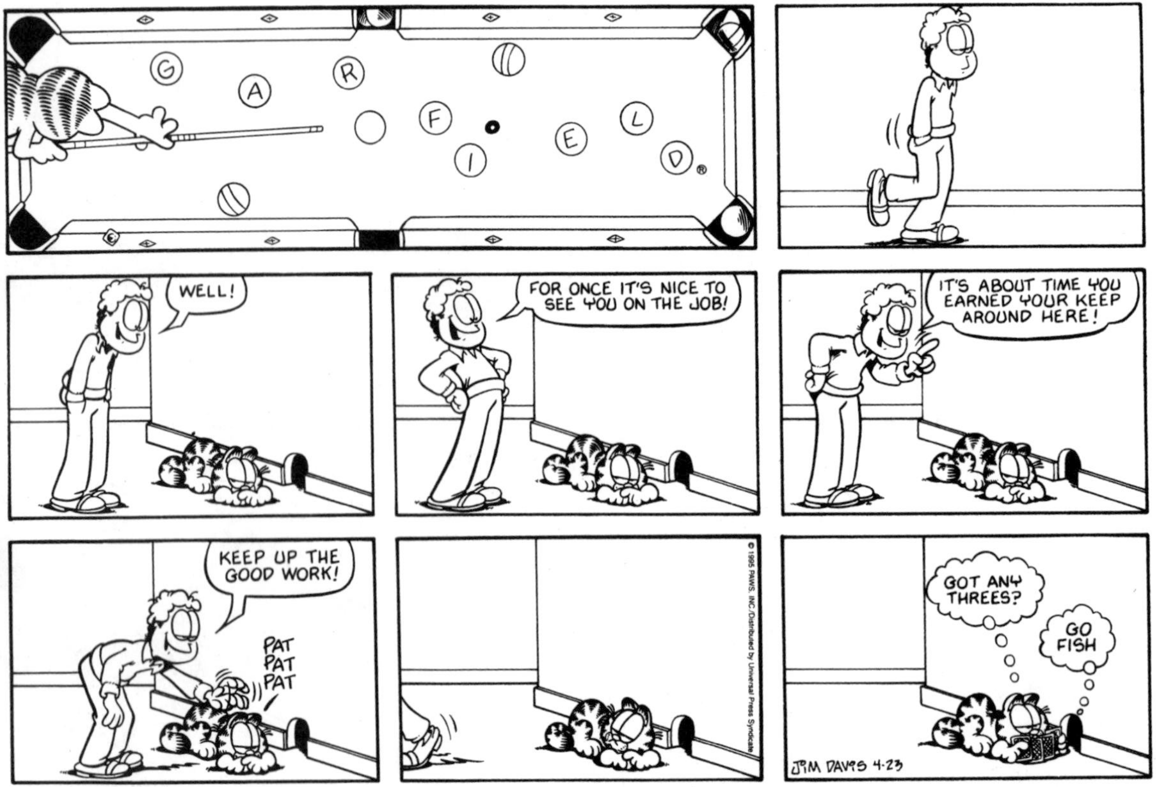
GARFIELD®
WELL!
FOR ONCE IT'S NICE TO SEE YOU ON THE JOB!
IT'S ABOUT TIME YOU EARNED YOUR KEEP AROUND HERE!
KEEP UP THE GOOD WORK!
PAT PAT PAT
© 1995 PAWS, INC./Distributed by Universal Press Syndicate
GOT ANY THREES?
GO FISH
JIM DAVIS 4-23

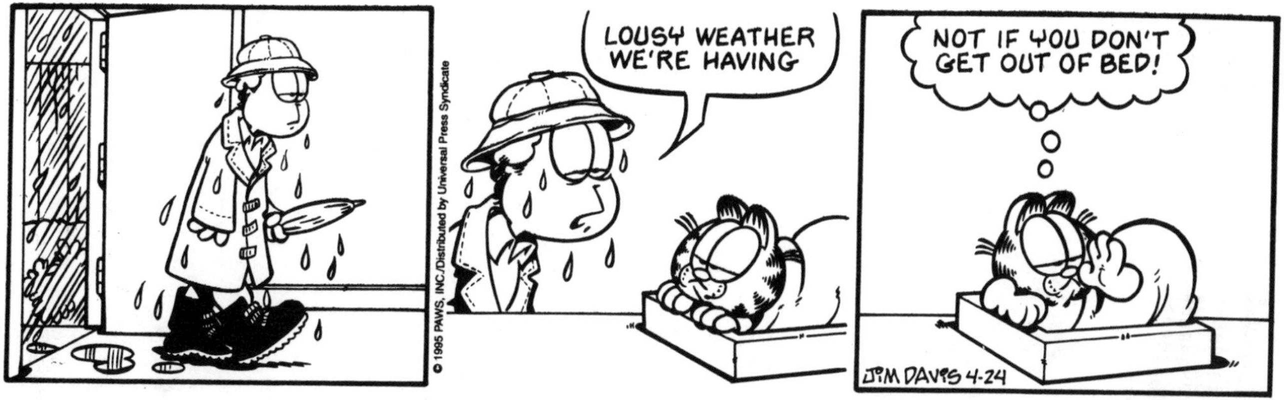
© 1995 PAWS, INC./Distributed by Universal Press Syndicate
LOUSY WEATHER WE'RE HAVING
NOT IF YOU DON'T GET OUT OF BED!
JIM DAVIS 4-24

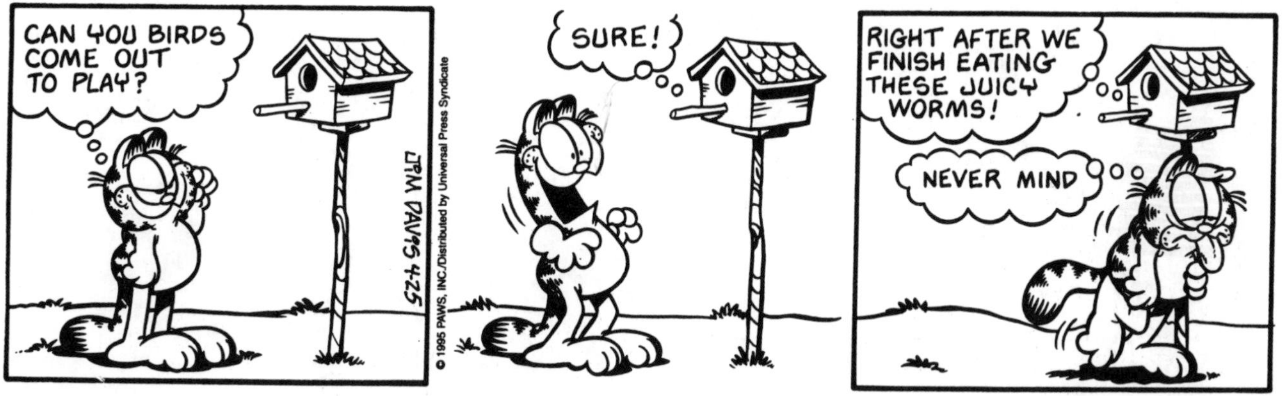
CAN YOU BIRDS COME OUT TO PLAY?
JIM DAVIS 4-25
© 1995 PAWS, INC./Distributed by Universal Press Syndicate
SURE!
RIGHT AFTER WE FINISH EATING THESE JUICY WORMS!
NEVER MIND

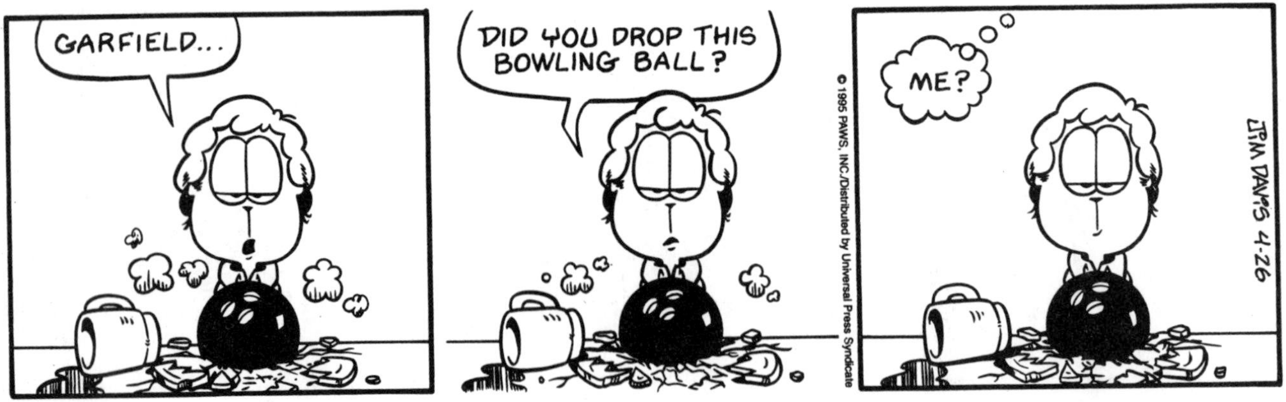
GARFIELD...
DID YOU DROP THIS BOWLING BALL?
© 1995 PAWS, INC./Distributed by Universal Press Syndicate
ME?
JIM DAVIS 4-26

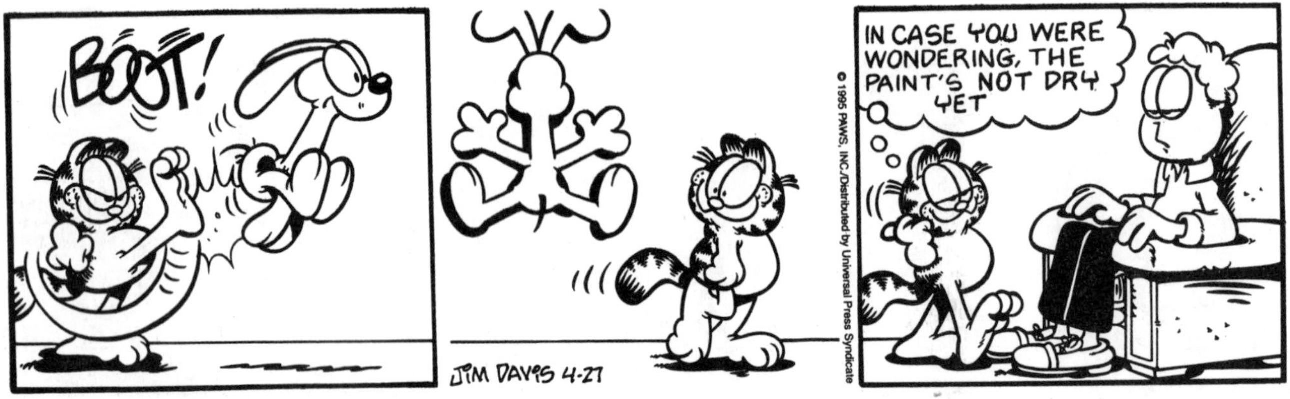
BOOT!
JIM DAVIS 4-27
© 1995 PAWS, INC./Distributed by Universal Press Syndicate
IN CASE YOU WERE WONDERING, THE PAINT'S NOT DRY YET

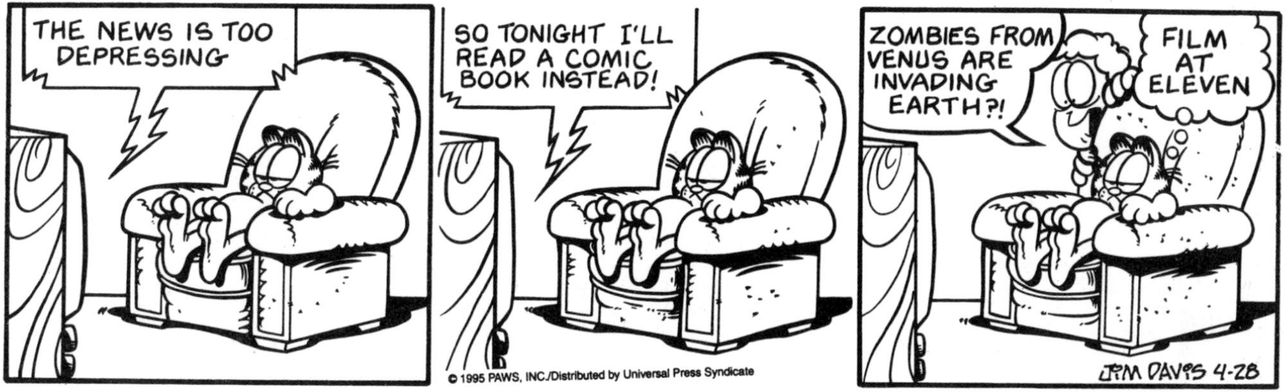
THE NEWS IS TOO DEPRESSING
SO TONIGHT I'LL READ A COMIC BOOK INSTEAD!
© 1995 PAWS, INC./Distributed by Universal Press Syndicate
ZOMBIES FROM VENUS ARE INVADING EARTH?!
FILM AT ELEVEN
JIM DAVIS 4-28

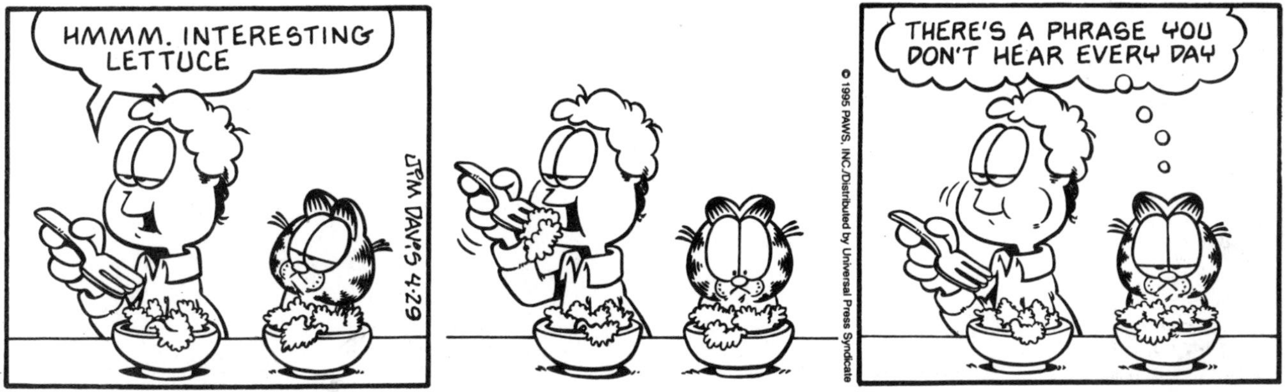
HMMM. INTERESTING LETTUCE
JIM DAVIS 4-29
© 1995 PAWS, INC./Distributed by Universal Press Syndicate
THERE'S A PHRASE YOU DON'T HEAR EVERY DAY

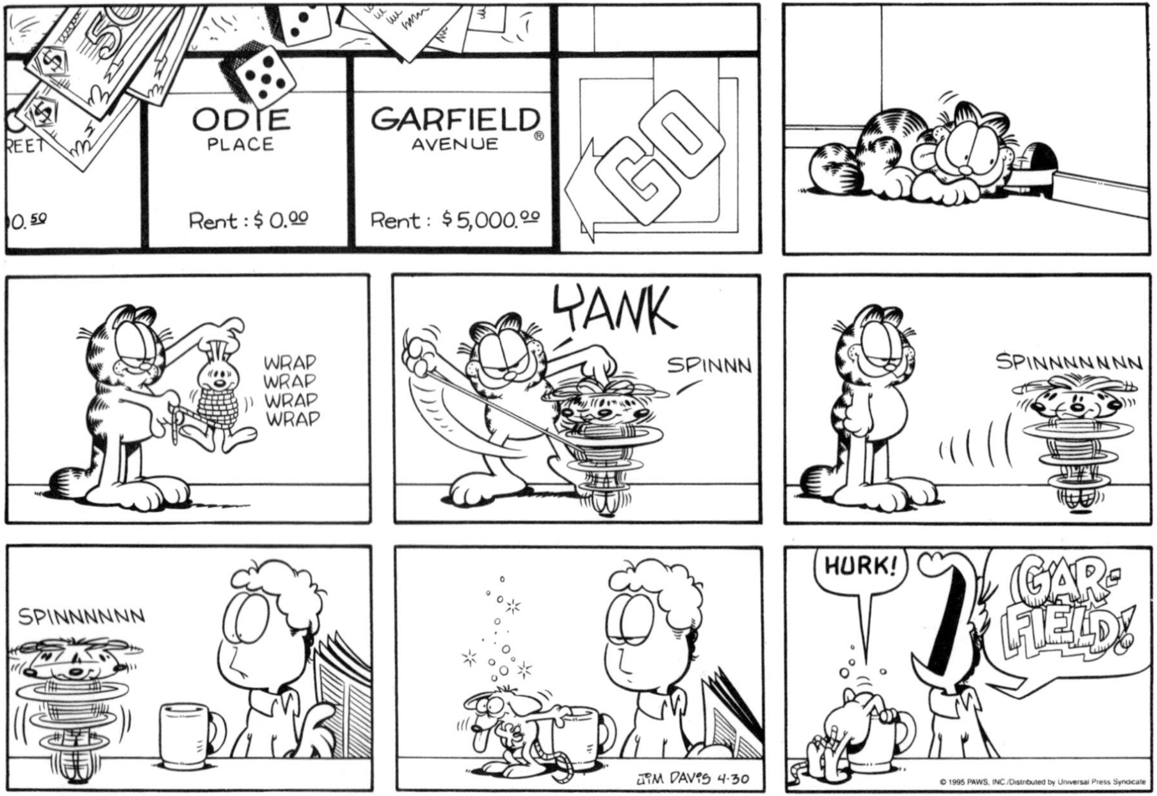

REET
0.50
ODIE
PLACE
Rent : $ 0.00
GARFIELD
AVENUE
Rent : $ 5,000.00
GO
WRAP
WRAP
WRAP
WRAP
YANK
SPINNN
SPINNNNNNNN
SPINNNNNNN
JIM DAVIS 4·30
HURK!
GAR-FIELD!
© 1995 PAWS, INC./Distributed by Universal Press Syndicate

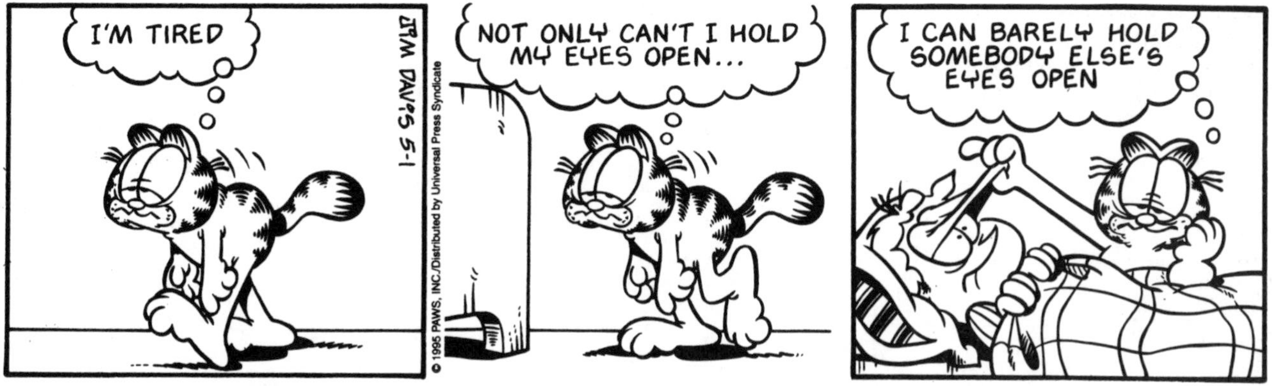
I'M TIRED
JIM DAVIS 5-1
© 1995 PAWS, INC./Distributed by Universal Press Syndicate
NOT ONLY CAN'T I HOLD MY EYES OPEN...
I CAN BARELY HOLD SOMEBODY ELSE'S EYES OPEN

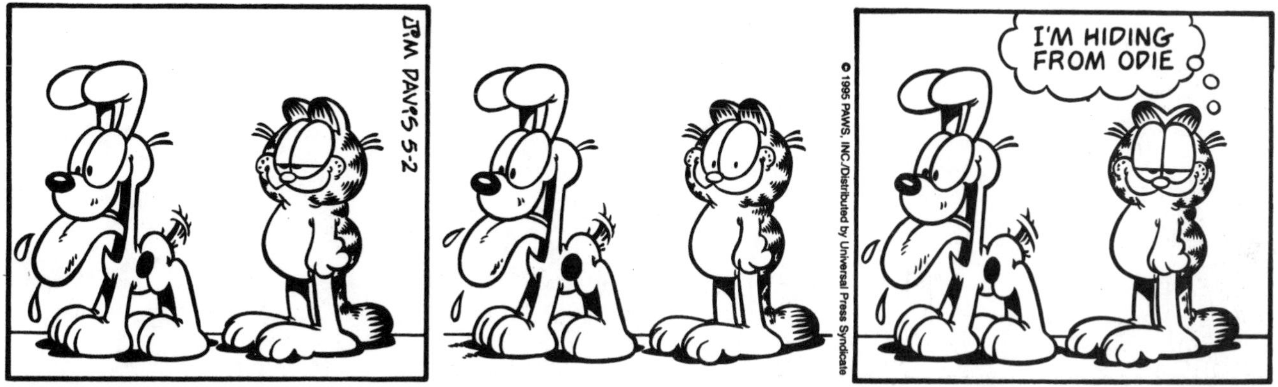
JIM DAVIS 5-2
© 1995 PAWS, INC./Distributed by Universal Press Syndicate
I'M HIDING FROM ODIE

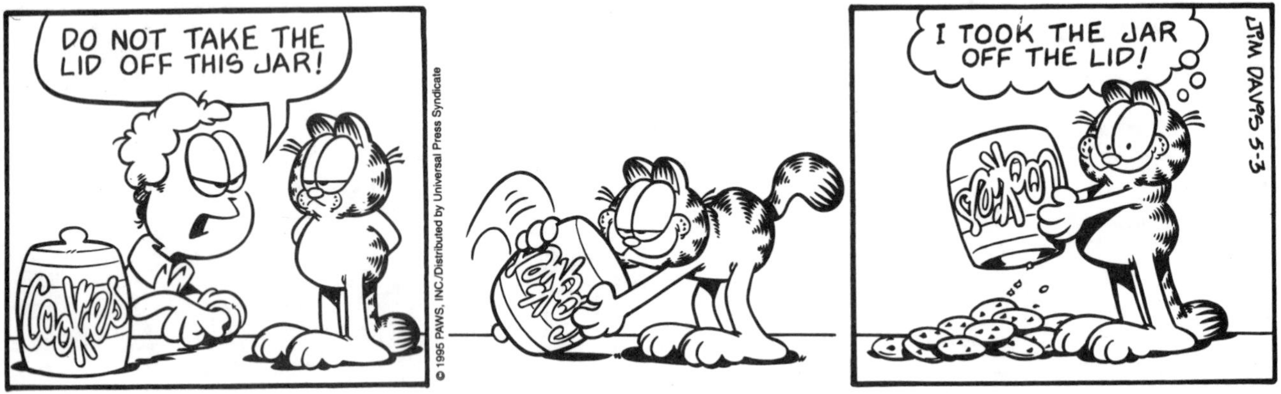
DO NOT TAKE THE LID OFF THIS JAR!
Cookies
© 1995 PAWS, INC./Distributed by Universal Press Syndicate
I TOOK THE JAR OFF THE LID!
JIM DAVIS 5-3

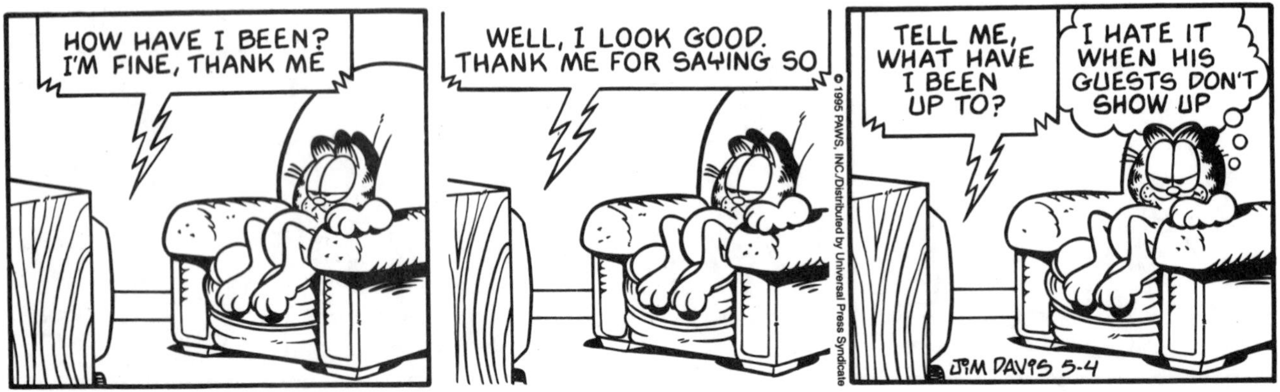
HOW HAVE I BEEN? I'M FINE, THANK ME
WELL, I LOOK GOOD. THANK ME FOR SAYING SO
© 1995 PAWS, INC./Distributed by Universal Press Syndicate
TELL ME, WHAT HAVE I BEEN UP TO?
I HATE IT WHEN HIS GUESTS DON'T SHOW UP
JIM DAVIS 5-4

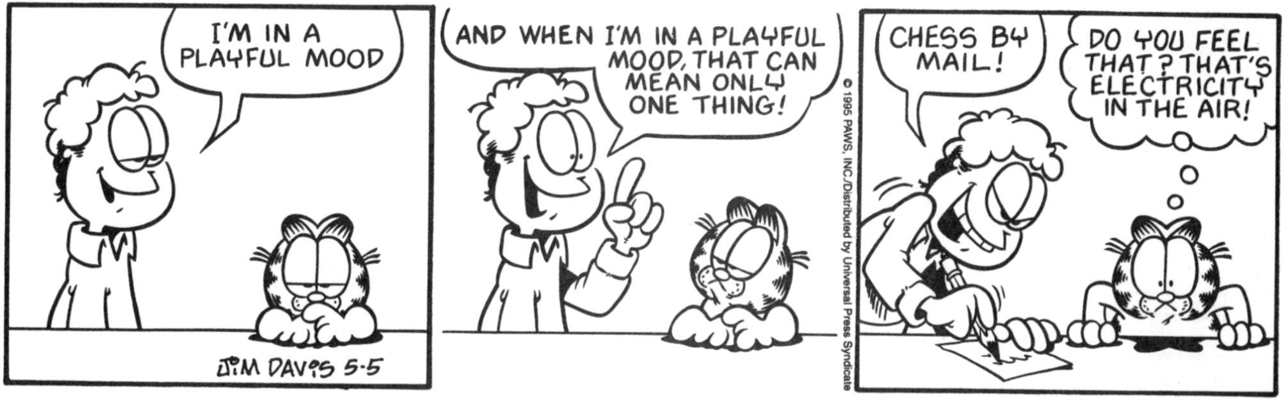
I'M IN A PLAYFUL MOOD
JIM DAVIS 5-5
AND WHEN I'M IN A PLAYFUL MOOD, THAT CAN MEAN ONLY ONE THING!
© 1995 PAWS, INC./Distributed by Universal Press Syndicate
CHESS BY MAIL!
DO YOU FEEL THAT? THAT'S ELECTRICITY IN THE AIR!

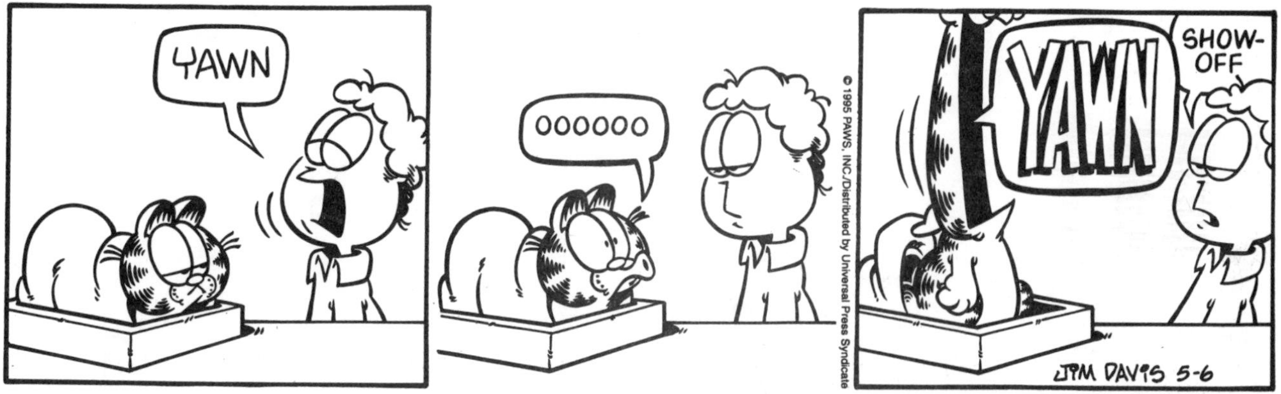
YAWN
OOOOOO
© 1995 PAWS, INC./Distributed by Universal Press Syndicate
YAWN
SHOW-OFF
JIM DAVIS 5-6

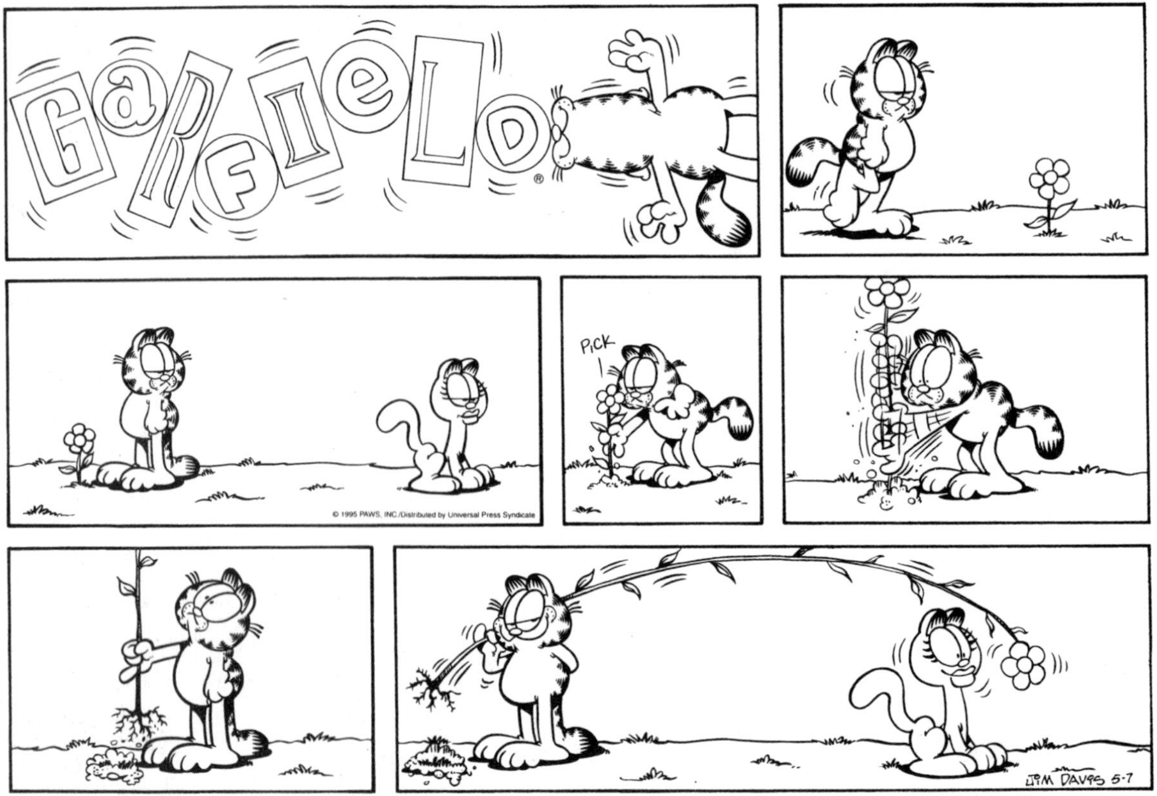
GARFIELD®
PICK
© 1995 PAWS, INC./Distributed by Universal Press Syndicate
JIM DAVIS 5-7

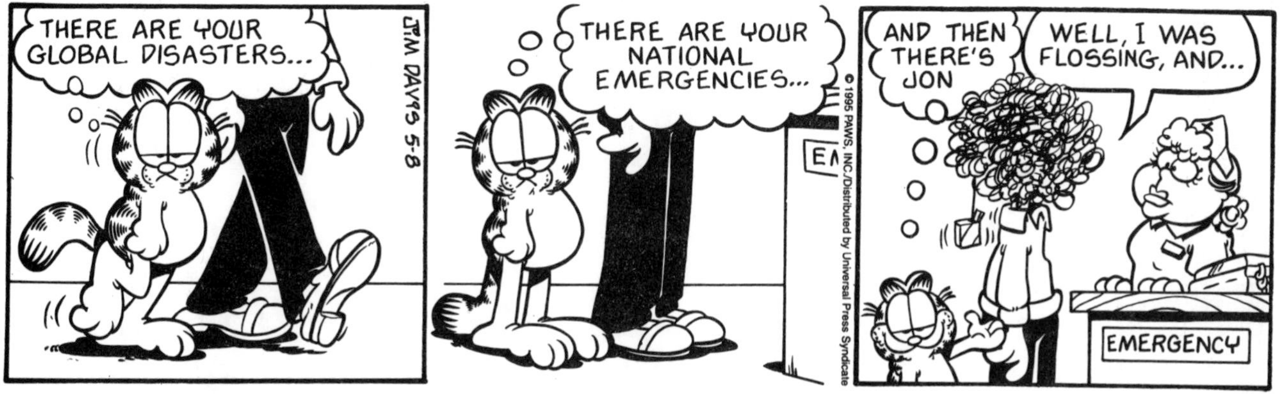
THERE ARE YOUR GLOBAL DISASTERS...
JIM DAVIS 5-8
THERE ARE YOUR NATIONAL EMERGENCIES...
EM
© 1995 PAWS, INC./Distributed by Universal Press Syndicate
AND THEN THERE'S JON
WELL, I WAS FLOSSING, AND...
EMERGENCY

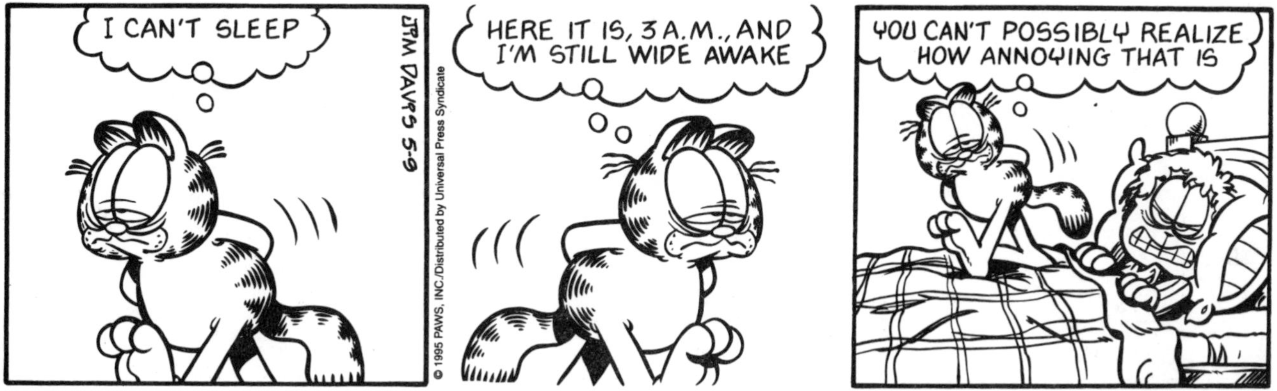
I CAN'T SLEEP
JIM DAVIS 5-9
© 1995 PAWS, INC./Distributed by Universal Press Syndicate
HERE IT IS, 3 A.M., AND I'M STILL WIDE AWAKE
YOU CAN'T POSSIBLY REALIZE HOW ANNOYING THAT IS

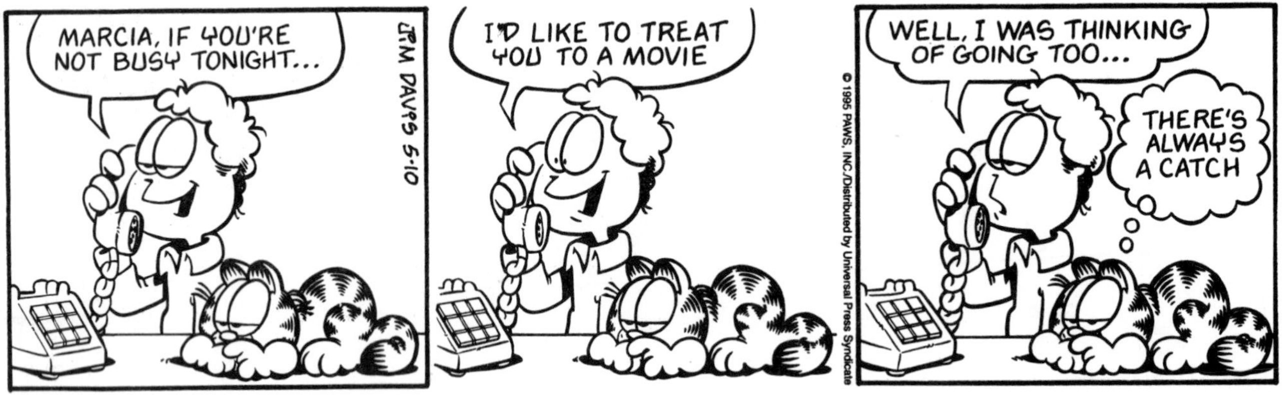
MARCIA, IF YOU'RE NOT BUSY TONIGHT...
JIM DAVIS 5-10
I'D LIKE TO TREAT YOU TO A MOVIE
© 1995 PAWS, INC./Distributed by Universal Press Syndicate
WELL, I WAS THINKING OF GOING TOO...
THERE'S ALWAYS A CATCH

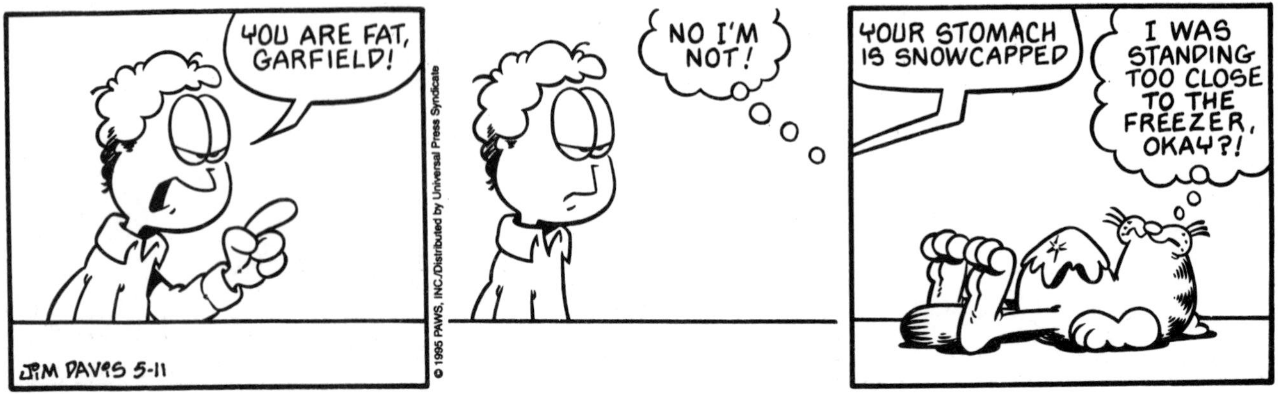
YOU ARE FAT, GARFIELD!
JIM DAVIS 5-11
© 1995 PAWS, INC./Distributed by Universal Press Syndicate
NO I'M NOT!
YOUR STOMACH IS SNOWCAPPED
I WAS STANDING TOO CLOSE TO THE FREEZER, OKAY?!

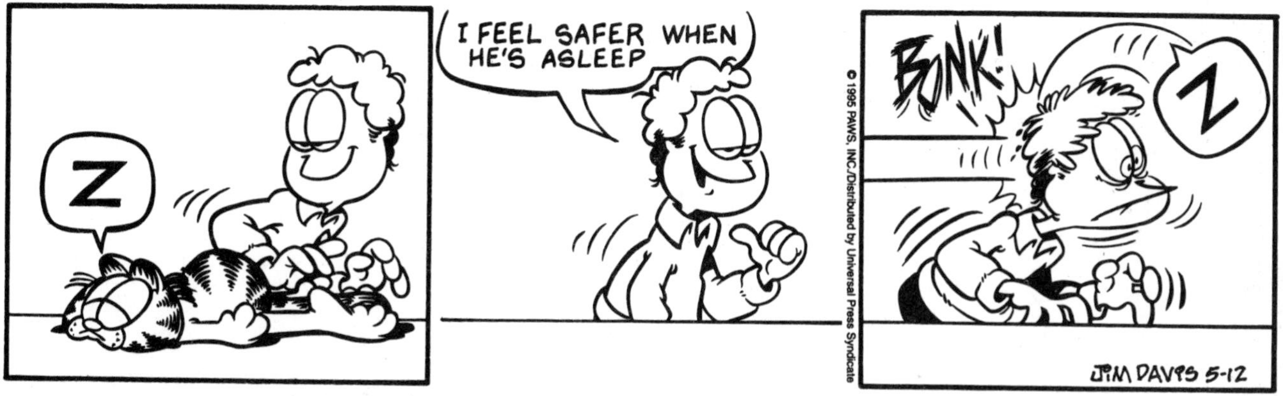
Z
I FEEL SAFER WHEN HE'S ASLEEP
BONK!
Z
JIM DAVIS 5-12
© 1995 PAWS, INC./Distributed by Universal Press Syndicate

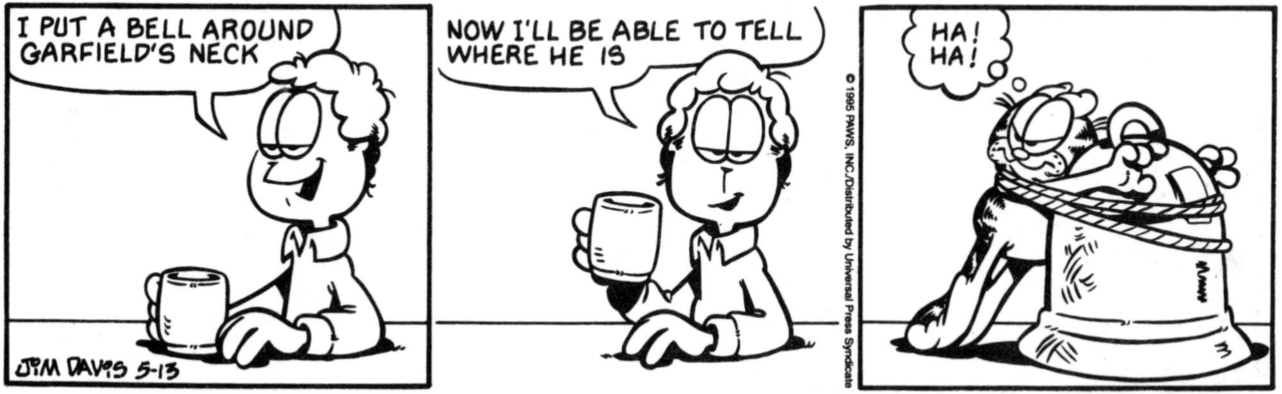
I PUT A BELL AROUND GARFIELD'S NECK
JIM DAVIS 5-13
NOW I'LL BE ABLE TO TELL WHERE HE IS
HA! HA!
© 1995 PAWS, INC./Distributed by Universal Press Syndicate

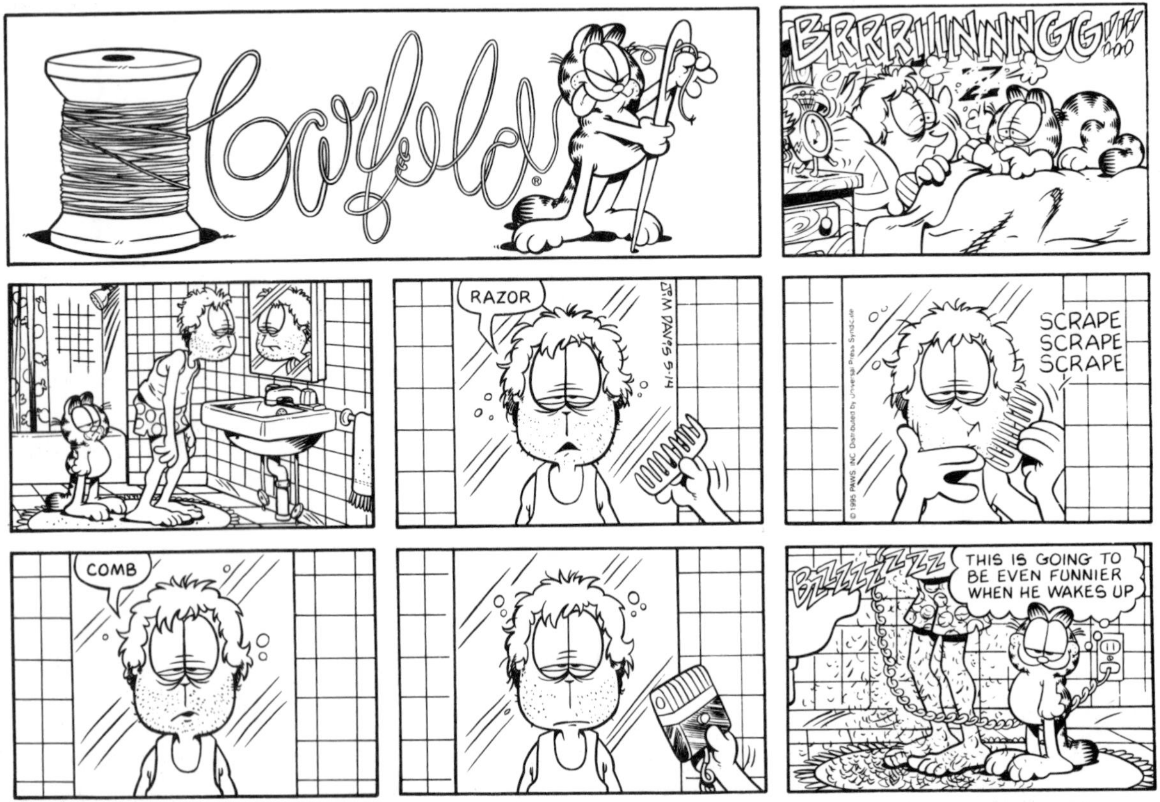
Garfield
BRRRIIINNNGG!!!
RAZOR
JIM DAVIS 5-14
© 1995 PAWS, INC. Distributed by Universal Press Syndicate
SCRAPE SCRAPE SCRAPE
COMB
BZZZZZZZZZ
THIS IS GOING TO BE EVEN FUNNIER WHEN HE WAKES UP

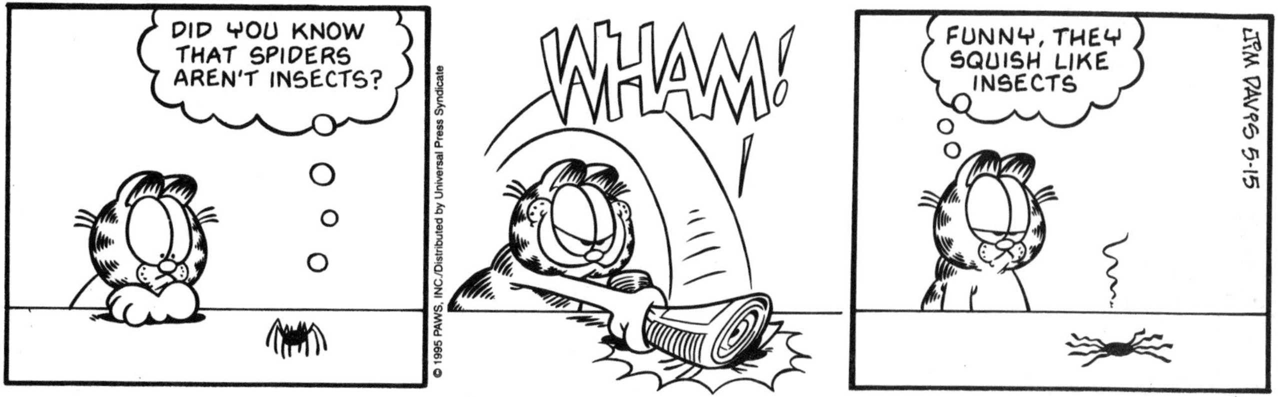
DID YOU KNOW THAT SPIDERS AREN'T INSECTS?
WHAM!
FUNNY, THEY SQUISH LIKE INSECTS
JIM DAVIS 5-15

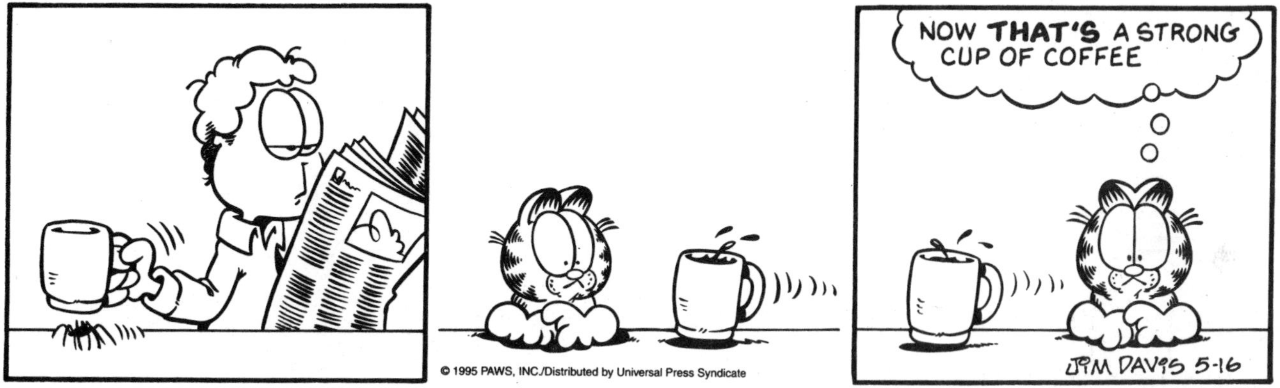
NOW **THAT'S** A STRONG CUP OF COFFEE
JIM DAVIS 5-16

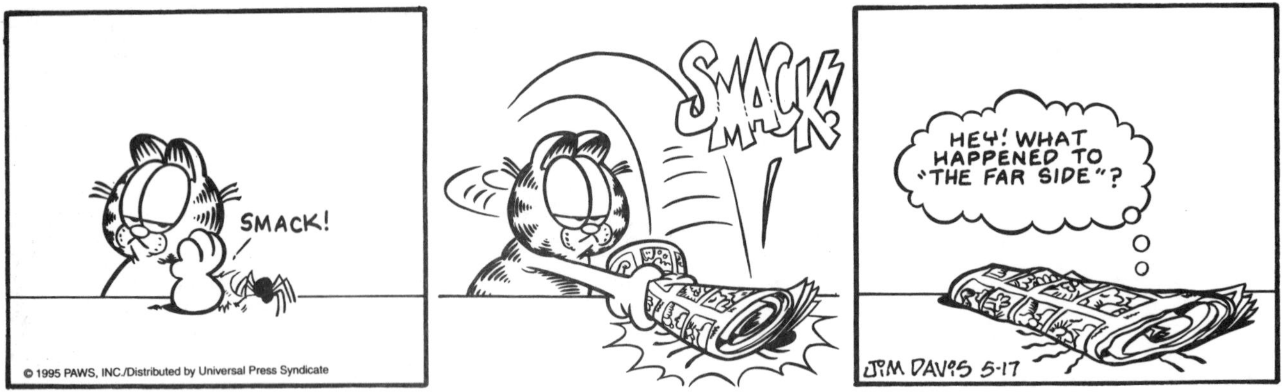
SMACK!
© 1995 PAWS, INC./Distributed by Universal Press Syndicate
SMACK
HEY! WHAT HAPPENED TO "THE FAR SIDE"?
JIM DAVIS 5-17

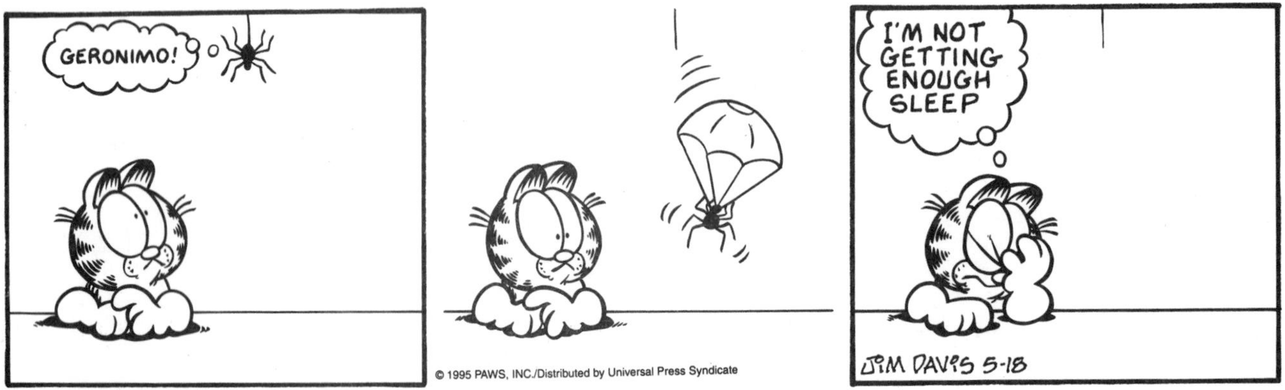
GERONIMO!
© 1995 PAWS, INC./Distributed by Universal Press Syndicate
I'M NOT GETTING ENOUGH SLEEP
JIM DAVIS 5-18

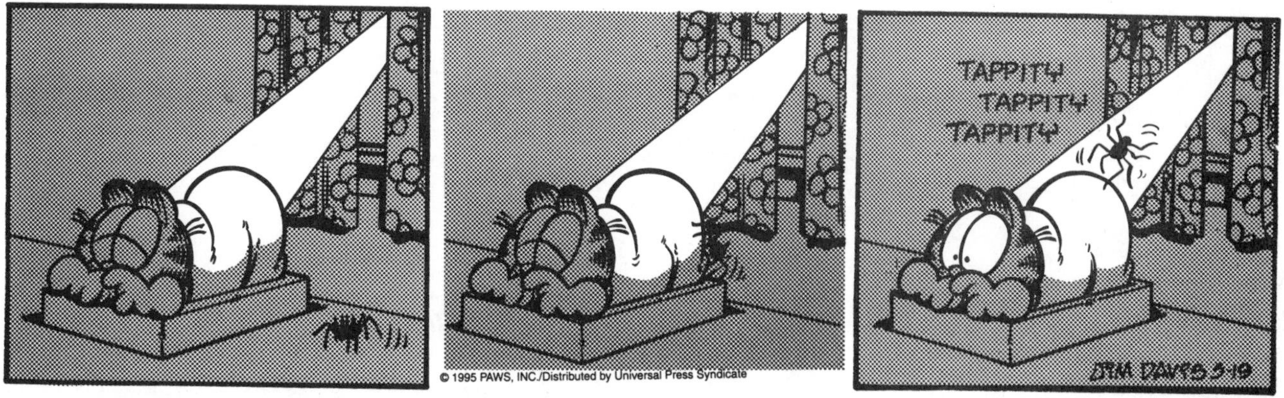
TAPPITY
TAPPITY
TAPPITY
© 1995 PAWS, INC./Distributed by Universal Press Syndicate
JIM DAVIS 5-19

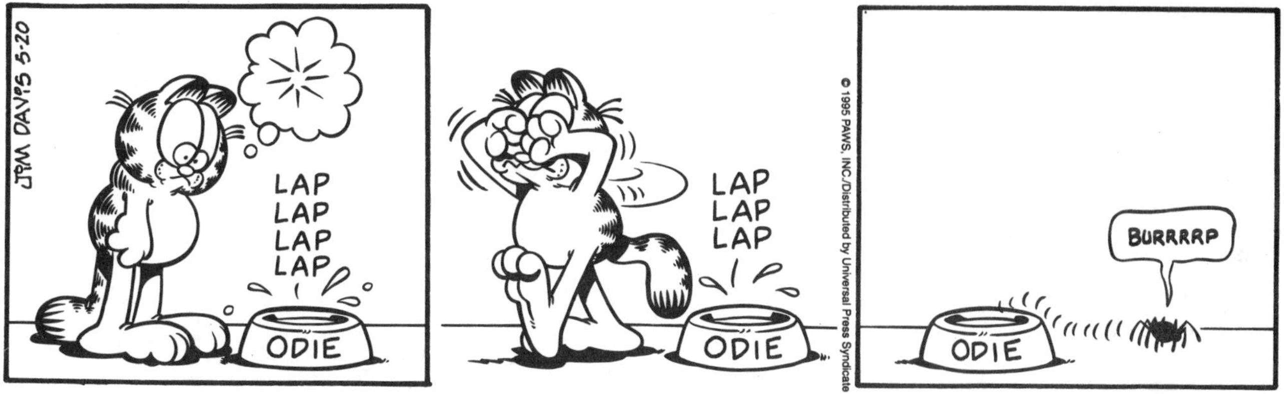
JIM DAVIS 5-20
LAP
LAP
LAP
LAP
ODIE
LAP
LAP
LAP
ODIE
© 1995 PAWS, INC./Distributed by Universal Press Syndicate
BURRRRP
ODIE

GARFIELD®
TAPPY TAPPY TAPPY
TAPPY TAPPY TAPPY
© 1995 PAWS, INC./Distributed by Universal Press Syndicate
CLAP CLAP CLAP
CLAP CLAP
CLAP CLAP CLAP
TAPPITY TAPPITY TAPPITY
TAPPITY TAPPITY TAPPITY TAPPITY
SPLUT!
SPLOT!
NEVER FOLLOW A DOG ACT
JIM DAVIS 5-21

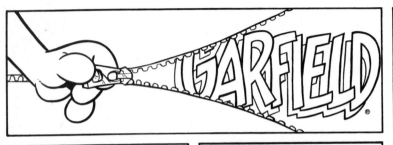

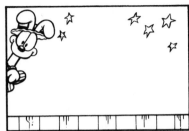

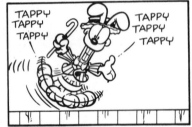

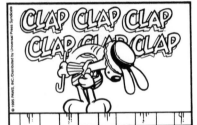

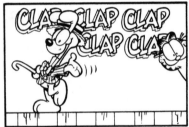

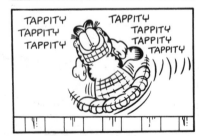

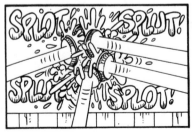

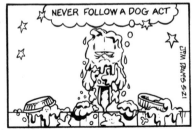

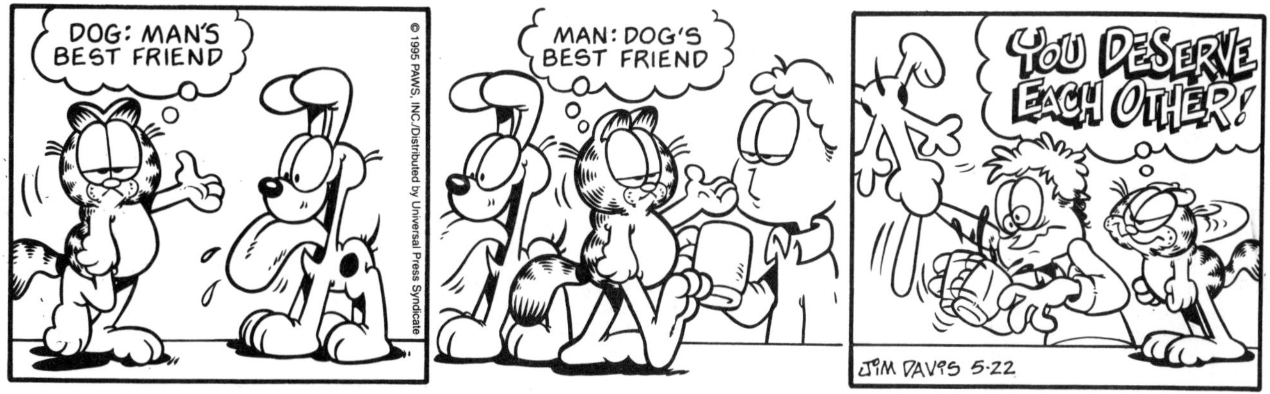
DOG: MAN'S BEST FRIEND
MAN: DOG'S BEST FRIEND
YOU DESERVE EACH OTHER!
JIM DAVIS 5-22

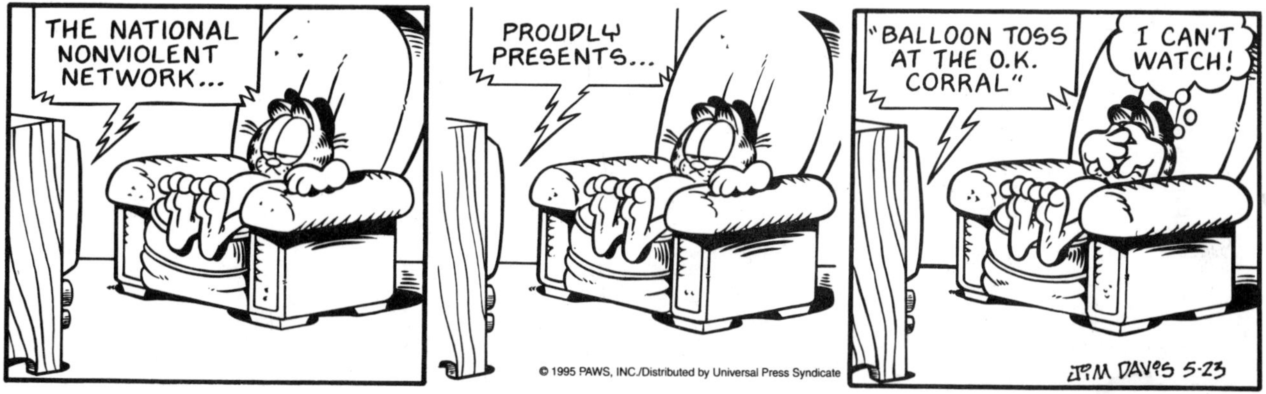
THE NATIONAL NONVIOLENT NETWORK...
PROUDLY PRESENTS...
"BALLOON TOSS AT THE O.K. CORRAL"
I CAN'T WATCH!
JIM DAVIS 5-23

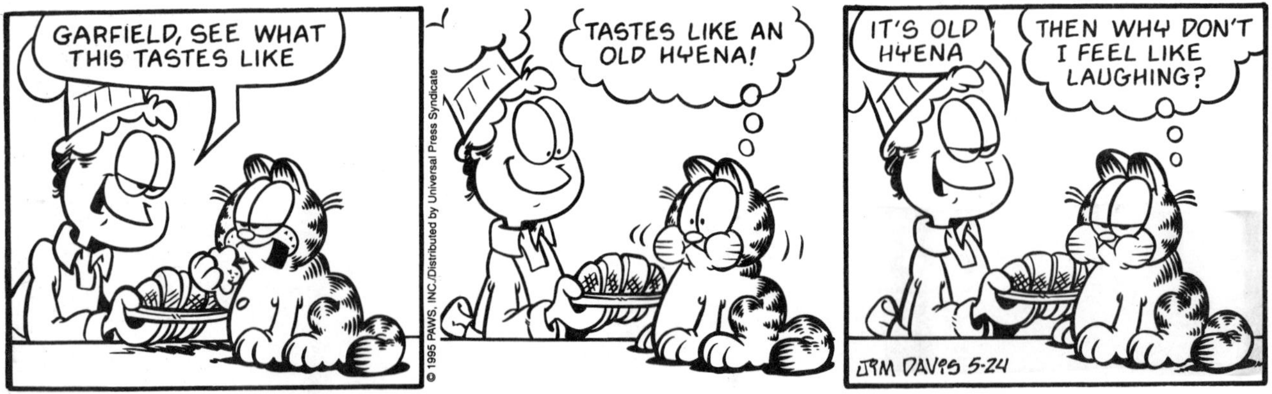
GARFIELD, SEE WHAT THIS TASTES LIKE
TASTES LIKE AN OLD HYENA!
IT'S OLD HYENA
THEN WHY DON'T I FEEL LIKE LAUGHING?
JIM DAVIS 5-24

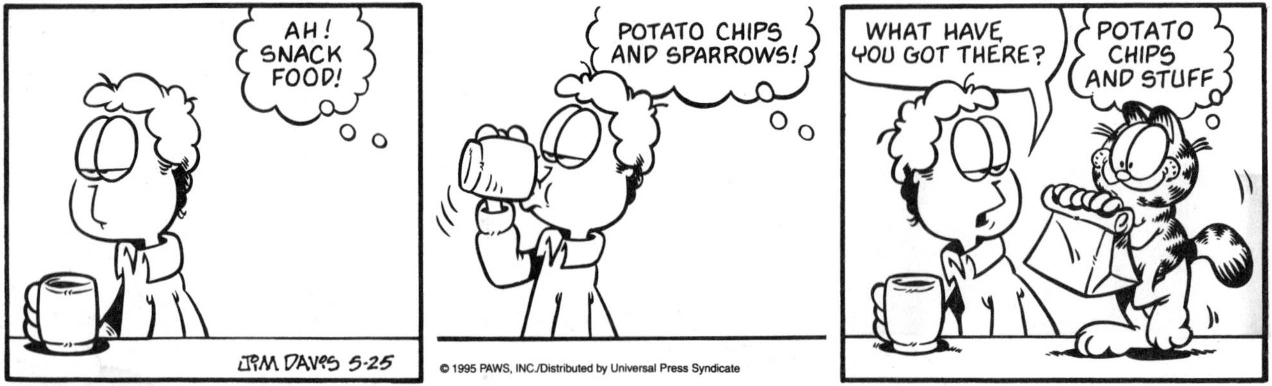
AH! SNACK FOOD!
POTATO CHIPS AND SPARROWS!
WHAT HAVE YOU GOT THERE?
POTATO CHIPS AND STUFF
JIM DAVIS 5-25

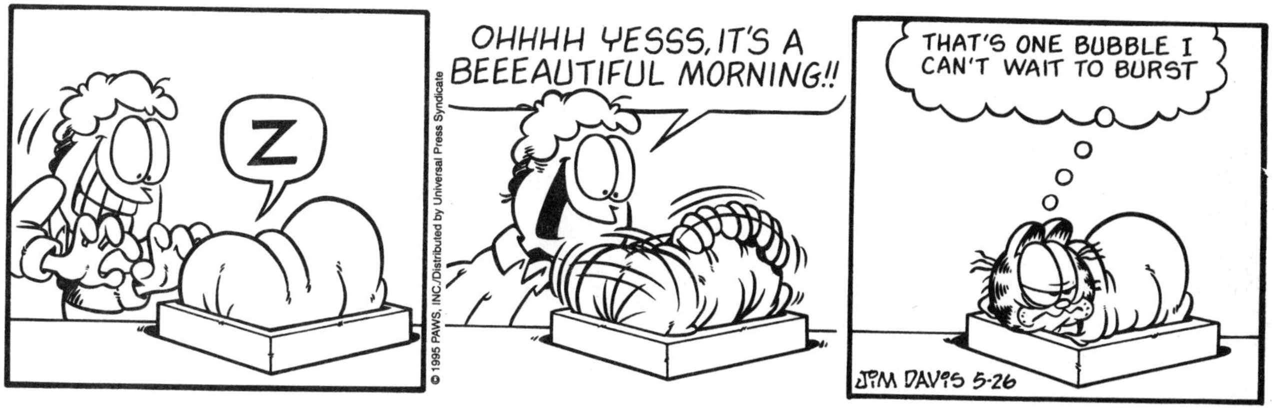
Z
OHHHH YESSS, IT'S A BEEEAUTIFUL MORNING!!
THAT'S ONE BUBBLE I CAN'T WAIT TO BURST
© 1995 PAWS, INC./Distributed by Universal Press Syndicate
JIM DAVIS 5-26

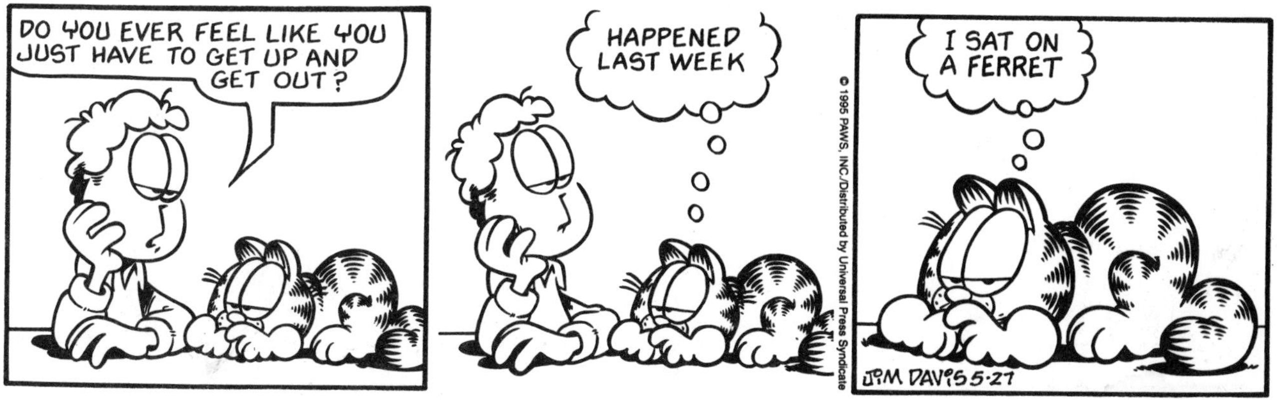
DO YOU EVER FEEL LIKE YOU JUST HAVE TO GET UP AND GET OUT?
HAPPENED LAST WEEK
I SAT ON A FERRET
© 1995 PAWS, INC./Distributed by Universal Press Syndicate
JIM DAVIS 5-27

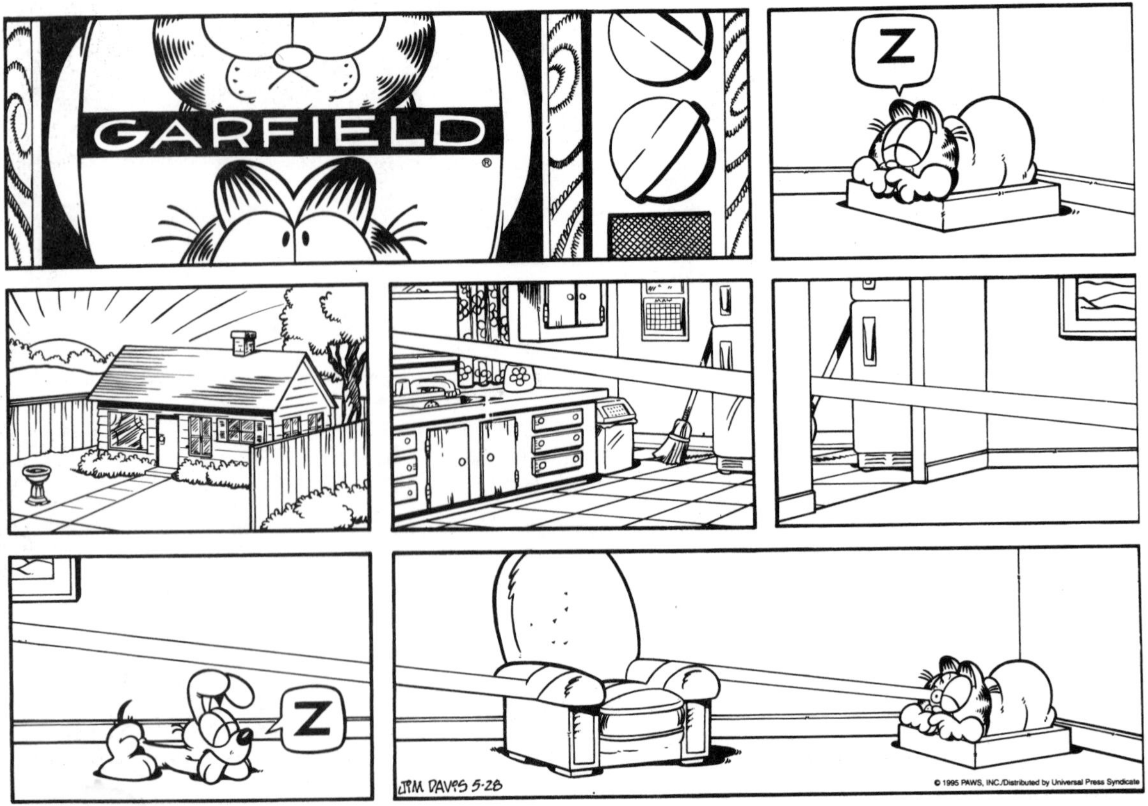
GARFIELD
Z
Z
JIM DAVIS 5-28
© 1995 PAWS, INC./Distributed by Universal Press Syndicate

GREETINGS, FOLKS! I... UM... UM...
NEVER HIRE A DOG AS A CUE CARD BOY
JIM DAVIS
© 1995 PAWS, INC./Distributed by Universal Press Syndicate
5-29

TAPPITY TAPPITY
TAPPITY TAPPITY
BONK!
© 1995 PAWS, INC./Distributed by Universal Press Syndicate
I WANT THAT USHER'S NAME!
JIM DAVIS
5-30

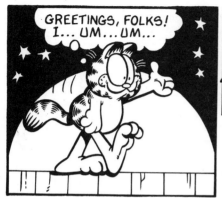

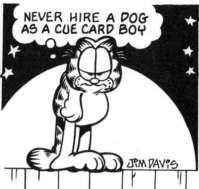

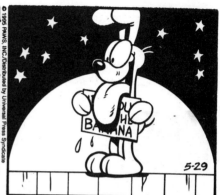

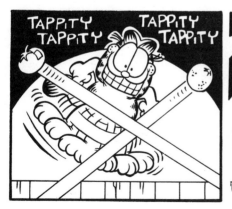

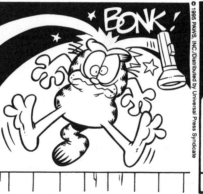

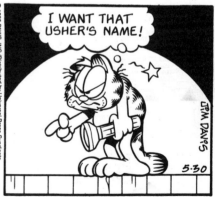

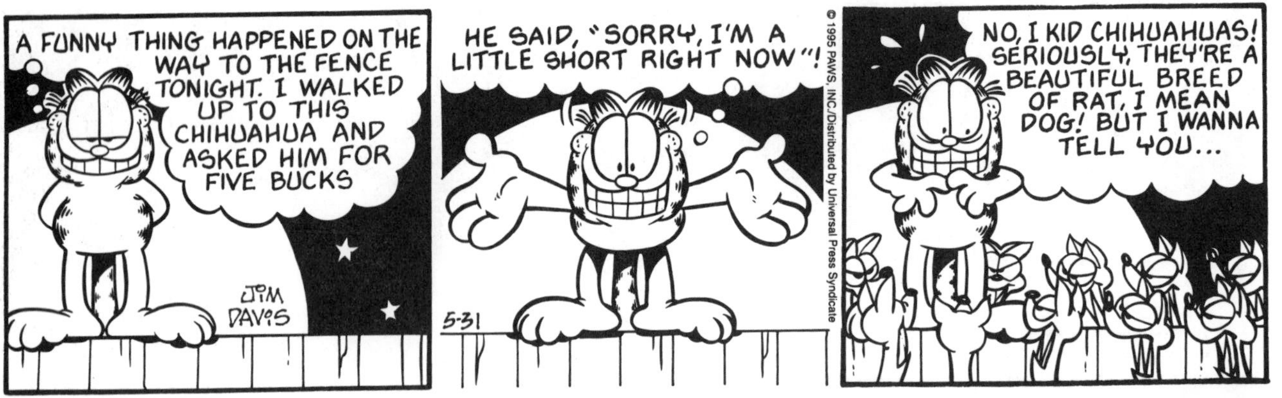
A FUNNY THING HAPPENED ON THE WAY TO THE FENCE TONIGHT. I WALKED UP TO THIS CHIHUAHUA AND ASKED HIM FOR FIVE BUCKS
JIM DAVIS
HE SAID, "SORRY, I'M A LITTLE SHORT RIGHT NOW"!
5-31
© 1995 PAWS, INC./Distributed by Universal Press Syndicate
NO, I KID CHIHUAHUAS! SERIOUSLY, THEY'RE A BEAUTIFUL BREED OF RAT, I MEAN DOG! BUT I WANNA TELL YOU...

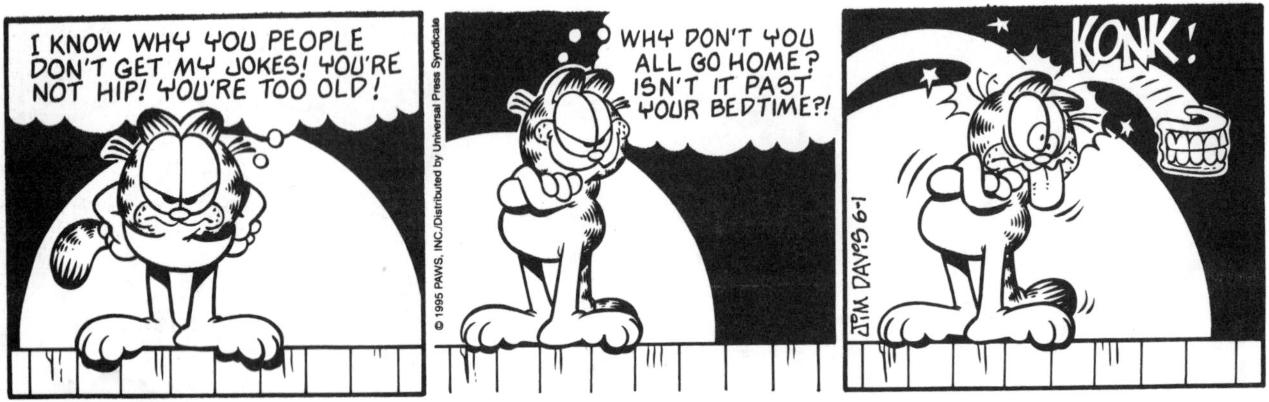
I KNOW WHY YOU PEOPLE DON'T GET MY JOKES! YOU'RE NOT HIP! YOU'RE TOO OLD!
© 1995 PAWS, INC./Distributed by Universal Press Syndicate
WHY DON'T YOU ALL GO HOME? ISN'T IT PAST YOUR BEDTIME?!
JIM DAVIS 6-1
KONK!

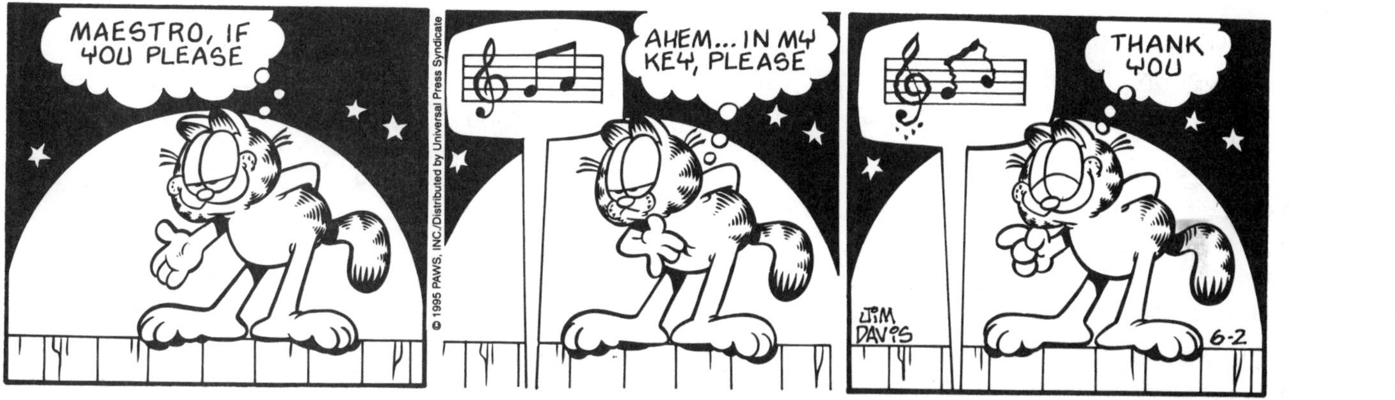
MAESTRO, IF YOU PLEASE
AHEM... IN MY KEY, PLEASE
THANK YOU
JIM DAVIS
6-2
© 1995 PAWS, INC./Distributed by Universal Press Syndicate

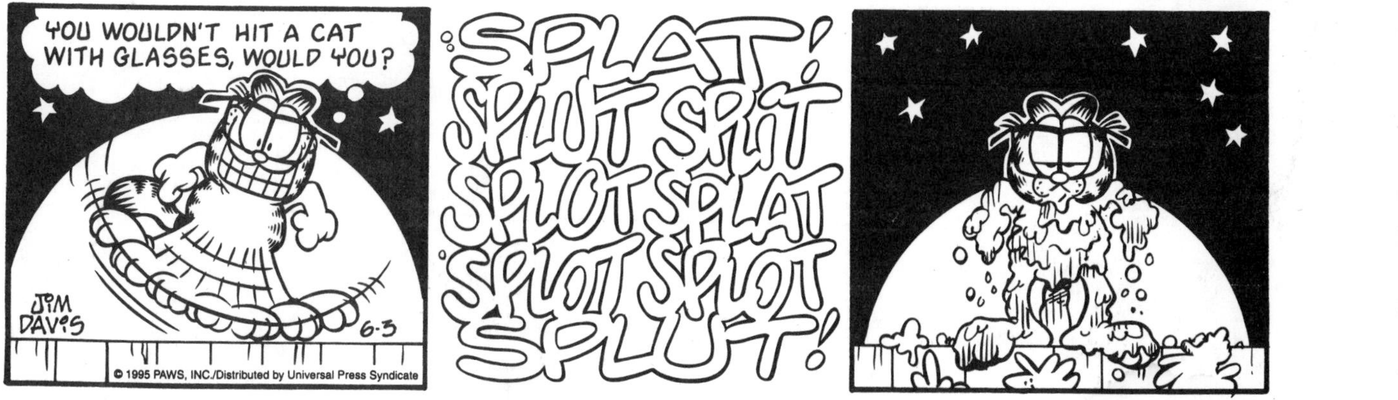
YOU WOULDN'T HIT A CAT WITH GLASSES, WOULD YOU?
JIM DAVIS
6-3
© 1995 PAWS, INC./Distributed by Universal Press Syndicate
SPLAT!
SPLUT SPLIT
SPLOT SPLAT
SPLUT SPLOT
SPLUT!

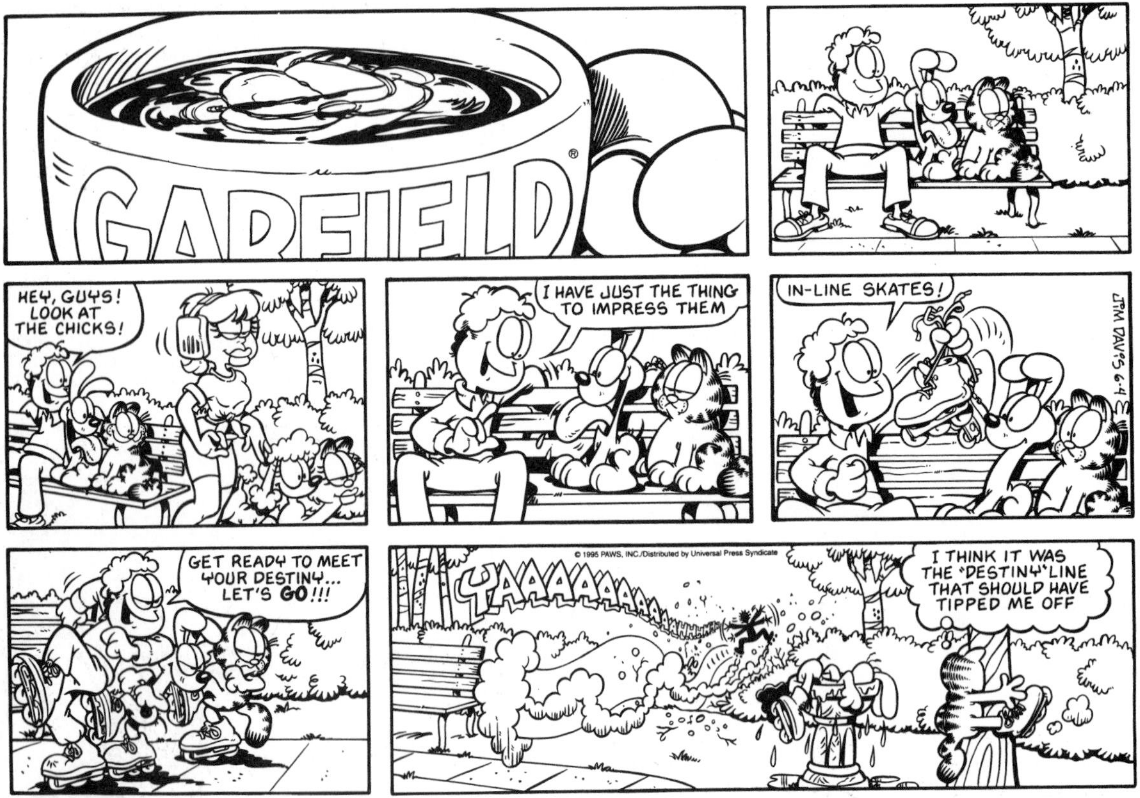

GARFIELD®
HEY, GUYS! LOOK AT THE CHICKS!
I HAVE JUST THE THING TO IMPRESS THEM
IN-LINE SKATES!
JIM DAVIS 6-4
GET READY TO MEET YOUR DESTINY... LET'S GO!!!
© 1995 PAWS, INC./Distributed by Universal Press Syndicate
YAAAAAAAAAAHHHHH
I THINK IT WAS THE "DESTINY" LINE THAT SHOULD HAVE TIPPED ME OFF

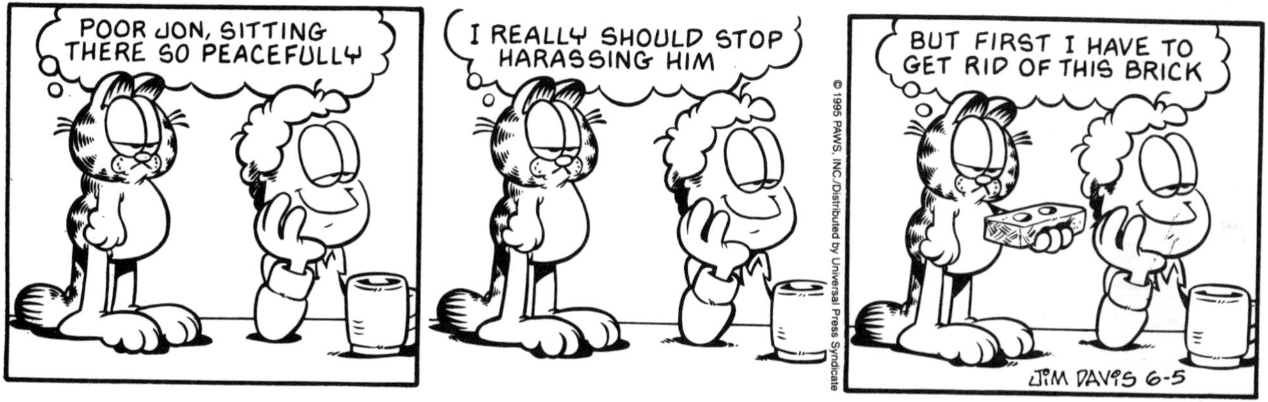
POOR JON, SITTING THERE SO PEACEFULLY
I REALLY SHOULD STOP HARASSING HIM
BUT FIRST I HAVE TO GET RID OF THIS BRICK
JIM DAVIS 6-5

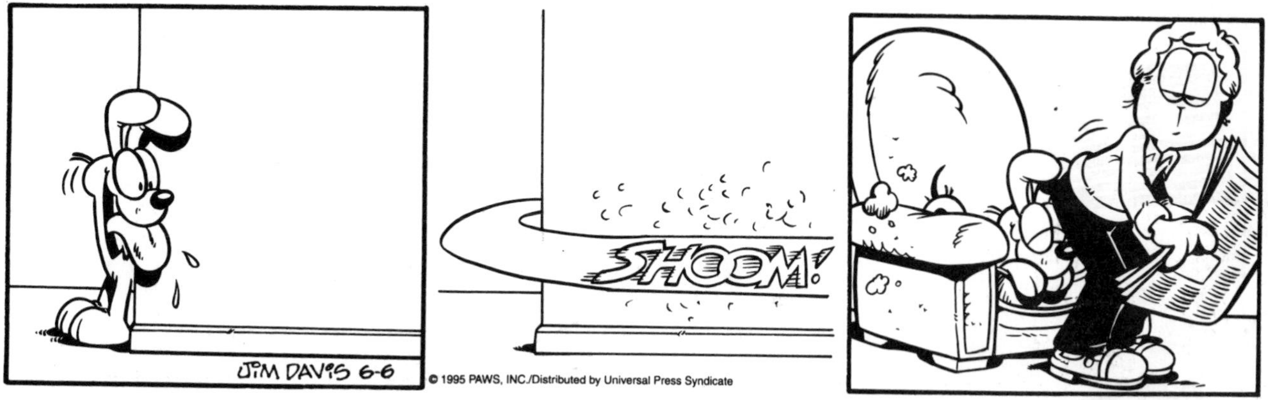
SHOOM!
JIM DAVIS 6-6

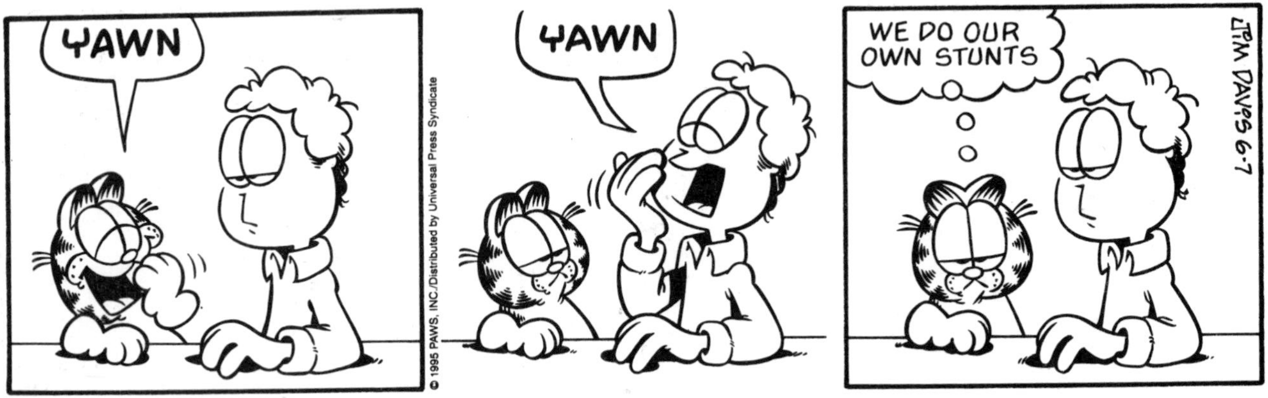
YAWN
YAWN
WE DO OUR OWN STUNTS
JIM DAVIS 6-7
© 1995 PAWS, INC./Distributed by Universal Press Syndicate

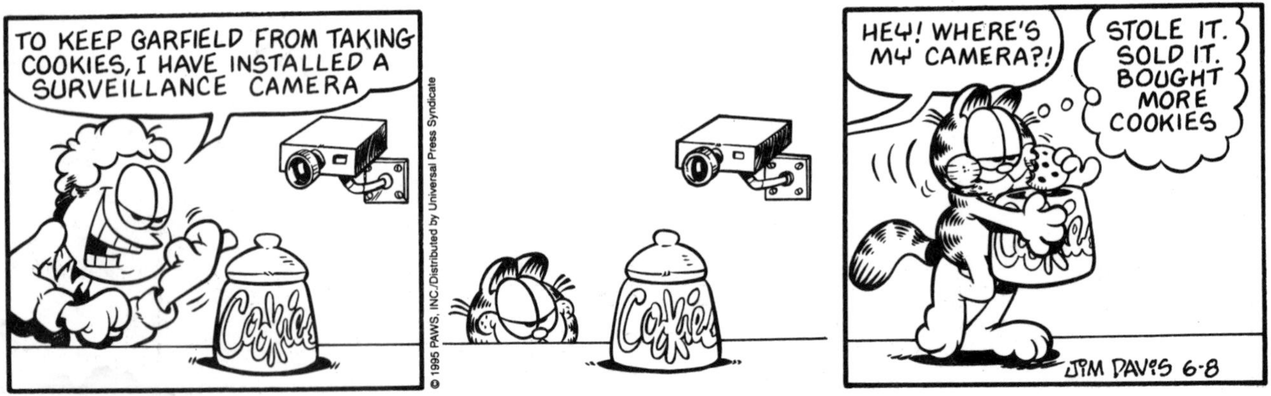
TO KEEP GARFIELD FROM TAKING COOKIES, I HAVE INSTALLED A SURVEILLANCE CAMERA
Cookies
Cookies
HEY! WHERE'S MY CAMERA?!
STOLE IT. SOLD IT. BOUGHT MORE COOKIES
JIM DAVIS 6-8
© 1995 PAWS, INC./Distributed by Universal Press Syndicate

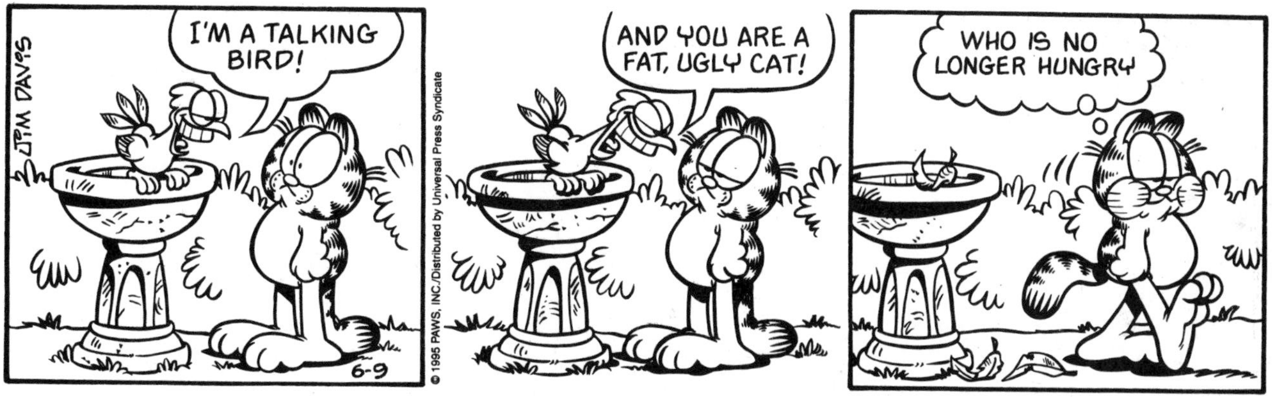
JIM DAVIS
I'M A TALKING BIRD!
6-9
© 1995 PAWS, INC./Distributed by Universal Press Syndicate
AND YOU ARE A FAT, UGLY CAT!
WHO IS NO LONGER HUNGRY

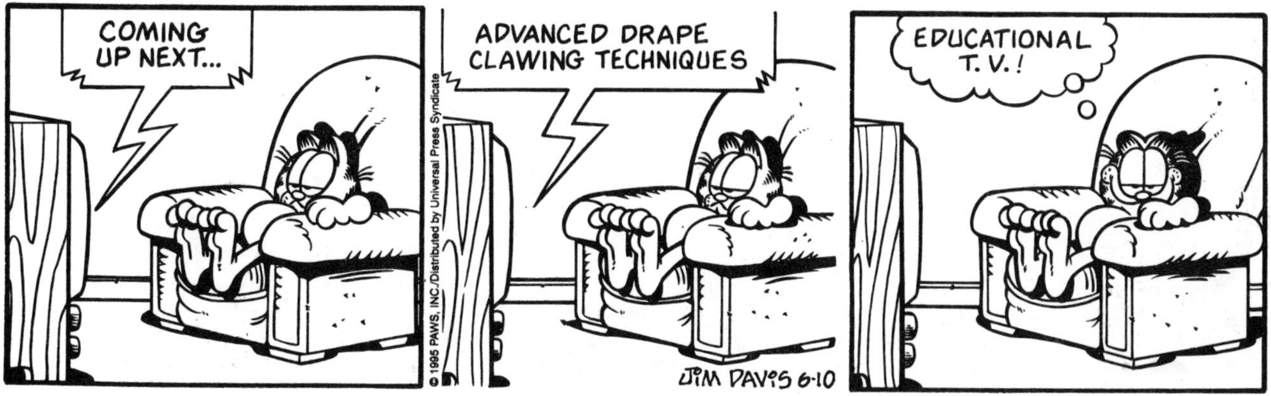
COMING UP NEXT...
© 1995 PAWS, INC./Distributed by Universal Press Syndicate
ADVANCED DRAPE CLAWING TECHNIQUES
JIM DAVIS 6-10
EDUCATIONAL T.V.!

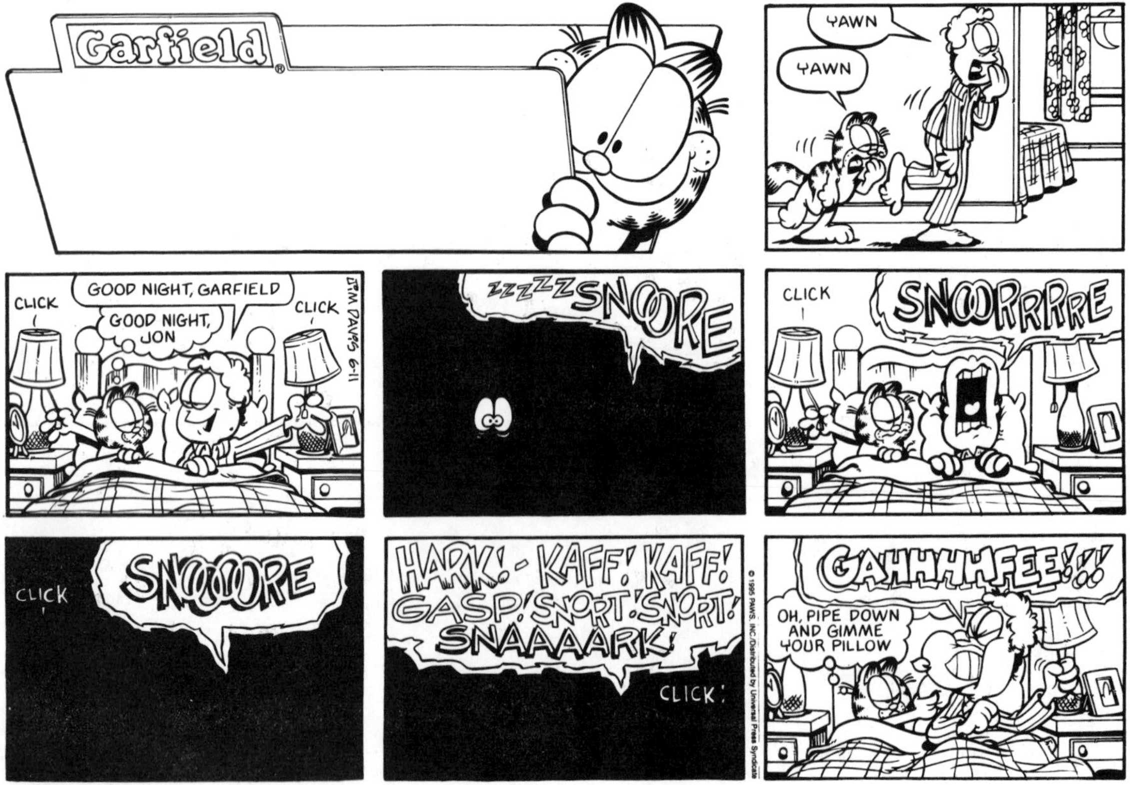
Garfield®
YAWN
YAWN
JIM DAVIS 6-11
CLICK
GOOD NIGHT, GARFIELD
GOOD NIGHT, JON
CLICK
ZZZZZSNOORE
CLICK
SNOORRRRRE
CLICK
SNOOOORE
HARK! - KAFF! KAFF!
GASP! SNORT! SNORT!
SNAAAAARK!
CLICK!
© 1995 PAWS, INC./Distributed by Universal Press Syndicate
GAHHHHFEE!!!
OH, PIPE DOWN AND GIMME YOUR PILLOW

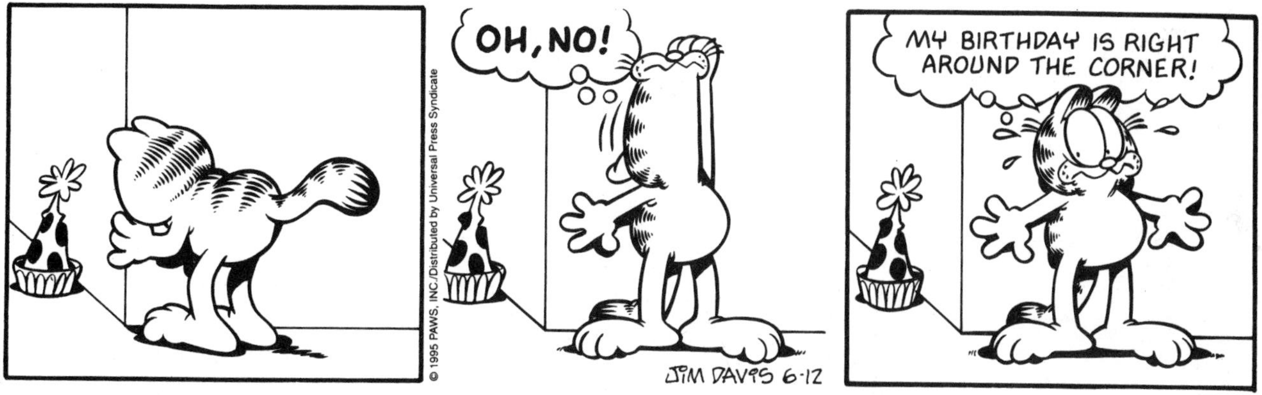
© 1995 PAWS, INC./Distributed by Universal Press Syndicate
OH, NO!
JIM DAVIS 6-12
MY BIRTHDAY IS RIGHT AROUND THE CORNER!

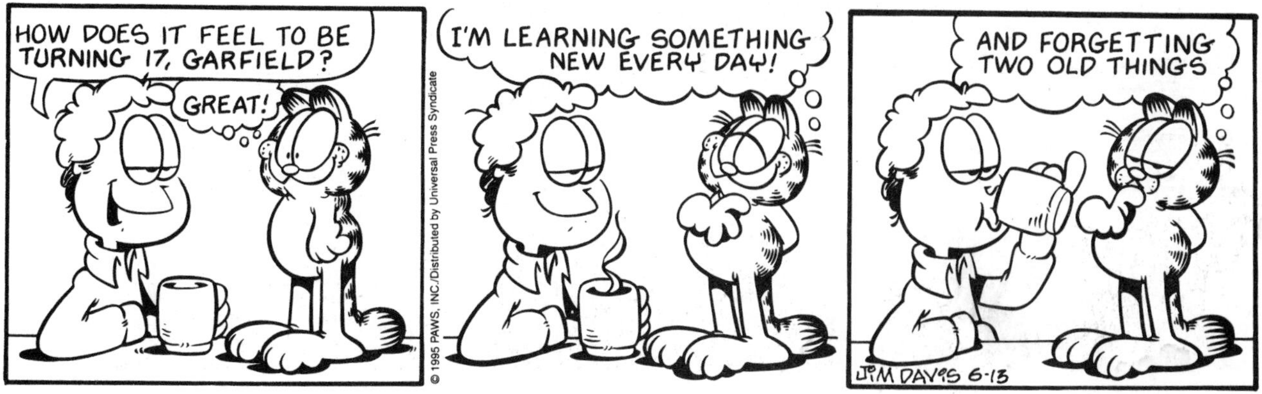
HOW DOES IT FEEL TO BE TURNING 17, GARFIELD?
GREAT!
© 1995 PAWS, INC./Distributed by Universal Press Syndicate
I'M LEARNING SOMETHING NEW EVERY DAY!
AND FORGETTING TWO OLD THINGS
JIM DAVIS 6-13

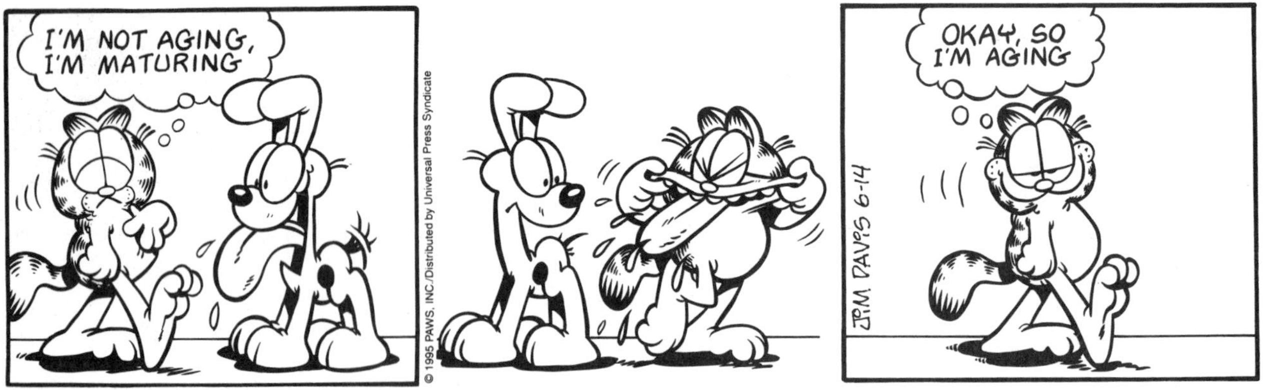
I'M NOT AGING, I'M MATURING
OKAY, SO I'M AGING
JIM DAVIS 6-14

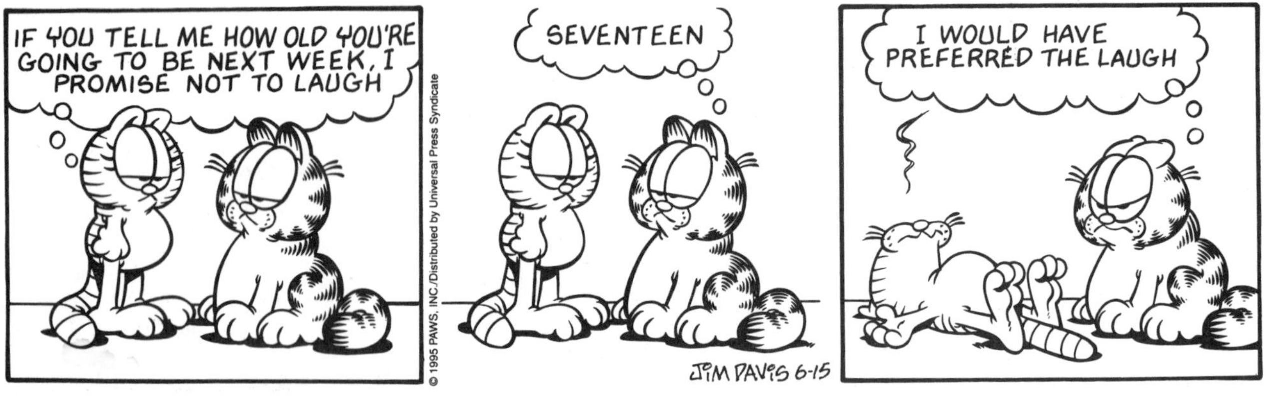
IF YOU TELL ME HOW OLD YOU'RE GOING TO BE NEXT WEEK, I PROMISE NOT TO LAUGH
SEVENTEEN
I WOULD HAVE PREFERRED THE LAUGH
JIM DAVIS 6-15

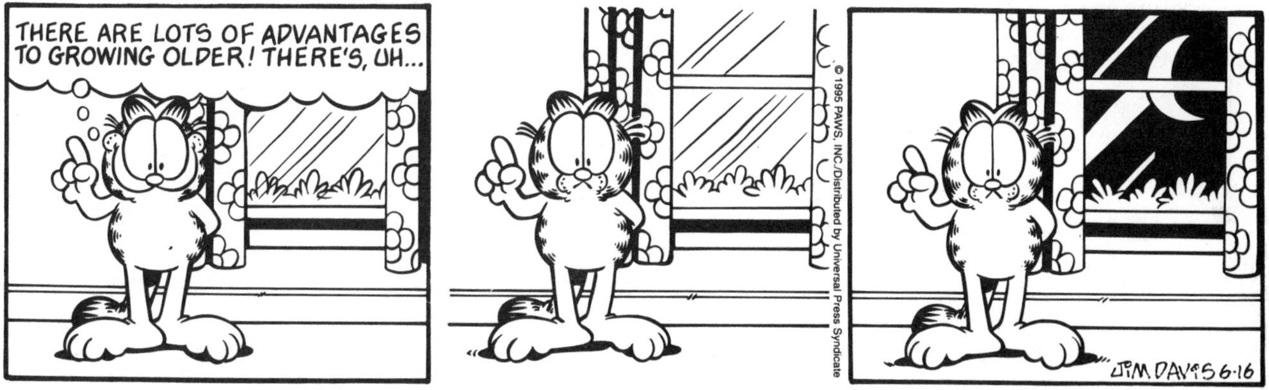
THERE ARE LOTS OF ADVANTAGES TO GROWING OLDER! THERE'S, UH...
© 1995 PAWS, INC./Distributed by Universal Press Syndicate
JIM DAVIS 6-16

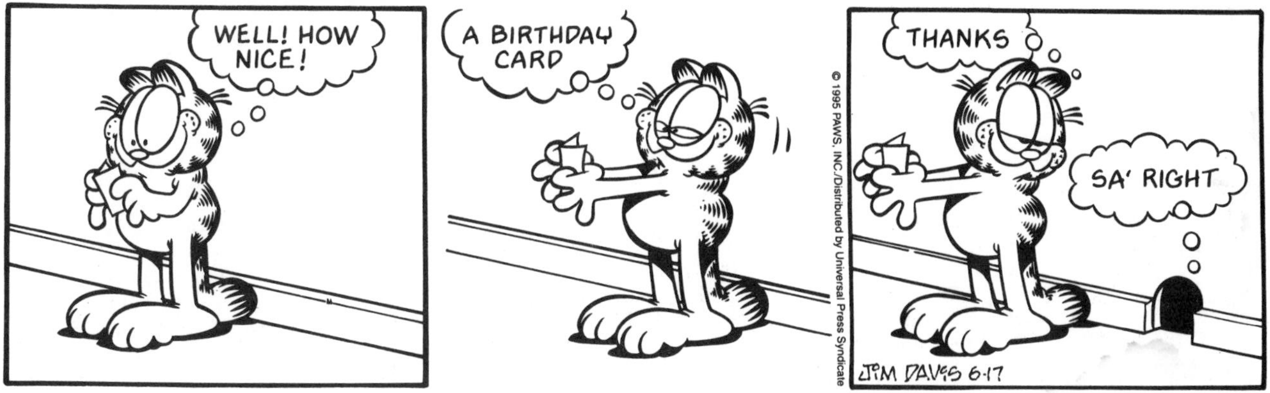
WELL! HOW NICE!
A BIRTHDAY CARD
THANKS
SA' RIGHT
© 1995 PAWS, INC./Distributed by Universal Press Syndicate
JIM DAVIS 6-17

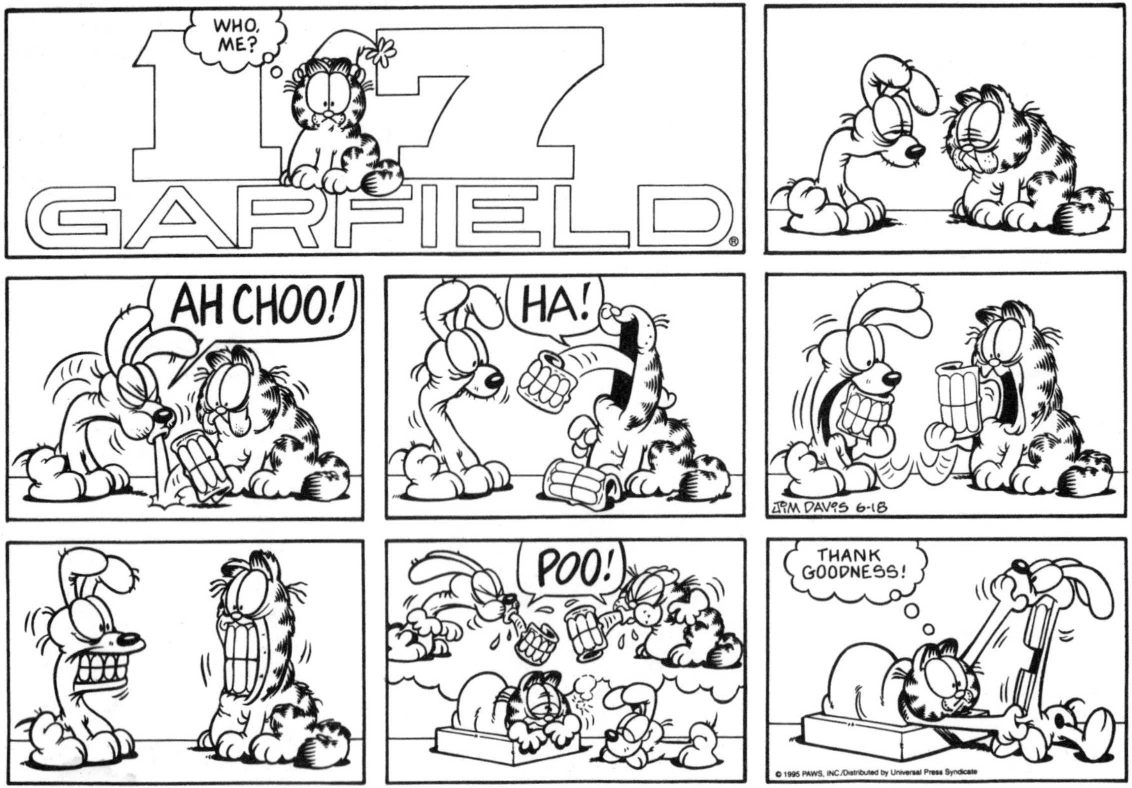
WHO, ME?
GARFIELD®
AH CHOO!
HA!
JIM DAVIS 6-18
POO!
THANK GOODNESS!
© 1995 PAWS, INC./Distributed by Universal Press Syndicate

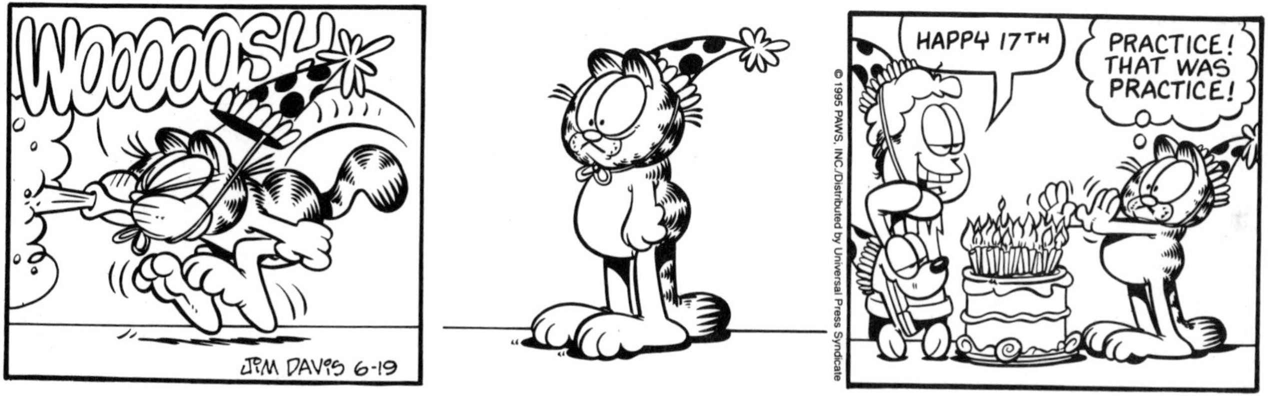
WOOOOOSH
JIM DAVIS 6-19
© 1995 PAWS, INC./Distributed by Universal Press Syndicate
HAPPY 17TH
PRACTICE! THAT WAS PRACTICE!

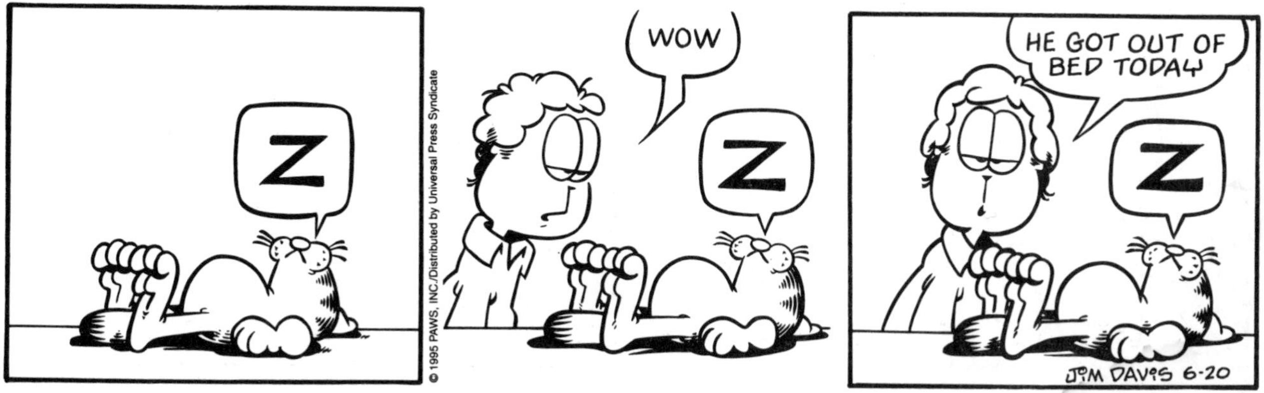
Z
© 1995 PAWS, INC./Distributed by Universal Press Syndicate
WOW
Z
HE GOT OUT OF BED TODAY
Z
JIM DAVIS 6-20

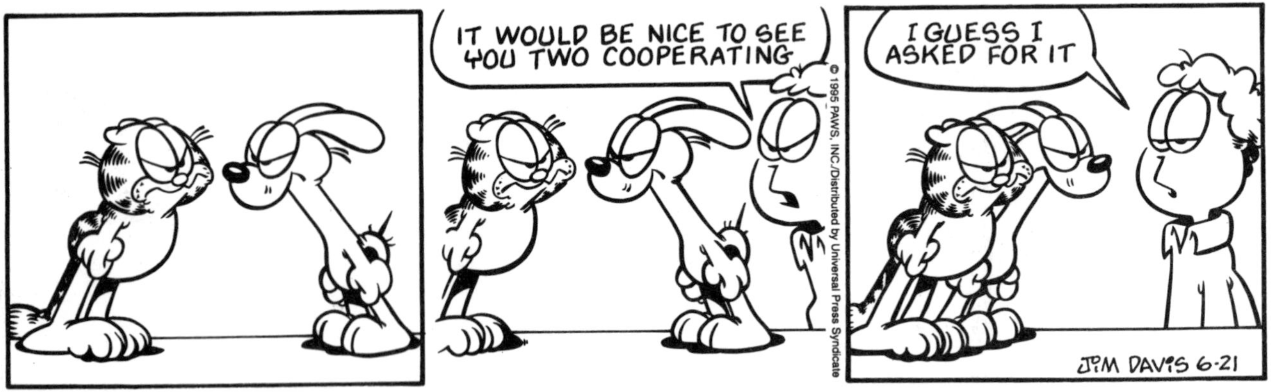
IT WOULD BE NICE TO SEE YOU TWO COOPERATING
I GUESS I ASKED FOR IT
© 1995 PAWS, INC./Distributed by Universal Press Syndicate
JIM DAVIS 6-21

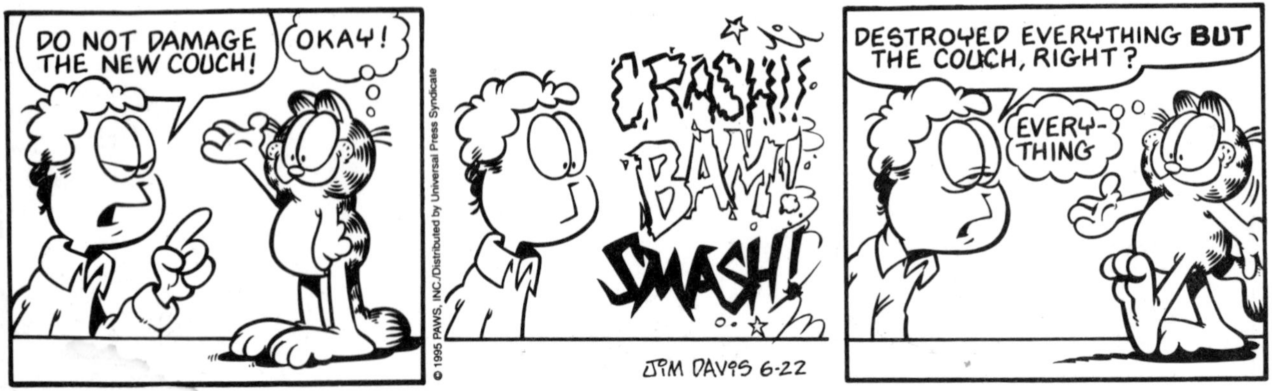
DO NOT DAMAGE THE NEW COUCH!
OKAY!
CRASH!! BAM! SMASH!
DESTROYED EVERYTHING **BUT** THE COUCH, RIGHT?
EVERY-THING
© 1995 PAWS, INC./Distributed by Universal Press Syndicate
JIM DAVIS 6-22

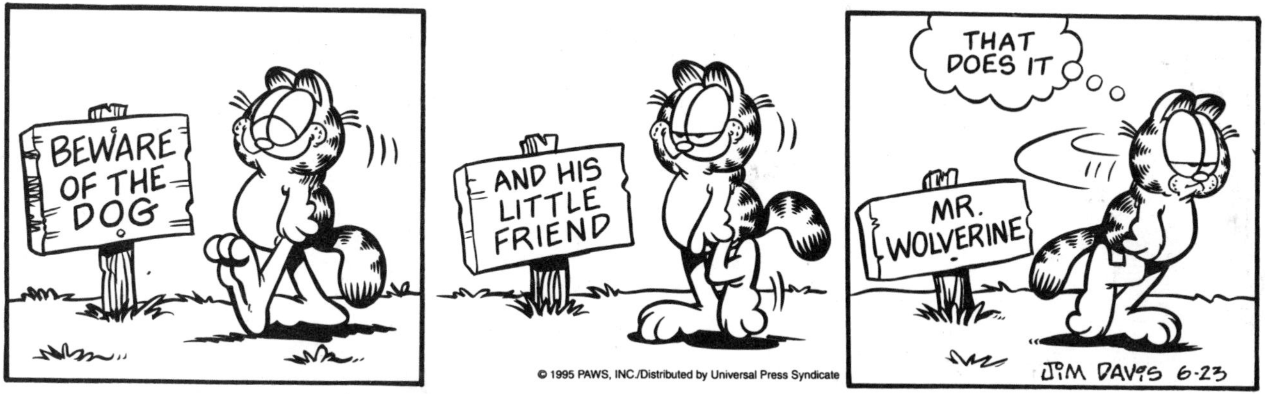
BEWARE OF THE DOG
AND HIS LITTLE FRIEND
MR. WOLVERINE
THAT DOES IT
JIM DAVIS 6-23

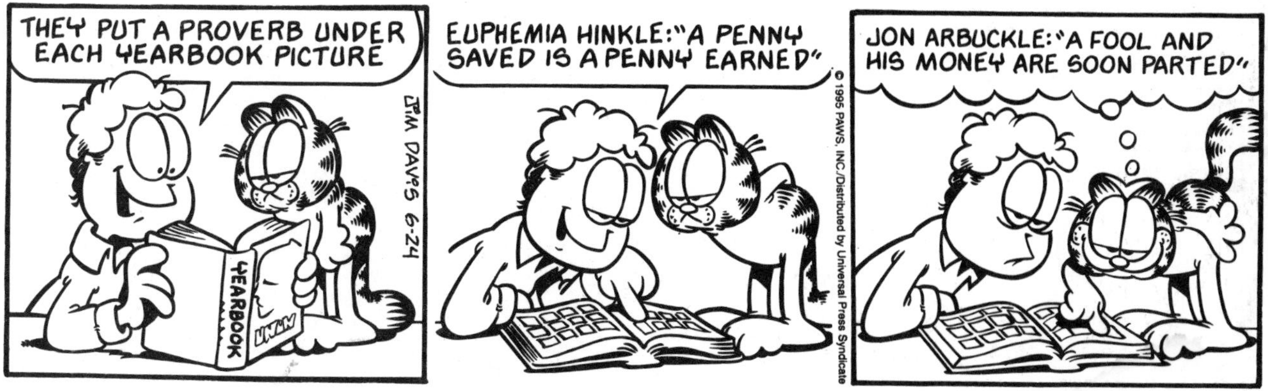
THEY PUT A PROVERB UNDER EACH YEARBOOK PICTURE
YEARBOOK
JIM DAVIS 6-24
EUPHEMIA HINKLE: "A PENNY SAVED IS A PENNY EARNED"
JON ARBUCKLE: "A FOOL AND HIS MONEY ARE SOON PARTED"

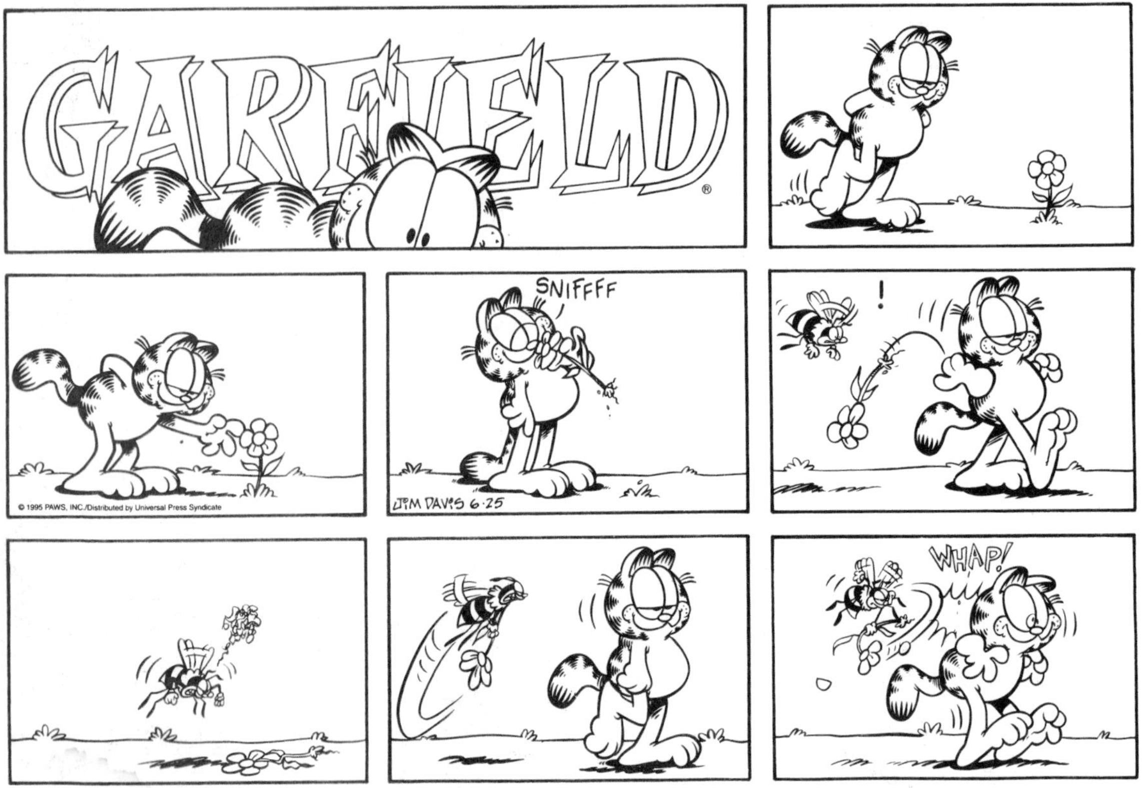
GARFIELD®
© 1995 PAWS, INC./Distributed by Universal Press Syndicate
SNIFFFF
JIM DAVIS 6·25
!
WHAP!

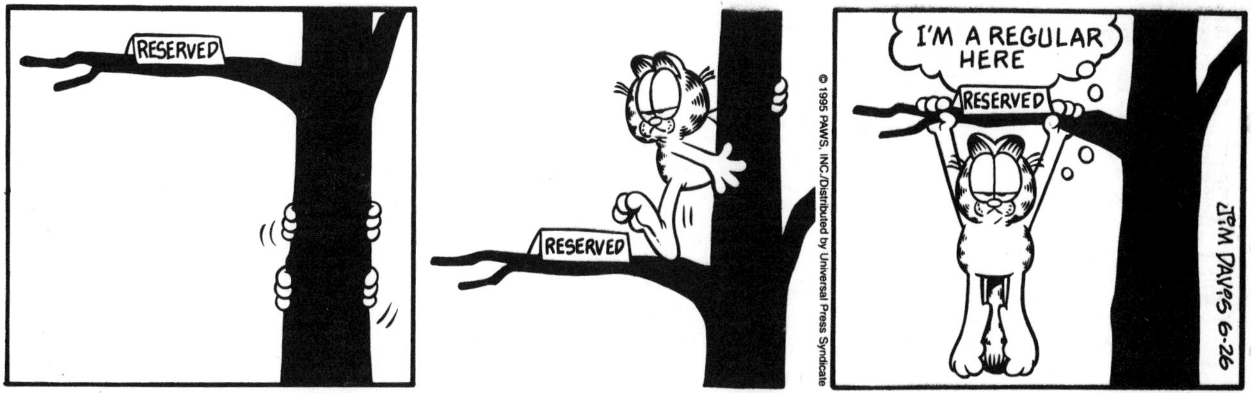
RESERVED
RESERVED
I'M A REGULAR HERE
RESERVED
JIM DAVIS 6-26
© 1995 PAWS, INC./Distributed by Universal Press Syndicate

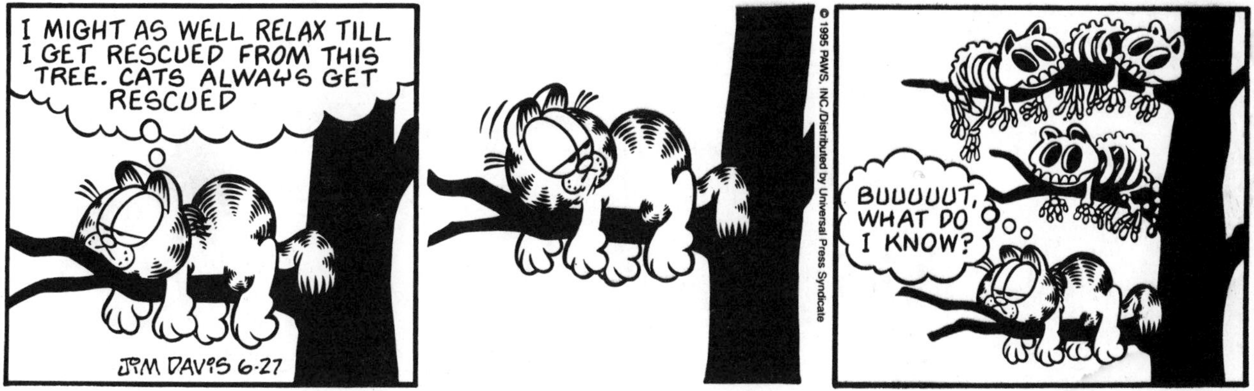
I MIGHT AS WELL RELAX TILL I GET RESCUED FROM THIS TREE. CATS ALWAYS GET RESCUED
JIM DAVIS 6-27
BUUUUUT, WHAT DO I KNOW?
© 1995 PAWS, INC./Distributed by Universal Press Syndicate

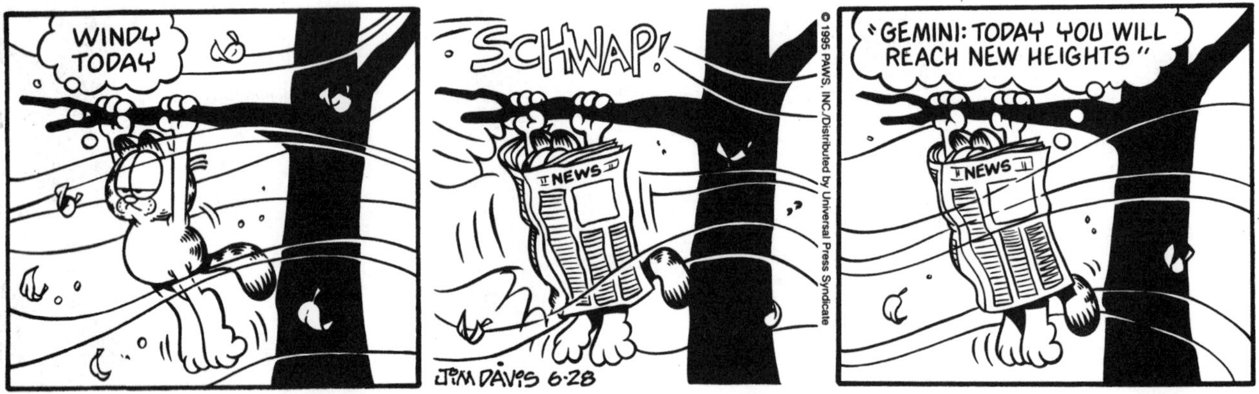
WINDY TODAY
SCHWAP!
JIM DAVIS 6-28
© 1995 PAWS, INC./Distributed by Universal Press Syndicate
"GEMINI: TODAY YOU WILL REACH NEW HEIGHTS"

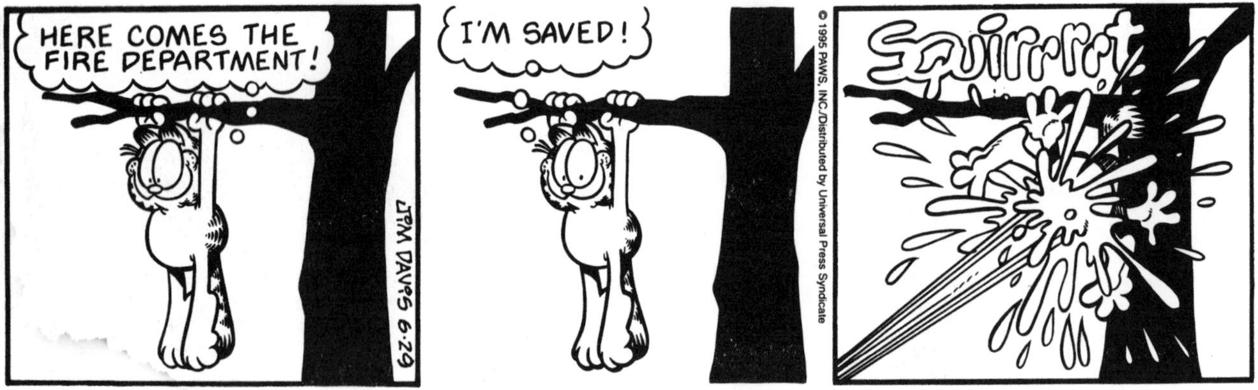
HERE COMES THE FIRE DEPARTMENT!
JIM DAVIS 6-29
I'M SAVED!
© 1995 PAWS, INC./Distributed by Universal Press Syndicate
Squirrrrt

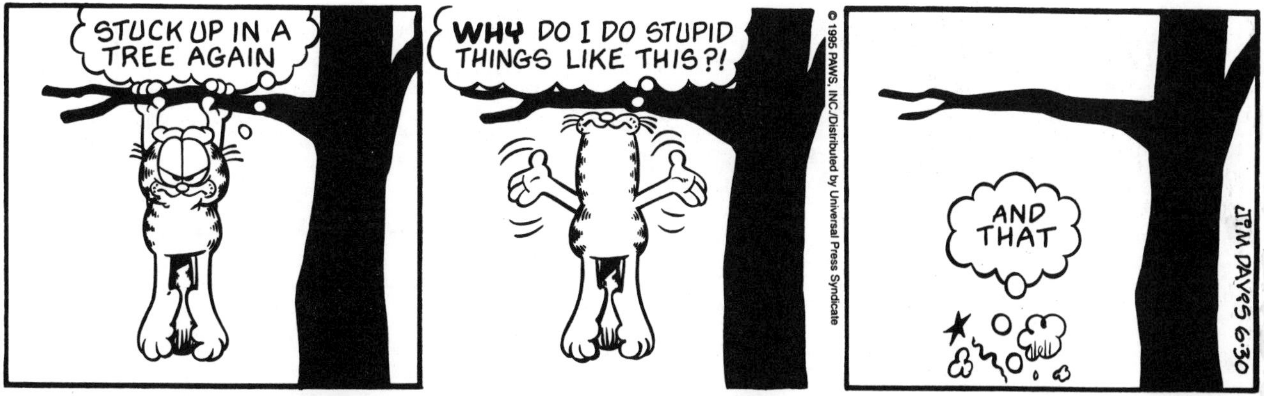
STUCK UP IN A TREE AGAIN
WHY DO I DO STUPID THINGS LIKE THIS?!
© 1995 PAWS, INC./Distributed by Universal Press Syndicate
AND THAT
JIM DAVIS 6-30

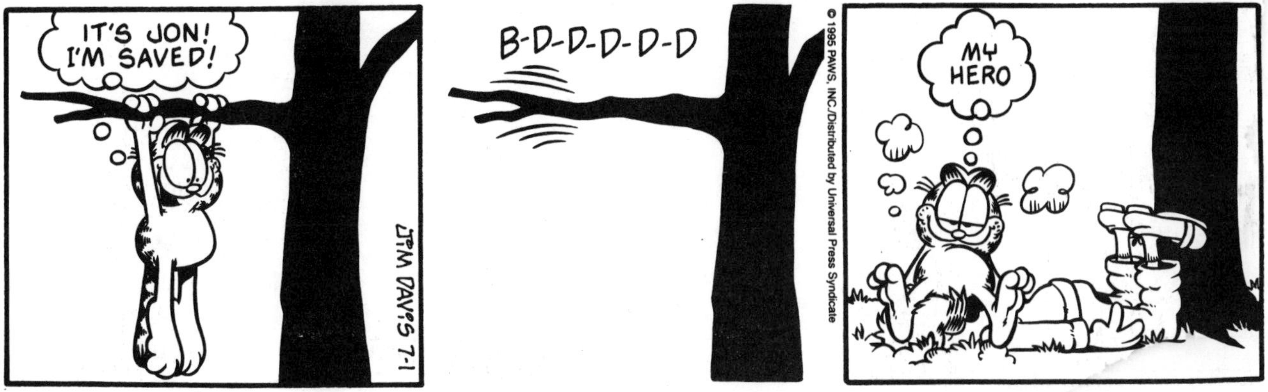
IT'S JON! I'M SAVED!
JIM DAVIS 7-1
B-D-D-D-D-D
© 1995 PAWS, INC./Distributed by Universal Press Syndicate
MY HERO

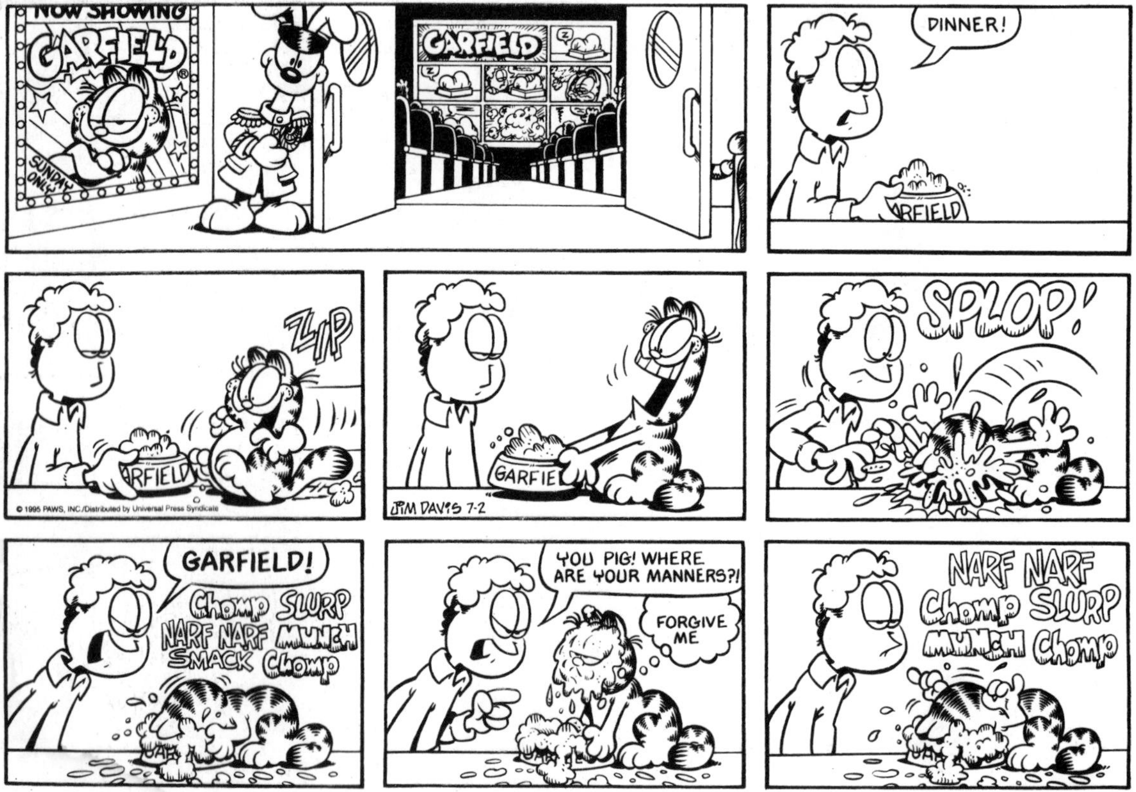
NOW SHOWING
GARFIELD
SUNDAY ONLY
GARFIELD
DINNER!
ZIP
© 1995 PAWS, INC./Distributed by Universal Press Syndicate
JIM DAVIS 7-2
SPLOP!
GARFIELD!
Chomp SLURP
NARF NARF MUNCH
SMACK Chomp
YOU PIG! WHERE ARE YOUR MANNERS?!
FORGIVE ME
NARF NARF
Chomp SLURP
MUNCH Chomp

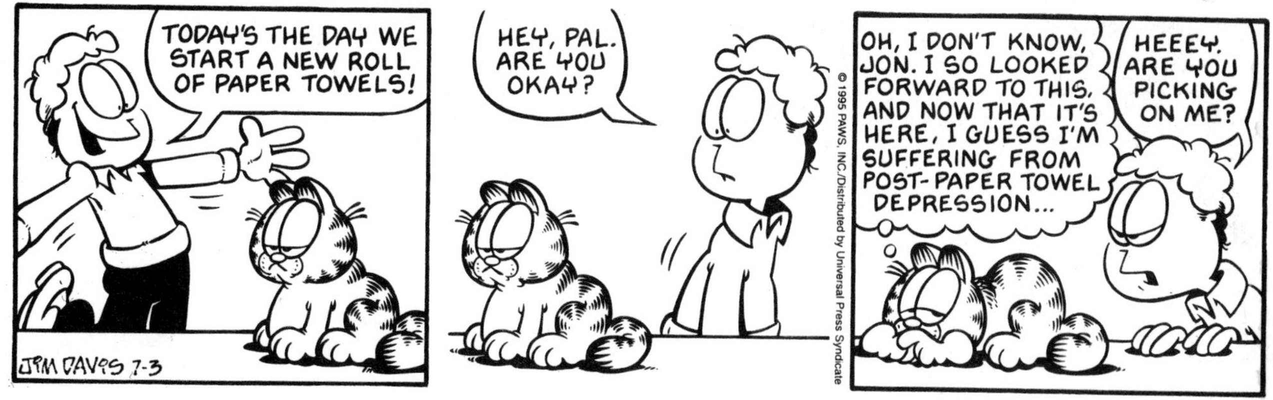
TODAY'S THE DAY WE START A NEW ROLL OF PAPER TOWELS!
HEY, PAL. ARE YOU OKAY?
OH, I DON'T KNOW, JON. I SO LOOKED FORWARD TO THIS, AND NOW THAT IT'S HERE, I GUESS I'M SUFFERING FROM POST-PAPER TOWEL DEPRESSION...
HEEEY. ARE YOU PICKING ON ME?
JIM DAVIS 7-3
© 1995 PAWS, INC./Distributed by Universal Press Syndicate

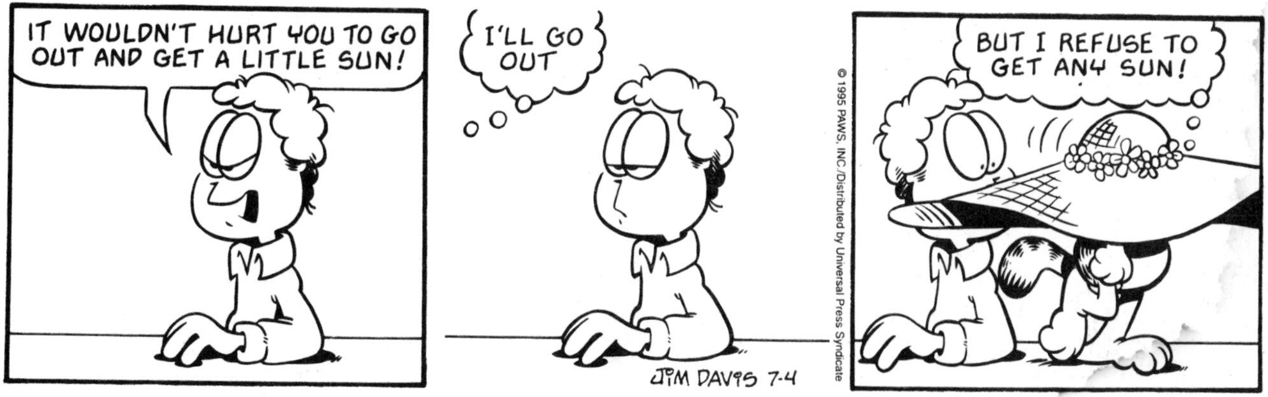
IT WOULDN'T HURT YOU TO GO OUT AND GET A LITTLE SUN!
I'LL GO OUT
BUT I REFUSE TO GET ANY SUN!
JIM DAVIS 7-4
© 1995 PAWS, INC./Distributed by Universal Press Syndicate

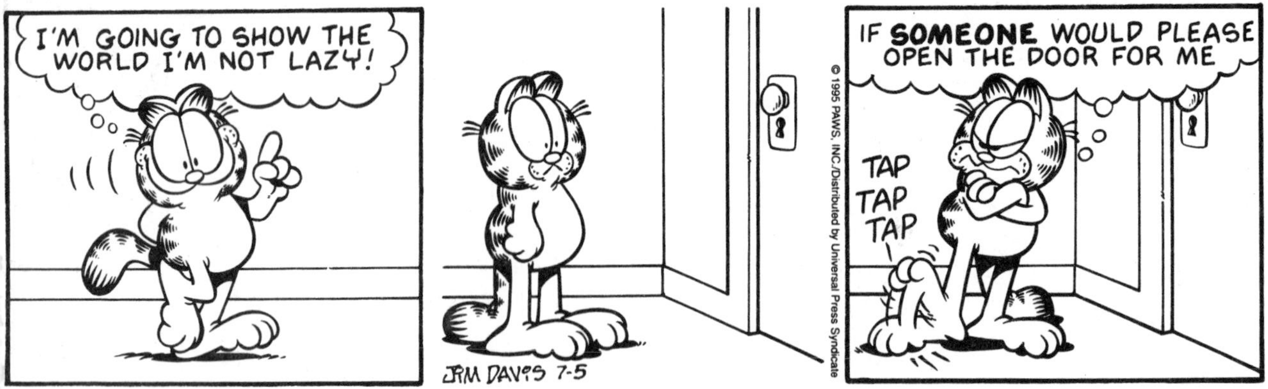
I'M GOING TO SHOW THE WORLD I'M NOT LAZY!
JIM DAVIS 7-5
IF SOMEONE WOULD PLEASE OPEN THE DOOR FOR ME
TAP TAP TAP
© 1995 PAWS, INC./Distributed by Universal Press Syndicate

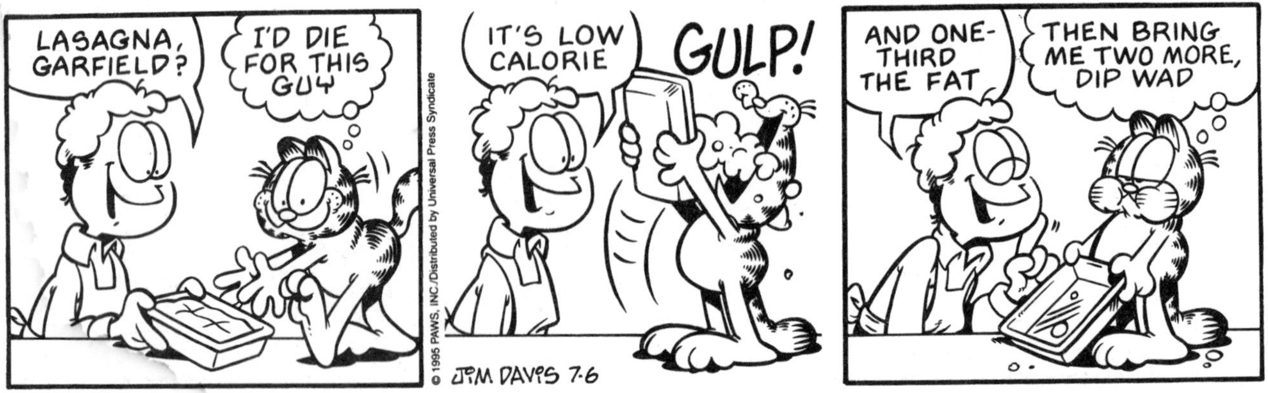
LASAGNA, GARFIELD?
I'D DIE FOR THIS GUY
© 1995 PAWS, INC./Distributed by Universal Press Syndicate
IT'S LOW CALORIE
GULP!
JIM DAVIS 7-6
AND ONE-THIRD THE FAT
THEN BRING ME TWO MORE, DIP WAD

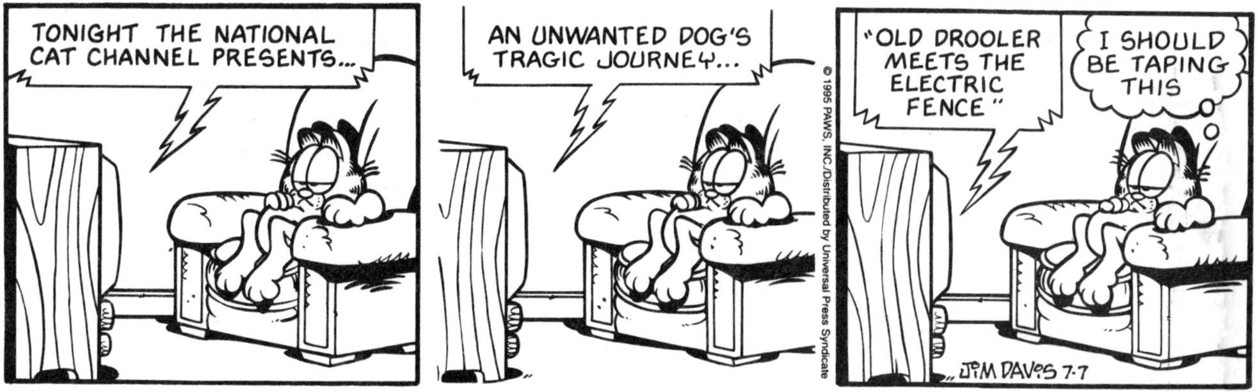
TONIGHT THE NATIONAL CAT CHANNEL PRESENTS...
AN UNWANTED DOG'S TRAGIC JOURNEY...
"OLD DROOLER MEETS THE ELECTRIC FENCE"
I SHOULD BE TAPING THIS
JIM DAVIS 7-7

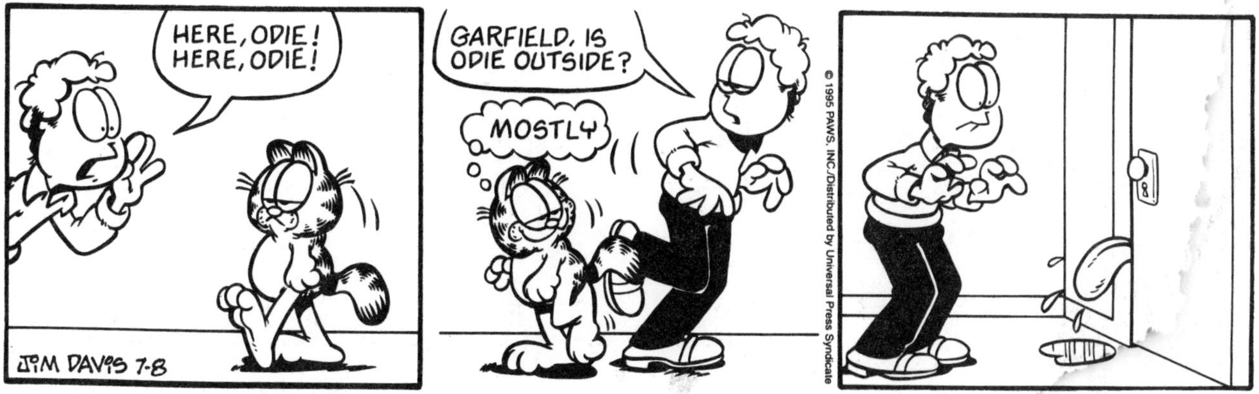
HERE, ODIE! HERE, ODIE!
JIM DAVIS 7-8
GARFIELD, IS ODIE OUTSIDE?
MOSTLY

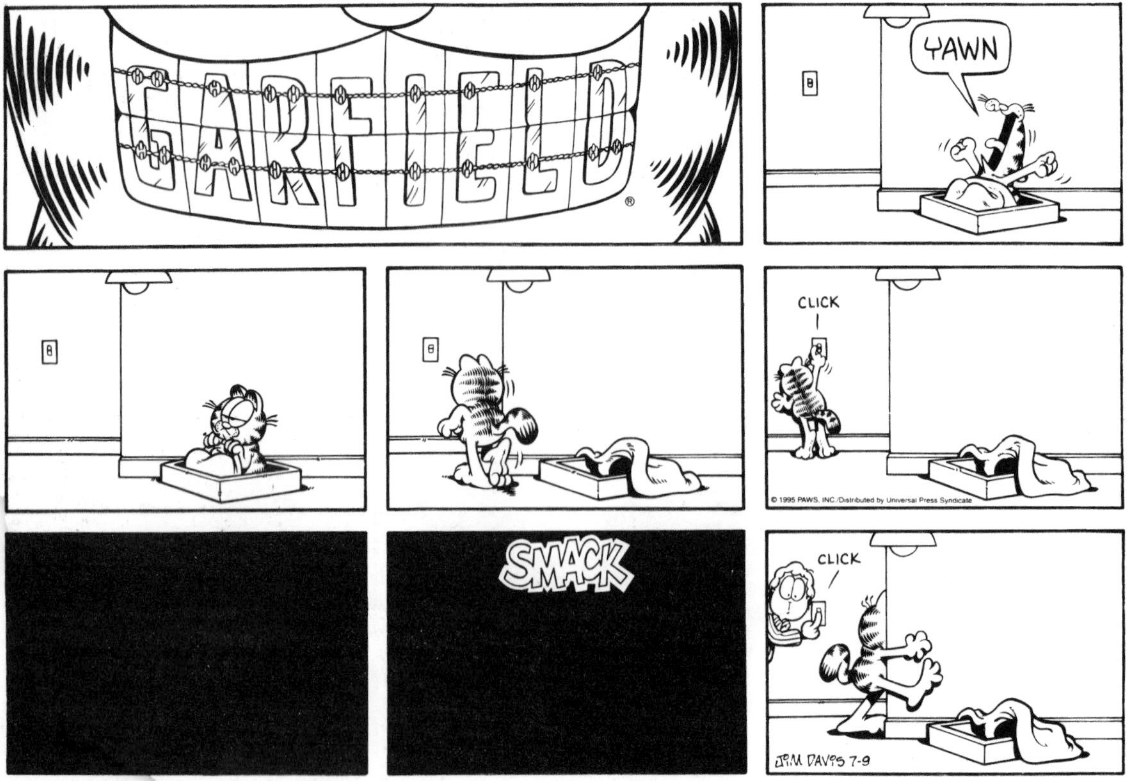
GARFIELD®
YAWN
CLICK
© 1995 PAWS, INC./Distributed by Universal Press Syndicate
SMACK
CLICK
JIM DAVIS 7-9

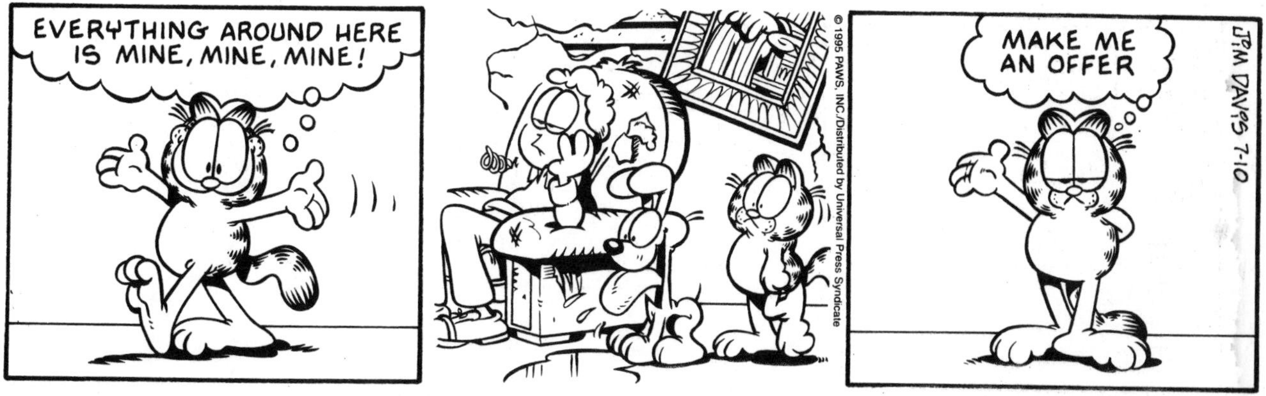
EVERYTHING AROUND HERE IS MINE, MINE, MINE!
© 1995 PAWS, INC./Distributed by Universal Press Syndicate
MAKE ME AN OFFER
JIM DAVIS 7-10

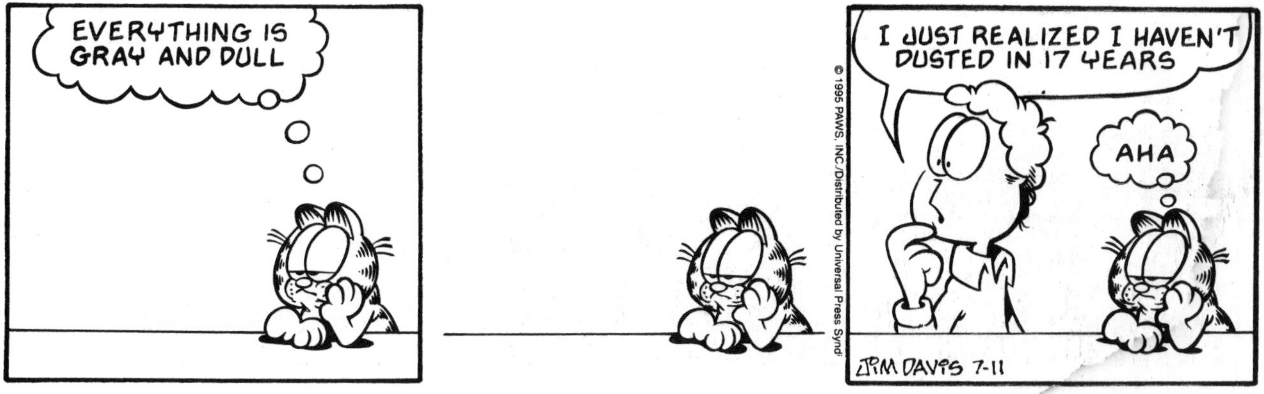
EVERYTHING IS GRAY AND DULL
© 1995 PAWS, INC./Distributed by Universal Press Syndi
I JUST REALIZED I HAVEN'T DUSTED IN 17 YEARS
AHA
JIM DAVIS 7-11

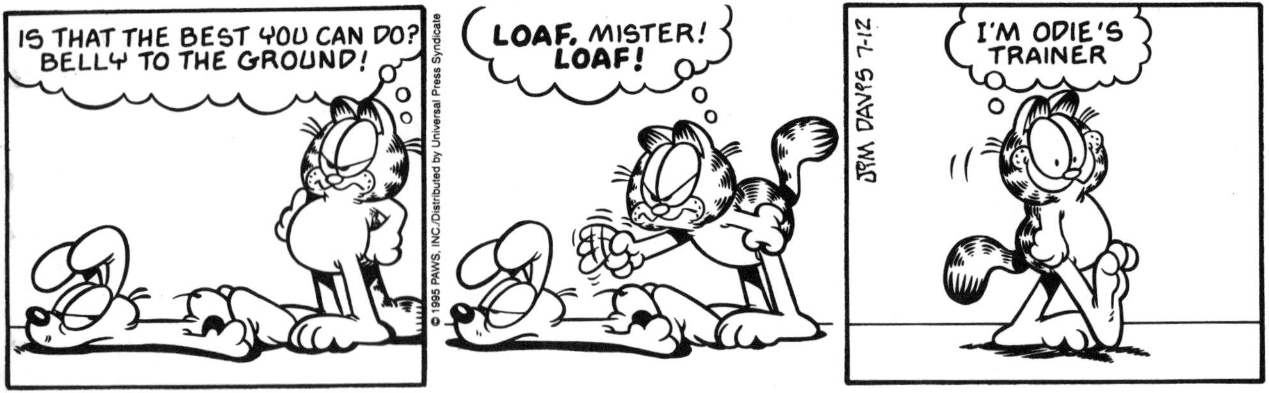
IS THAT THE BEST YOU CAN DO? BELLY TO THE GROUND!
© 1995 PAWS, INC./Distributed by Universal Press Syndicate
LOAF, MISTER! LOAF!
JIM DAVIS 7-12
I'M ODIE'S TRAINER

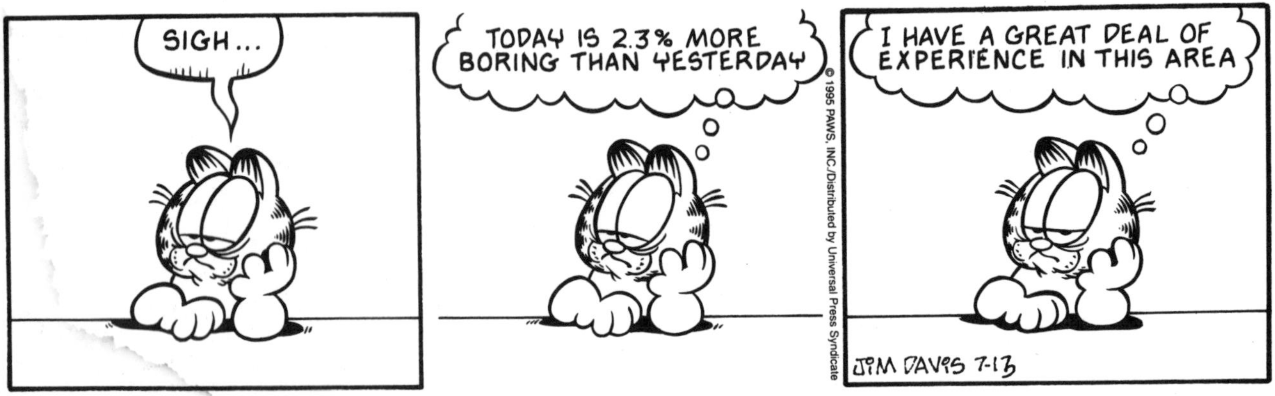
SIGH...
TODAY IS 2.3% MORE BORING THAN YESTERDAY
© 1995 PAWS, INC./Distributed by Universal Press Syndicate
I HAVE A GREAT DEAL OF EXPERIENCE IN THIS AREA
JIM DAVIS 7-13

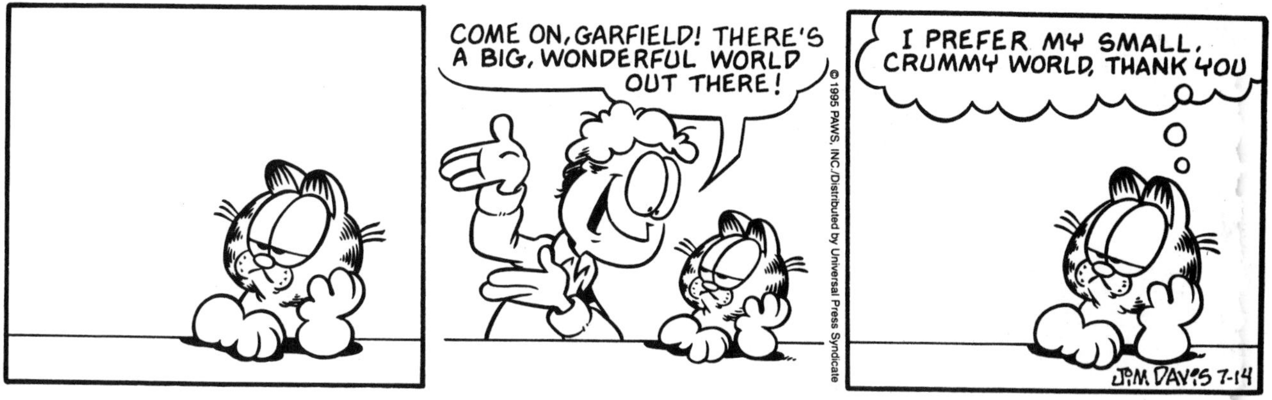
COME ON, GARFIELD! THERE'S A BIG, WONDERFUL WORLD OUT THERE!
I PREFER MY SMALL, CRUMMY WORLD, THANK YOU
© 1995 PAWS, INC./Distributed by Universal Press Syndicate
JIM DAVIS 7-14

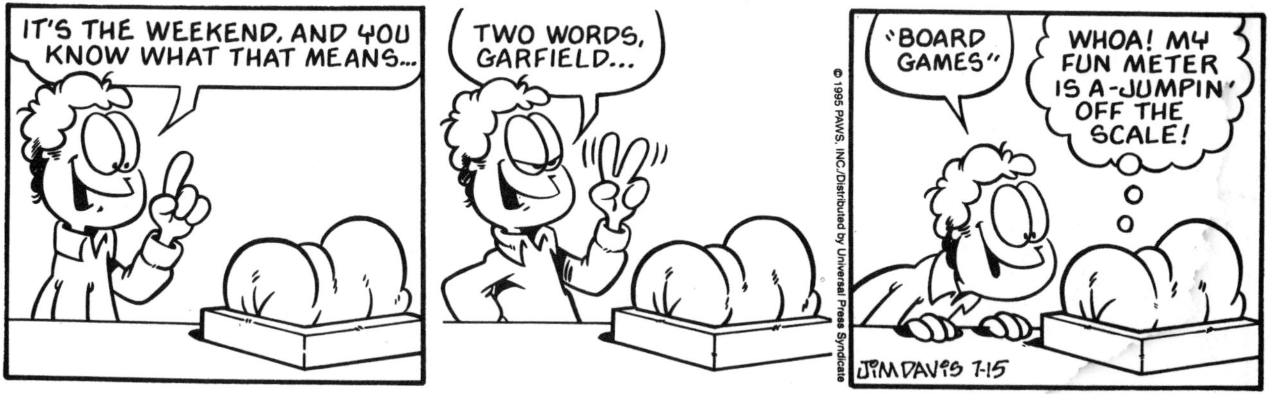
IT'S THE WEEKEND, AND YOU KNOW WHAT THAT MEANS...
TWO WORDS, GARFIELD...
"BOARD GAMES"
WHOA! MY FUN METER IS A-JUMPIN' OFF THE SCALE!
© 1995 PAWS, INC./Distributed by Universal Press Syndicate
JIM DAVIS 7-15

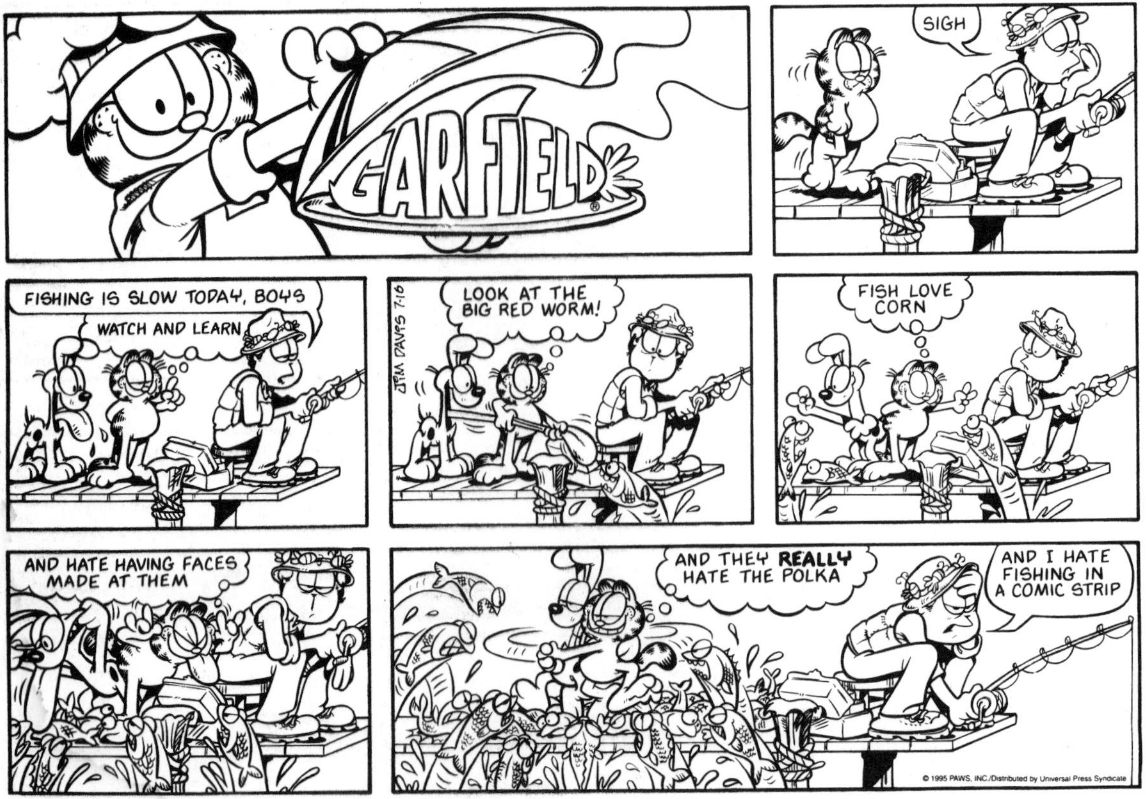
GARFIELD®
SIGH
FISHING IS SLOW TODAY, BOYS
WATCH AND LEARN
JIM DAVIS 7-16
LOOK AT THE BIG RED WORM!
FISH LOVE CORN
AND HATE HAVING FACES MADE AT THEM
AND THEY REALLY HATE THE POLKA
AND I HATE FISHING IN A COMIC STRIP
© 1995 PAWS, INC./Distributed by Universal Press Syndicate

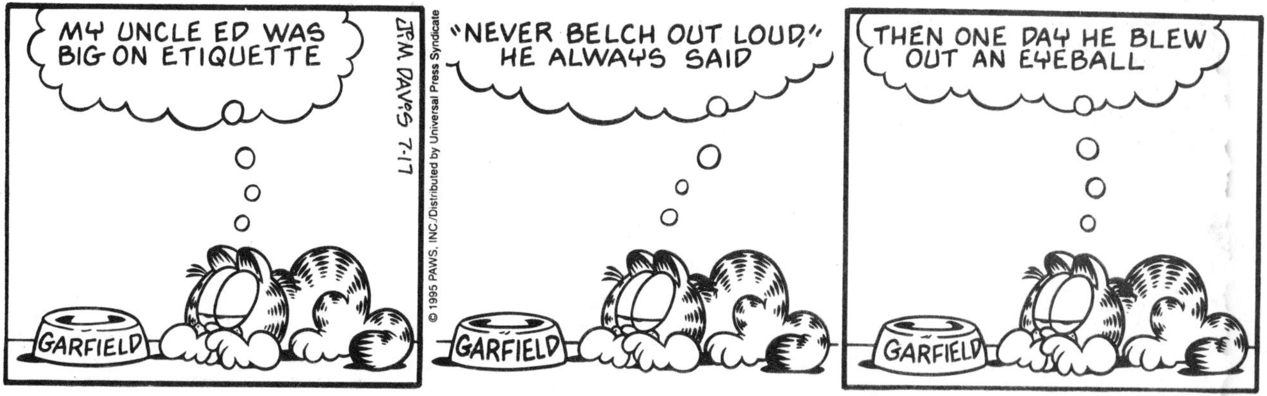
MY UNCLE ED WAS BIG ON ETIQUETTE
JIM DAVIS 7-17
"NEVER BELCH OUT LOUD," HE ALWAYS SAID
THEN ONE DAY HE BLEW OUT AN EYEBALL
GARFIELD
GARFIELD
GARFIELD

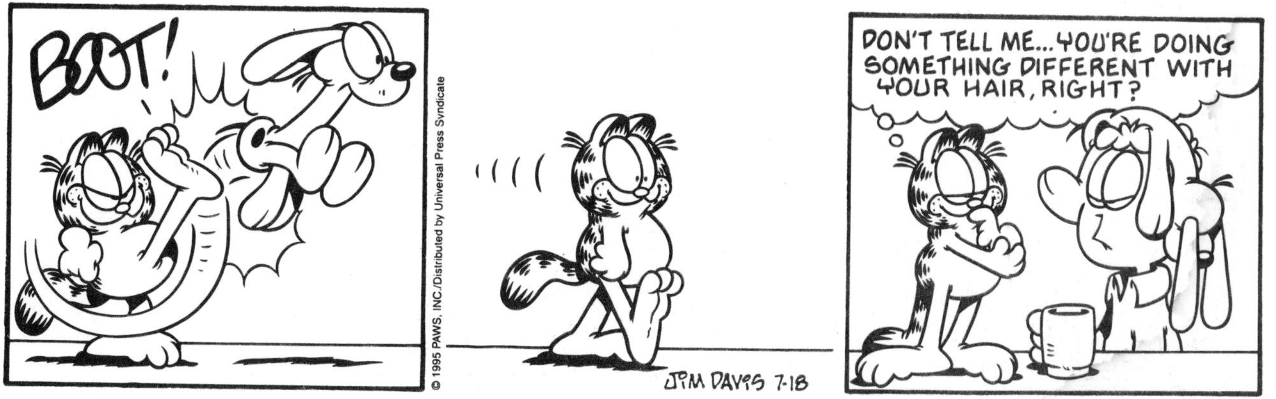
BOOT!
DON'T TELL ME...YOU'RE DOING SOMETHING DIFFERENT WITH YOUR HAIR, RIGHT?
JIM DAVIS 7-18

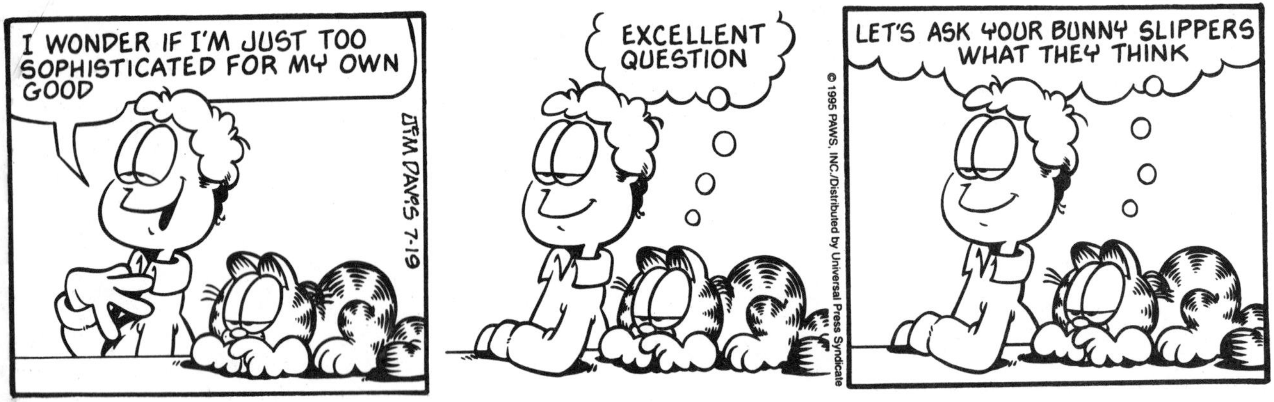
I WONDER IF I'M JUST TOO SOPHISTICATED FOR MY OWN GOOD
JIM DAVIS 7-19
EXCELLENT QUESTION
© 1995 PAWS, INC./Distributed by Universal Press Syndicate
LET'S ASK YOUR BUNNY SLIPPERS WHAT THEY THINK

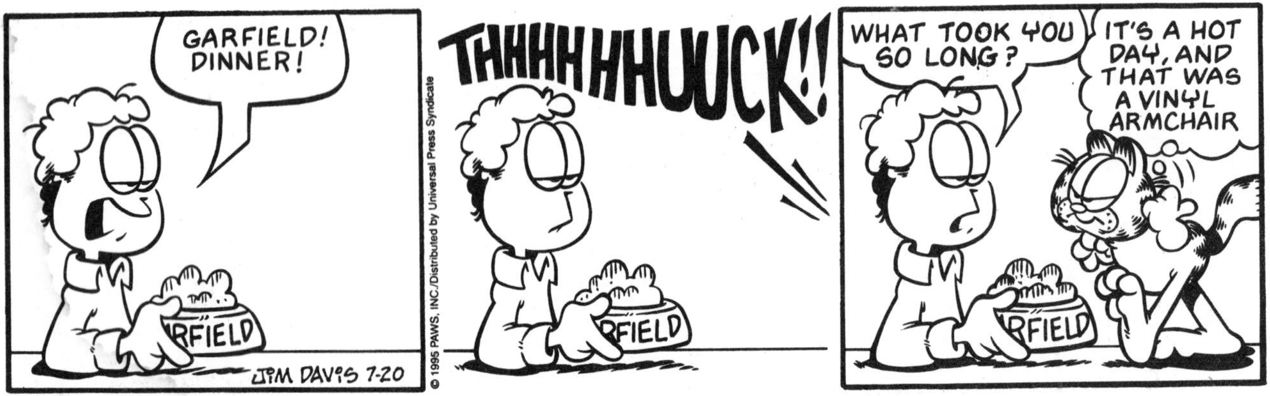
GARFIELD! DINNER!
RFIELD
JIM DAVIS 7-20
© 1995 PAWS, INC./Distributed by Universal Press Syndicate
THHHHHHUUCK!!
RFIELD
WHAT TOOK YOU SO LONG?
IT'S A HOT DAY, AND THAT WAS A VINYL ARMCHAIR
RFIELD

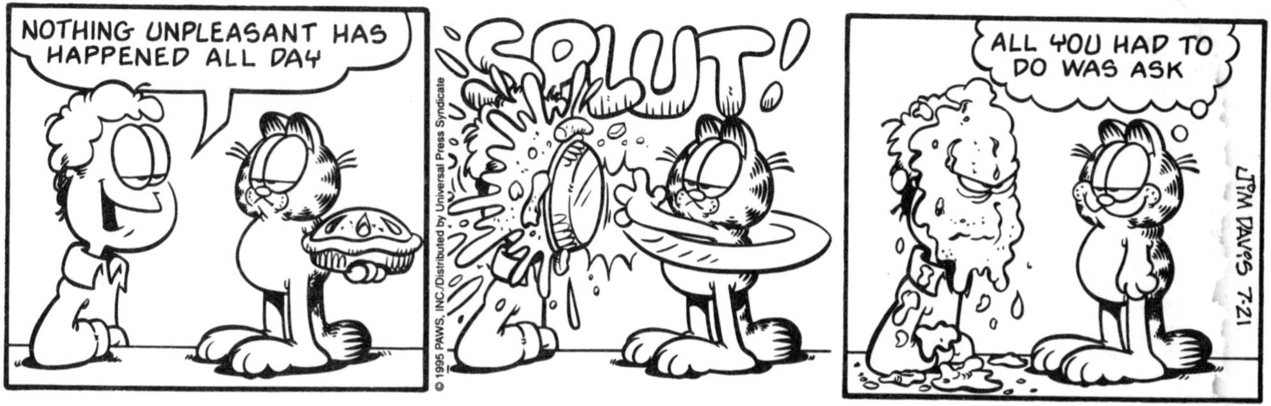
NOTHING UNPLEASANT HAS HAPPENED ALL DAY
SPLUT!
ALL YOU HAD TO DO WAS ASK
JIM DAVIS 7-21
© 1995 PAWS, INC./Distributed by Universal Press Syndicate

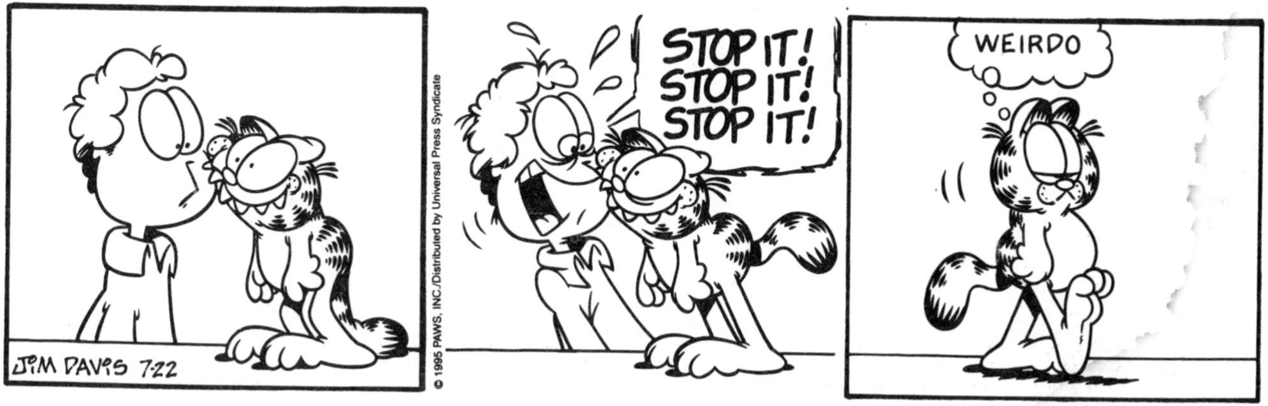
JIM DAVIS 7-22
STOP IT! STOP IT! STOP IT!
WEIRDO
© 1995 PAWS, INC./Distributed by Universal Press Syndicate

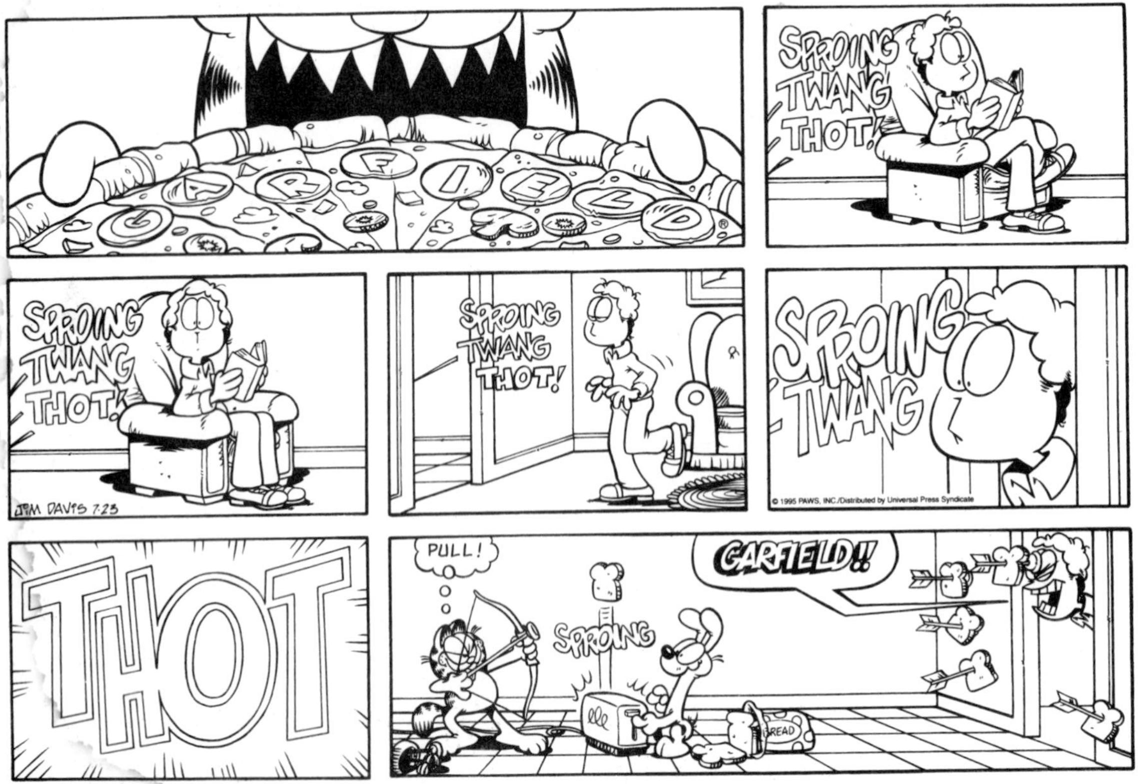
GARFIELD®
SPROING
TWANG
THOT!
SPROING
TWANG
THOT!
JIM DAVIS 7-23
SPROING
TWANG
THOT!
SPROING
TWANG
© 1995 PAWS, INC./Distributed by Universal Press Syndicate
THOT
PULL!
SPROING
GARFIELD!!
BREAD

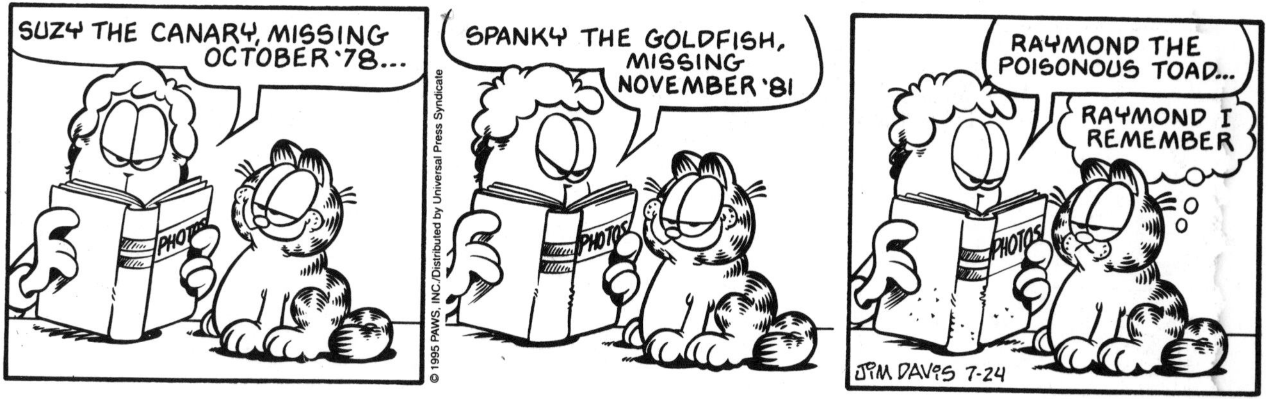
SUZY THE CANARY, MISSING OCTOBER '78...
SPANKY THE GOLDFISH, MISSING NOVEMBER '81
RAYMOND THE POISONOUS TOAD...
RAYMOND I REMEMBER
PHOTOS
© 1995 PAWS, INC./Distributed by Universal Press Syndicate
JIM DAVIS 7-24

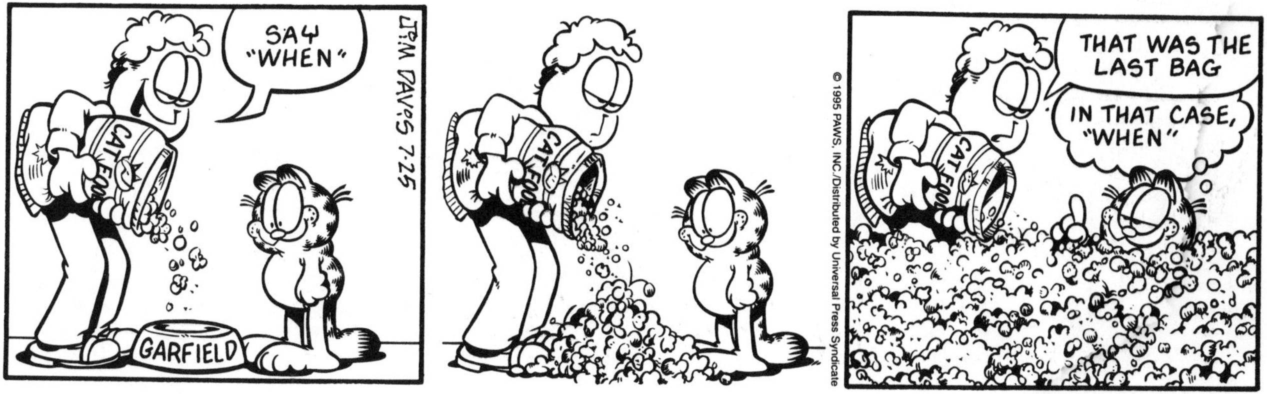
SAY "WHEN"
CAT FOOD
GARFIELD
THAT WAS THE LAST BAG
IN THAT CASE, "WHEN"
JIM DAVIS 7-25
© 1995 PAWS, INC./Distributed by Universal Press Syndicate

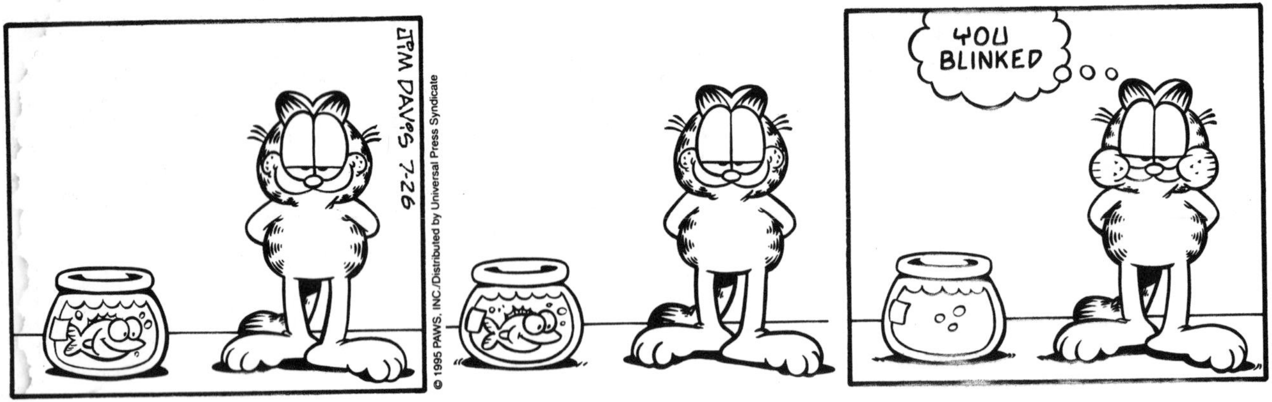
JIM DAVIS 7-26
YOU BLINKED

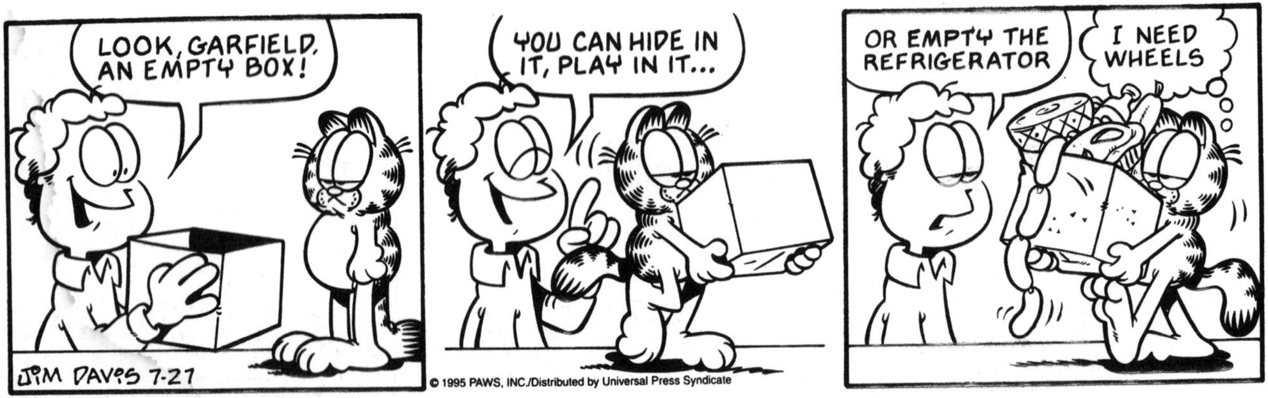
LOOK, GARFIELD, AN EMPTY BOX!
JIM DAVIS 7-27
YOU CAN HIDE IN IT, PLAY IN IT...
OR EMPTY THE REFRIGERATOR
I NEED WHEELS

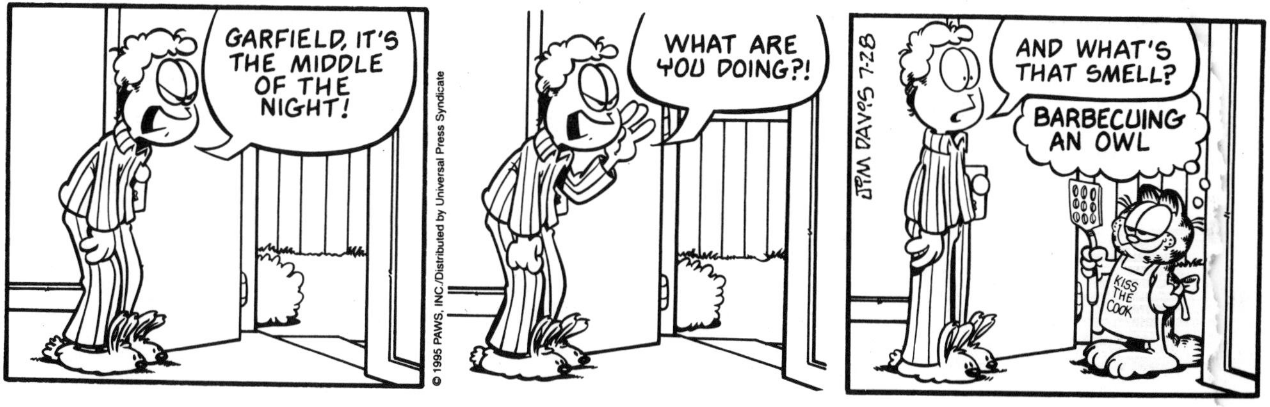
GARFIELD, IT'S THE MIDDLE OF THE NIGHT!
© 1995 PAWS, INC./Distributed by Universal Press Syndicate
WHAT ARE YOU DOING?!
JIM DAVIS 7-28
AND WHAT'S THAT SMELL?
BARBECUING AN OWL
KISS THE COOK

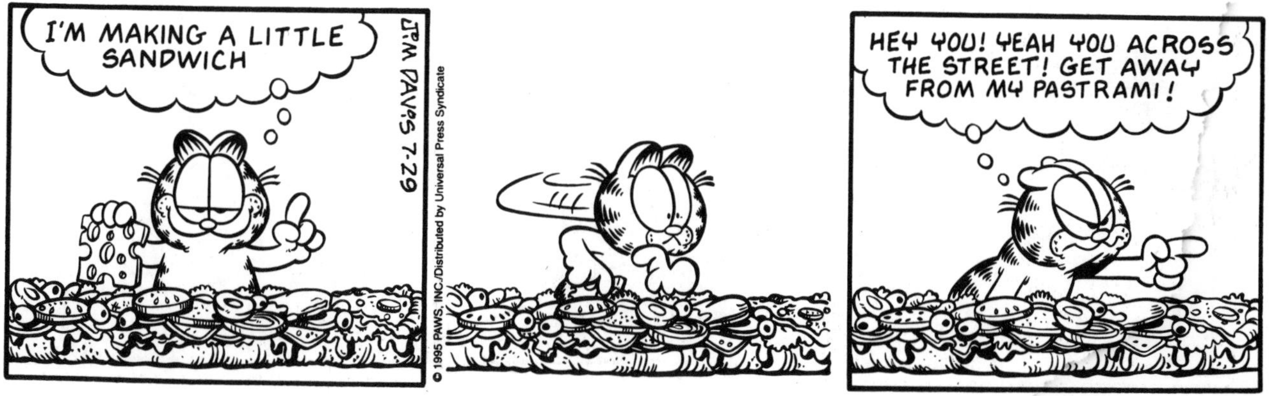
I'M MAKING A LITTLE SANDWICH
JIM DAVIS 7-29
© 1995 PAWS, INC./Distributed by Universal Press Syndicate
HEY YOU! YEAH YOU ACROSS THE STREET! GET AWAY FROM MY PASTRAMI!

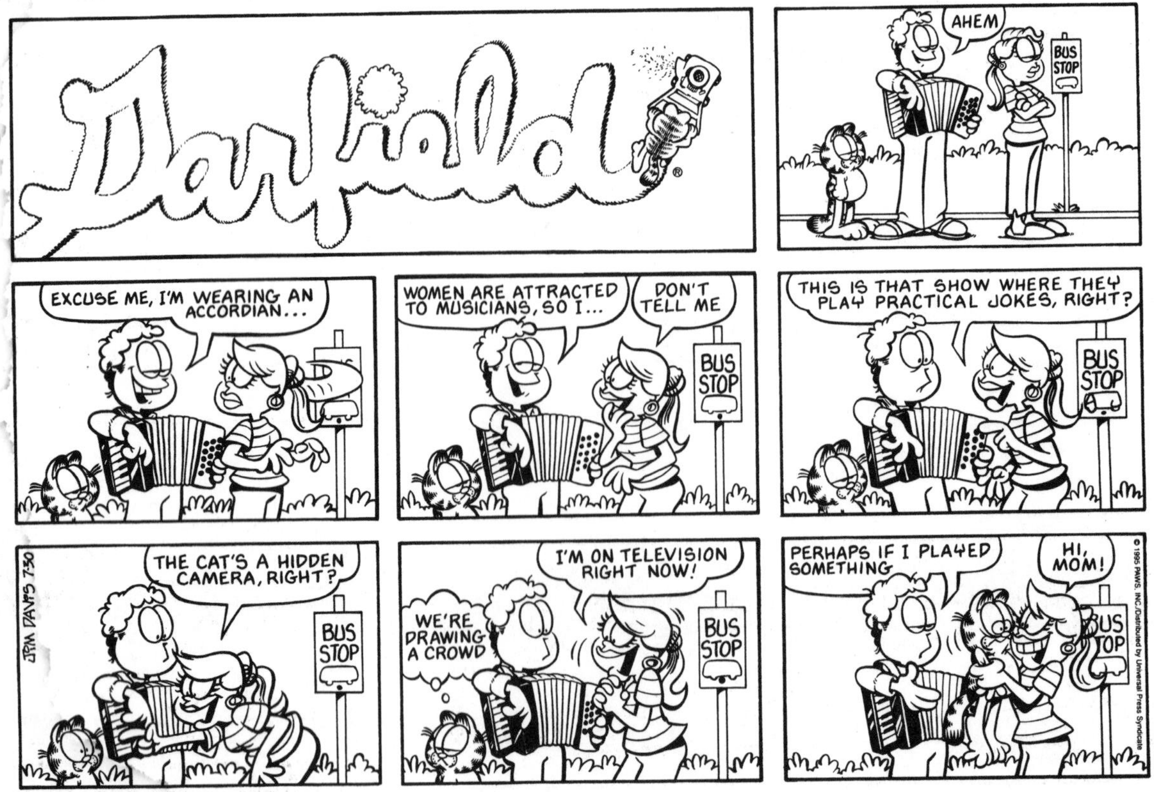
Garfield®
AHEM
BUS STOP
EXCUSE ME, I'M WEARING AN ACCORDIAN...
WOMEN ARE ATTRACTED TO MUSICIANS, SO I...
DON'T TELL ME
BUS STOP
THIS IS THAT SHOW WHERE THEY PLAY PRACTICAL JOKES, RIGHT?
BUS STOP
JIM DAVIS 7-30
THE CAT'S A HIDDEN CAMERA, RIGHT?
BUS STOP
I'M ON TELEVISION RIGHT NOW!
WE'RE DRAWING A CROWD
BUS STOP
PERHAPS IF I PLAYED SOMETHING
HI, MOM!
© 1995 PAWS, INC./Distributed by Universal Press Syndicate

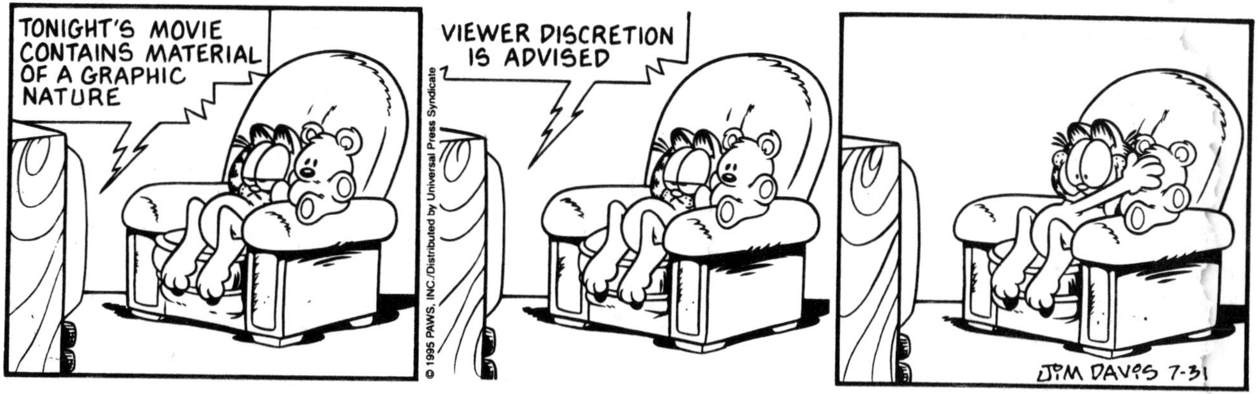
TONIGHT'S MOVIE CONTAINS MATERIAL OF A GRAPHIC NATURE
VIEWER DISCRETION IS ADVISED
JIM DAVIS 7-31

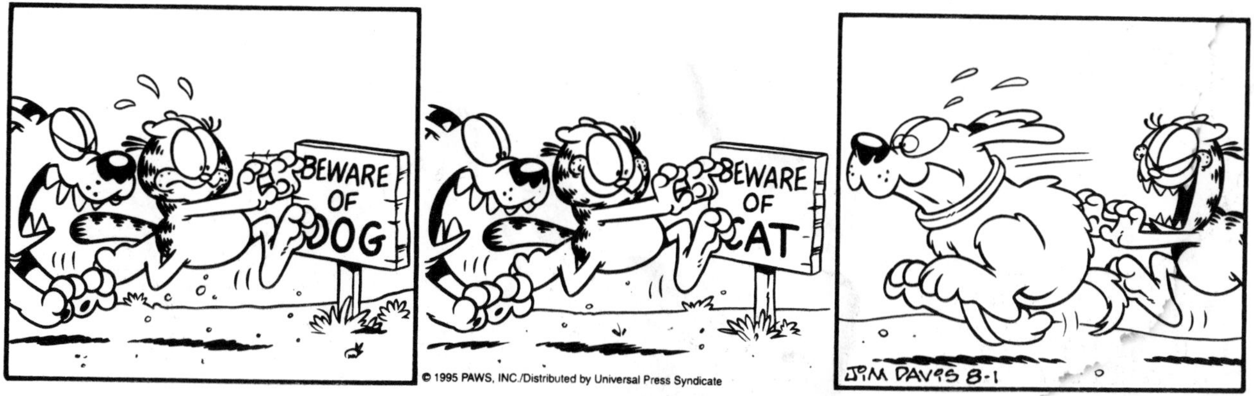
BEWARE OF DOG
BEWARE OF CAT
JIM DAVIS 8-1

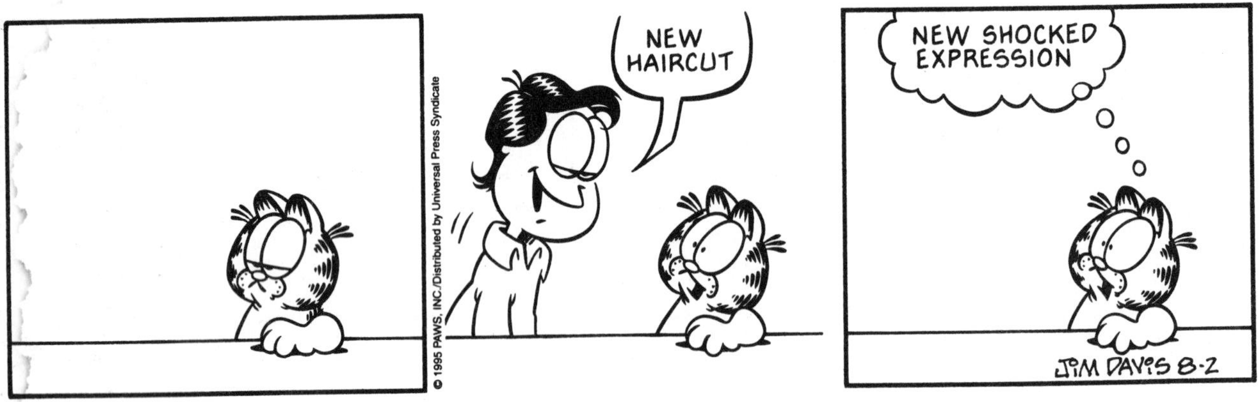

NEW HAIRCUT
NEW SHOCKED EXPRESSION
JIM DAVIS 8-2
© 1995 PAWS, INC./Distributed by Universal Press Syndicate

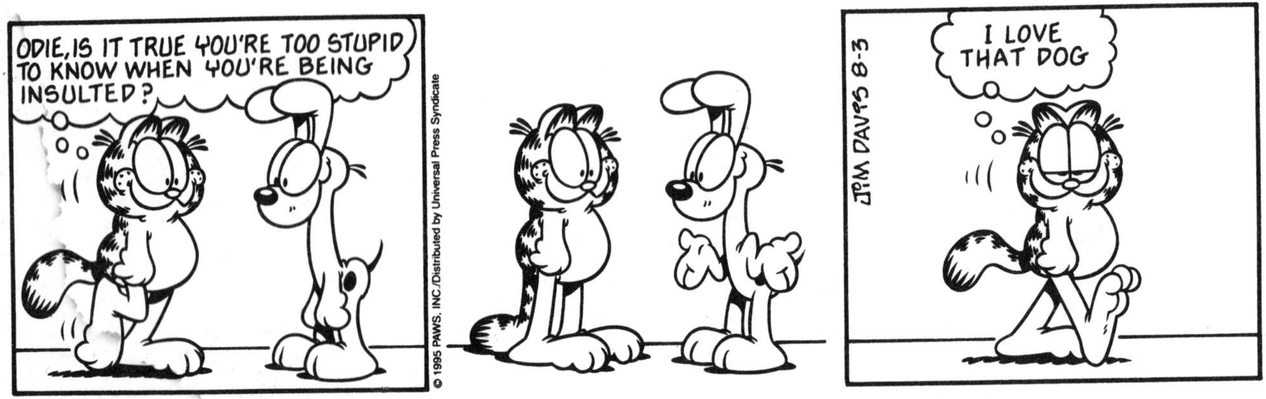

ODIE, IS IT TRUE YOU'RE TOO STUPID TO KNOW WHEN YOU'RE BEING INSULTED?
I LOVE THAT DOG
JIM DAVIS 8-3
© 1995 PAWS, INC./Distributed by Universal Press Syndicate

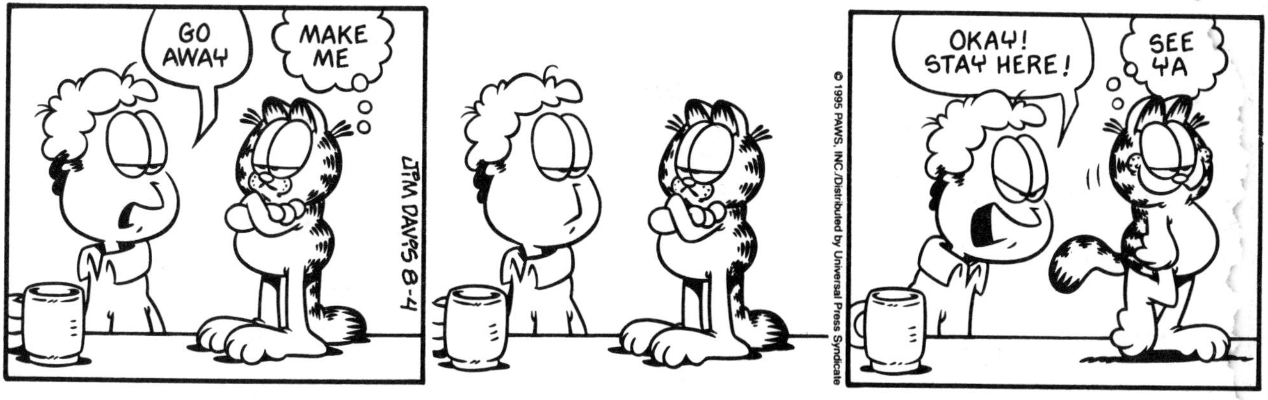
GO AWAY
MAKE ME
JIM DAVIS 8-4
OKAY! STAY HERE!
SEE YA
© 1995 PAWS, INC./Distributed by Universal Press Syndicate

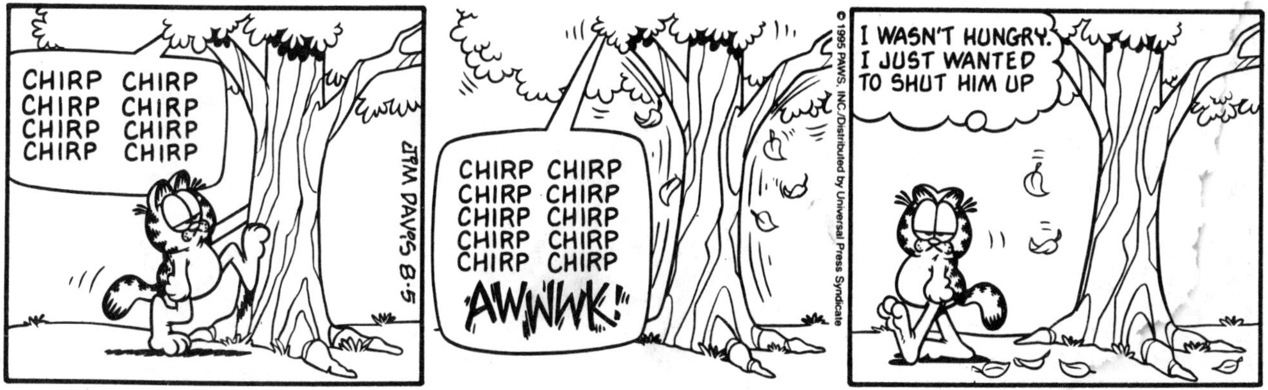
CHIRP CHIRP CHIRP CHIRP CHIRP CHIRP CHIRP CHIRP
JIM DAVIS 8-5
CHIRP CHIRP CHIRP CHIRP CHIRP CHIRP CHIRP CHIRP CHIRP CHIRP
AWWWK!
© 1995 PAWS, INC./Distributed by Universal Press Syndicate
I WASN'T HUNGRY. I JUST WANTED TO SHUT HIM UP

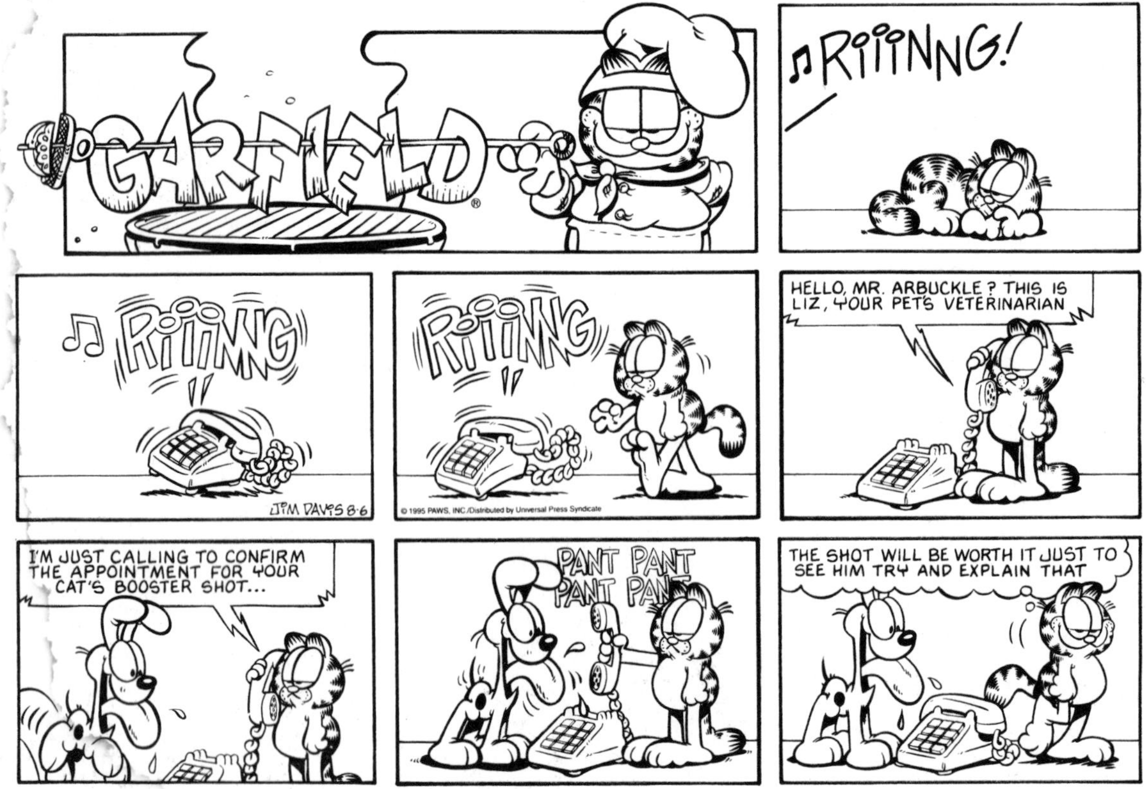
GARFIELD®
♫ RIIINNG!
♫ RIIINNG
RIIINNG
JIM DAVIS 8-6
© 1995 PAWS, INC./Distributed by Universal Press Syndicate
HELLO, MR. ARBUCKLE? THIS IS LIZ, YOUR PET'S VETERINARIAN
I'M JUST CALLING TO CONFIRM THE APPOINTMENT FOR YOUR CAT'S BOOSTER SHOT...
PANT PANT PANT PANT
THE SHOT WILL BE WORTH IT JUST TO SEE HIM TRY AND EXPLAIN THAT

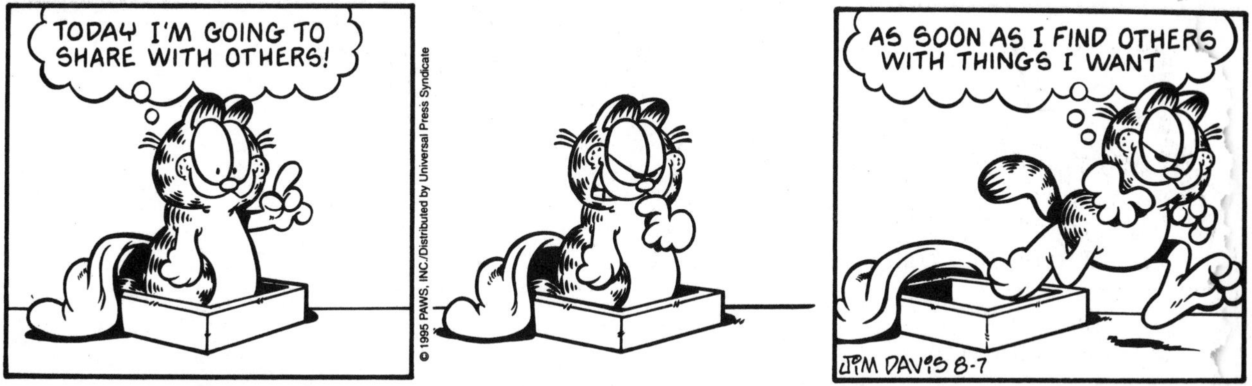
TODAY I'M GOING TO SHARE WITH OTHERS!
AS SOON AS I FIND OTHERS WITH THINGS I WANT
JIM DAVIS 8-7
© 1995 PAWS, INC./Distributed by Universal Press Syndicate

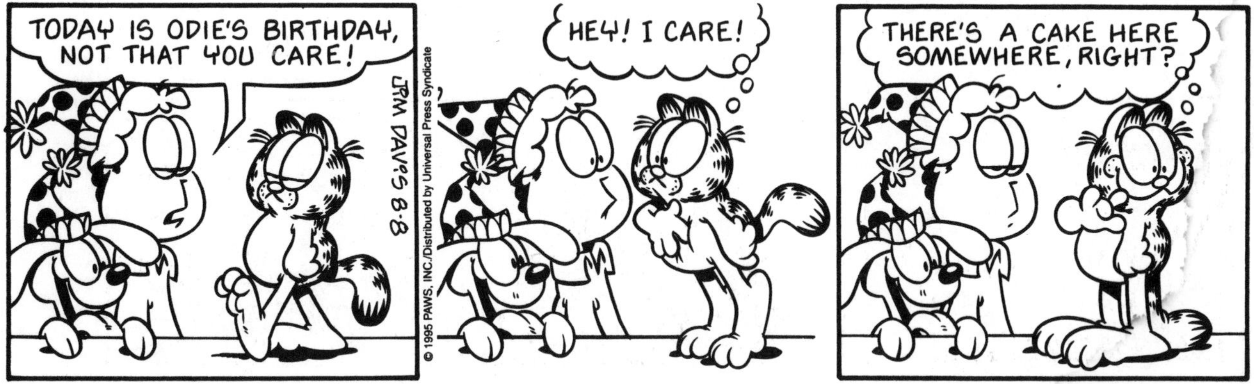
TODAY IS ODIE'S BIRTHDAY, NOT THAT YOU CARE!
HEY! I CARE!
THERE'S A CAKE HERE SOMEWHERE, RIGHT?
JIM DAVIS 8-8
© 1995 PAWS, INC./Distributed by Universal Press Syndicate

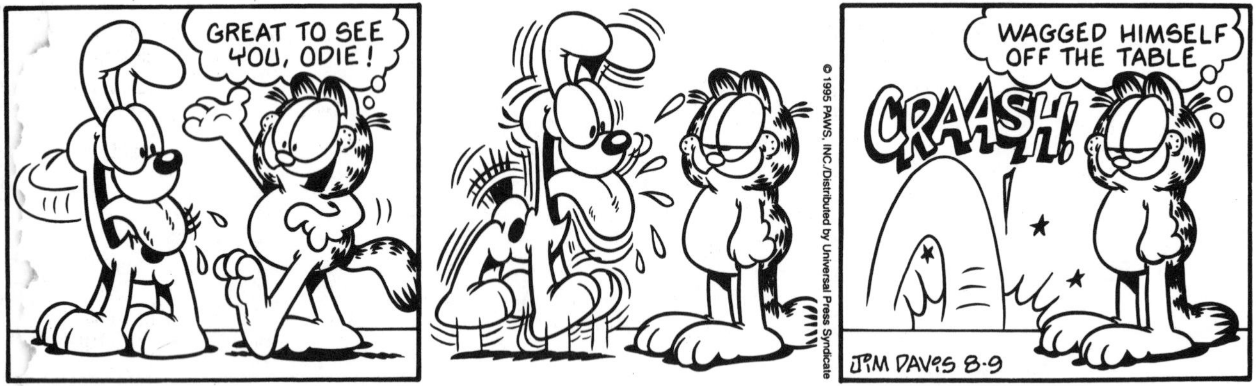
GREAT TO SEE YOU, ODIE!
CRAASH!
WAGGED HIMSELF OFF THE TABLE
JIM DAVIS 8-9
© 1995 PAWS, INC./Distributed by Universal Press Syndicate

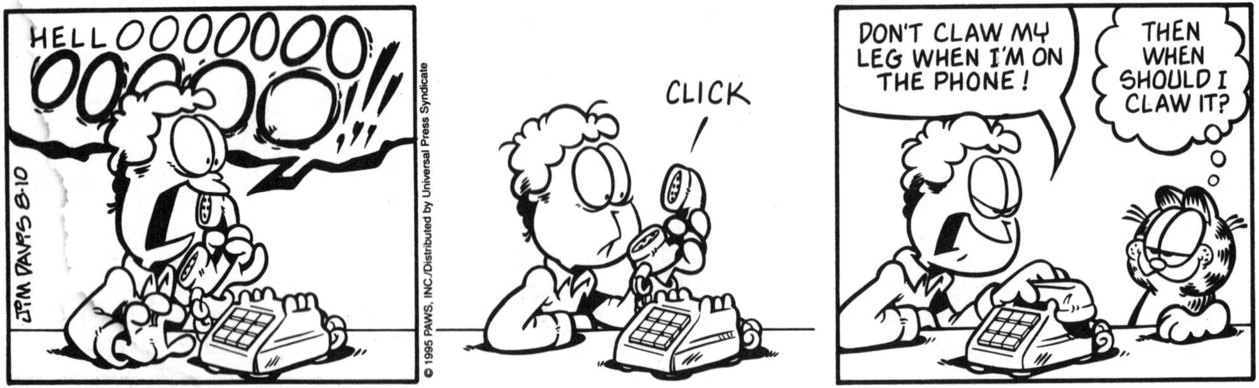
HELLOOOOOOO
OOOOO!!!
JIM DAVIS 8-10
© 1995 PAWS, INC./Distributed by Universal Press Syndicate
CLICK
DON'T CLAW MY LEG WHEN I'M ON THE PHONE!
THEN WHEN SHOULD I CLAW IT?

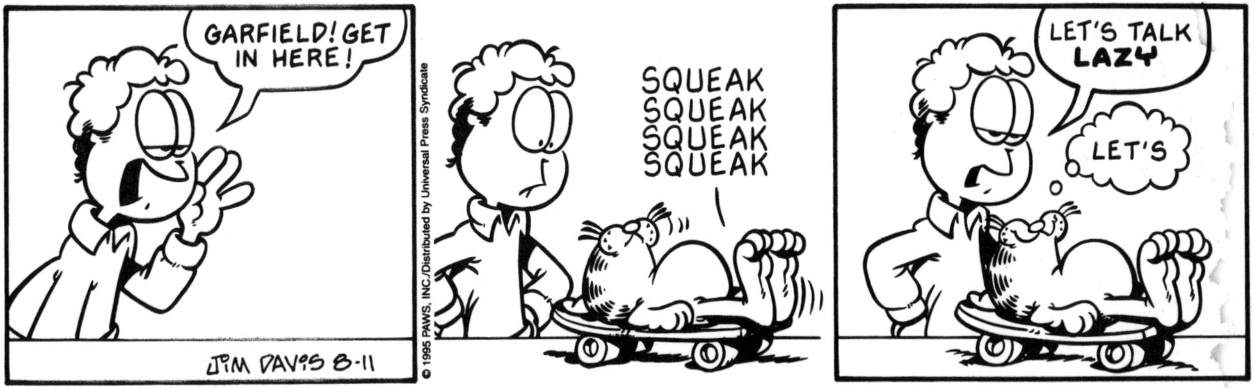
GARFIELD! GET IN HERE!
JIM DAVIS 8-11
© 1995 PAWS, INC./Distributed by Universal Press Syndicate
SQUEAK SQUEAK SQUEAK SQUEAK
LET'S TALK LAZY
LET'S

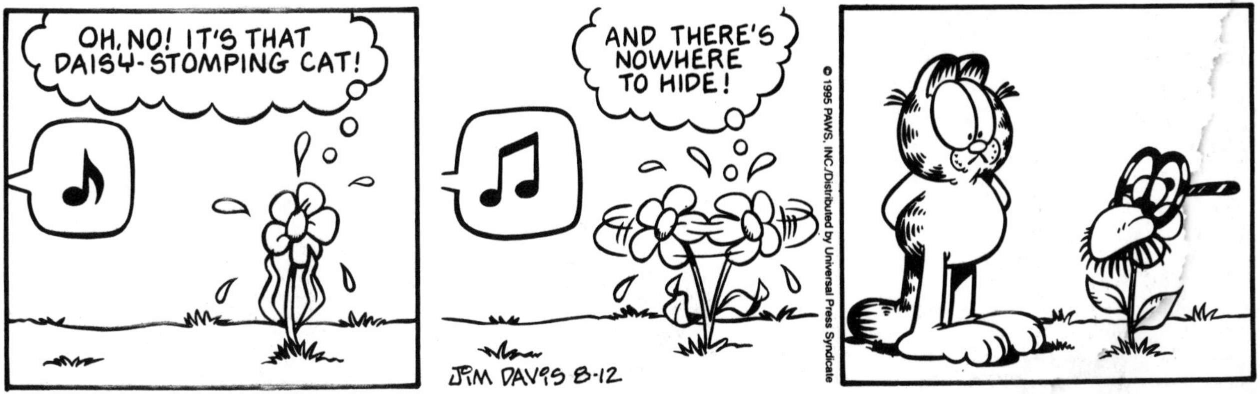
OH, NO! IT'S THAT DAISY-STOMPING CAT!
AND THERE'S NOWHERE TO HIDE!
JIM DAVIS 8-12
© 1995 PAWS, INC./Distributed by Universal Press Syndicate

How lazy is Garfield?

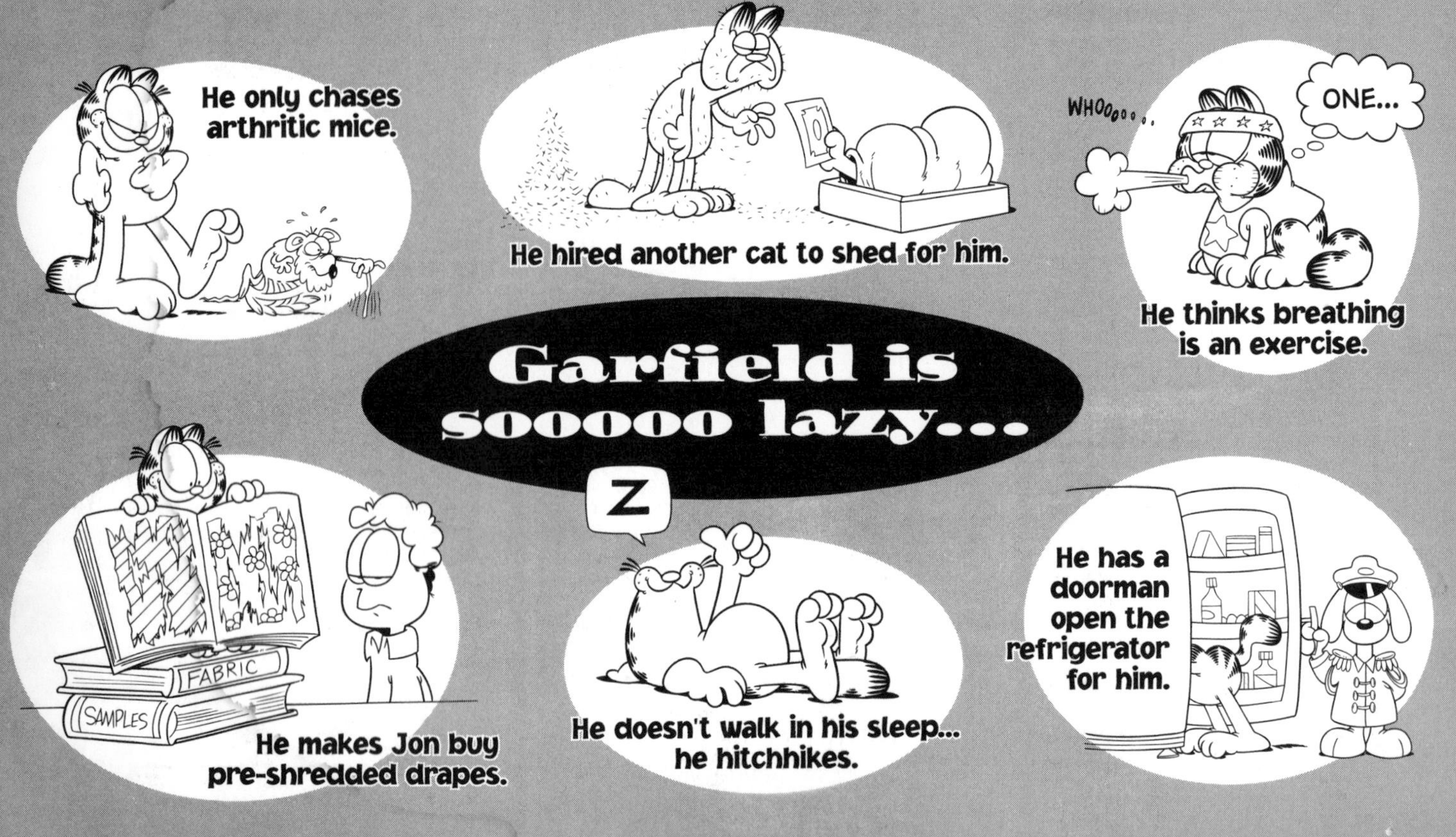

Garfield is sooooo lazy...
He only chases arthritic mice.
He hired another cat to shed for him.
WHOOooo...
ONE...
He thinks breathing is an exercise.
FABRIC
SAMPLES
He makes Jon buy pre-shredded drapes.
Z
He doesn't walk in his sleep... he hitchhikes.
He has a doorman open the refrigerator for him.

STRIPS, SPECIALS, OR BESTSELLING BOOKS . . .
GARFIELD'S ON EVERYONE'S MENU
Don't miss even one episode in the Tubby Tabby's hilarious series!

__GARFIELD AT LARGE (#1)   32013/$6.95
__GARFIELD GAINS WEIGHT (#2)   32008/$6.95
__GARFIELD BIGGER THAN LIFE (#3)   32007/$6.95
__GARFIELD WEIGHS IN (#4)   32010/$6.95
__GARFIELD TAKES THE CAKE (#5)   32009/$6.95
__GARFIELD EATS HIS HEART OUT (#6)   32018/$6.95
__GARFIELD SITS AROUND THE HOUSE (#7)   32011/$6.95
__GARFIELD TIPS THE SCALES (#8)   33580/$6.95
__GARFIELD LOSES HIS FEET (#9)   31805/$6.95
__GARFIELD MAKES IT BIG (#10)   31928/$6.95
__GARFIELD ROLLS ON (#11)   32634/$6.95
__GARFIELD OUT TO LUNCH (#12)   33118/$6.95
__GARFIELD FOOD FOR THOUGHT (#13)   34129/$6.95
__GARFIELD SWALLOWS HIS PRIDE (#14)   34725/$6.95
__GARFIELD WORLDWIDE (#15)   35158/$6.95
__GARFIELD ROUNDS OUT (#16)   35388/$6.95

__GARFIELD CHEWS THE FAT (#17)   35956/$6.95
__GARFIELD GOES TO WAIST (#18)   36430/$6.95
__GARFIELD HANGS OUT (#19)   36835/$6.95
__GARFIELD TAKES UP SPACE (#20)   37029/$6.95
__GARFIELD SAYS A MOUTHFUL (#21)   37368/$6.95
__GARFIELD BY THE POUND (#22)   37579/$6.95
__GARFIELD KEEPS HIS CHINS UP (#23)   37959/$6.95
__GARFIELD TAKES HIS LICKS (#24)   38170/$6.95
__GARFIELD HITS THE BIG TIME (#25)   38332/$6.95
__GARFIELD PULLS HIS WEIGHT (#26)   38666/$6.95
__GARFIELD DISHES IT OUT (#27)   39287/$6.95
__GARFIELD LIFE IN THE FAT LANE (#28)   39776/$6.95
__GARFIELD TONS OF FUN (#29)   40386/$6.95

GARFIELD AT HIS SUNDAY BEST!
__GARFIELD TREASURY   32106/$11.95
__THE SECOND GARFIELD TREASURY   33276/$10.95
__THE THIRD GARFIELD TREASURY   32635/$11.00
__THE FOURTH GARFIELD TREASURY   34726/$10.95
__THE FIFTH GARFIELD TREASURY   36268/$12.00
__THE SIXTH GARFIELD TREASURY   37367/$10.95
__THE SEVENTH GARFIELD TREASURY   38427/$10.95
__THE EIGHTH GARFIELD TREASURY   39778/$12.00

Please send me the BALLANTINE BOOKS I have checked above. I am enclosing $_____. (Please add $2.00 for the first book and $.50 for each additional book for postage and handling and include the appropriate state sales tax.) Send check or money order (no cash or C.O.D.'s) to Ballantine Mail Sales Dept. TA, 400 Hahn Road, Westminster, MD 21157.

To order by phone, call 1-800-733-3000 and use your major credit card.

Prices and numbers are subject to change without notice. Valid in the U.S. only. All orders are subject to availability.

Name_____

Address_____

City_____ State_____ Zip_____

30   Allow at least 4 weeks for delivery   7/93

BIRTHDAYS, HOLIDAYS, OR ANY DAY . . .

Keep GARFIELD on your calendar all year 'round!

GARFIELD TV SPECIALS
__BABES & BULLETS   36339/$5.95
__GARFIELD GOES HOLLYWOOD   34580/$6.95
__GARFIELD'S HALLOWEEN ADVENTURE   33045/$6.95
  (formerly GARFIELD IN DISGUISE)
__GARFIELD'S FELINE FANTASY   36902/$6.95
__GARFIELD IN PARADISE   33796/$6.95
__GARFIELD IN THE ROUGH   32242/$6.95
__GARFIELD ON THE TOWN   31542/$6.95
__GARFIELD'S THANKSGIVING   35650/$6.95
__HERE COMES GARFIELD   32021/$6.95
__GARFIELD GETS A LIFE   37375/$6.95
__A GARFIELD CHRISTMAS   35368/$5.95

Please send me the BALLANTINE BOOKS I have checked above. I am enclosing $_____. (Please add $2.00 for the first book and $.50 for each additional book for postage and handling and include the appropriate state sales tax.) Send check or money order (no cash or C.O.D.'s) to Ballantine Mail Sales Dept. TA, 400 Hahn Road, Westminster, MD 21157.

To order by phone, call 1-800-733-3000 and use your major credit card.

Prices and numbers are subject to change without notice. Valid in the U.S. only. All orders are subject to availability.

GREETINGS FROM GARFIELD!
GARFIELD POSTCARD BOOKS FOR ALL OCCASIONS.
__GARFIELD THINKING OF YOU   36516/$6.95
__GARFIELD WORDS TO LIVE BY   36679/$6.95
__GARFIELD BIRTHDAY GREETINGS   36771/$7.95
__GARFIELD BE MY VALENTINE   37121/$7.95
__GARFIELD SEASON'S GREETINGS   37435/$8.95
__GARFIELD VACATION GREETINGS   37774/$10.00
__GARFIELD'S THANK YOU POSTCARD BOOK   37893/$10.00
ALSO FROM GARFIELD:
__GARFIELD: HIS NINE LIVES   32061/$9.95
__THE GARFIELD BOOK OF CAT NAMES   35082/$5.95
__THE GARFIELD TRIVIA BOOK   33771/$6.95
__THE UNABRIDGED UNCENSORED
  UNBELIEVABLE GARFIELD   33772/$5.95
__GARFIELD: THE ME BOOK   36545/$7.95
__GARFIELD'S JUDGMENT DAY   36755/$6.95
__THE TRUTH ABOUT CATS   37226/$6.95

Name_____

Address_____

City_____ State_____ Zip_____